EDUCATION AND PUBLIC POLICY

By Seymour E. Harris and Others

EDUCATION
AND PUBLIC POLICY

Edited by

SEYMOUR E. HARRIS

*(Littauer Professor of Political Economy Emeritus,
Harvard University and Chairman, Department of
Economics, University of California, San Diego)*

and

ALAN LEVENSOHN

Introduction by SEYMOUR E. HARRIS

McCutchan Publishing Corporation
2526 Grove Street
Berkeley, California 94704

Preface

The present volume is the third of a series based on seminars given at Harvard; the first, *Higher Education: The Economic Problems,* (1962); the second, *Challenge and Change in American Education,* McCutchan Publishing Corporation, Berkeley, California (1965).

In 1962-63, Dean (now United States Commissioner of Education) Frank Keppel and the writer gave a seminar on *Education and Public Policy* at Harvard. Unfortunately Commissioner Keppel had to leave at midyears, but he contributed much to the seminar during the first semester. Our loss at his departure is compensated; for from all reports Keppel has performed brilliantly in Washington. At a number of places we have had to modify our statements here as a result of his performance there.

The Ford Foundation provided the necessary finance. This volume gives the results of that seminar, with some updating when necessary.

As a rule 2 or 3 experts prepared papers for the seminar, followed by comments of invited guests and students. Alan Levensohn is responsible for what I consider an excellent summary of the discussion from recordings of the seminar and he contributed indispensable general editorial help. This help was so important that I have put his name on the title page. I owe much also to Robert Repetto and Glenn Miller who did the preliminary job of organizing the discussion material.

We assembled experts from relevant fields—two University and College Presidents, one Vice President (M.I.T.), a Provost and one College Dean, the President of the American Council of Education (the major association in higher education), two State Commissioners of Education, two top Accreditation officials, high officials of the Federal Government (two from the Office of Education and three from other departments), three Foundation Officers, one Congressional Staff Officer, a Monsignor of the Catholic Church and Editor, the Budget Officer and head of the Senate of the Massachusetts Government and nine professors of Law, Education, Government, Sociology, Psychology and Economics at Harvard and M.I.T.

Our objective was to invite experts from relevant fields and interests who might throw light on problems that seemed to us to be important. We did not try to cover the whole field. What determined our coverage was the discovery of areas not treated adequately in our earlier volumes that seemed to us in need of study, and of the experts to perform the necessary tasks.

Part I (*Political Issues*) covers such problems as Who Controls the Schools? Political and Religious Issues of Federal Aid (a discussion among a Monsignor, a Harvard Law Professor and the Massachusetts Assistant Attorney General), Federal Relations to (1) Higher Education (2) contributions to Student Aid and (3) Educational Planning.

Under Part II (*Qualitative Issues*) we concentrated on Research in Education, Accreditation of Universities and Colleges, and College Admissions.

The subjects under consideration in Part III (*Economic Issues: The Cost of Education*) are primarily: how economical are school and college operations, and what can be done to improve management and raise productivity.

Under Part IV (*Economic Issues: Government and Education*) the problems discussed are the allocation of resources to education (what determines how much goes to education?), how can we more effectively use our man- and womanpower through improved and extended education, and what does education add to income, and how can this contribution be increased.

In my introduction the reader will find a summary, some updating when it seemed necessary and an occasional attempt to fill some gaps.

Miss Marian Wilson, Mrs. Priscilla White, Mrs. Beth Shaw and Mrs. Myrtle Williams provided indispensable secretarial and typing help. I have a special obligation to my former colleague and friend Dean Don Price of the Graduate School of Public Administration at Harvard, who helped us plan both this and an earlier seminar.

Seymour E. Harris

La Jolla, California

CONTRIBUTORS
(In order of their contributions)

Neal Gross, Professor of Education, Harvard University.

James Q. Wilson, Associate Professor of Government, Harvard University.

Mark DeWolfe Howe, Professor of Law, Harvard University.

Gerald A. Berlin, Assistant Attorney General, Commonwealth of Massachusetts.

Monsignor Francis J. Lally, Editor, *The Pilot* (Archdiocese of Boston).

Logan Wilson, President, American Council on Education.

Vernon Alden, President, Ohio University; Former Associate Dean, Harvard University Business School, and Associate Director, School for College Presidents.

General James McCormack, Vice President, Massachusetts Institute of Technology.

John F. Morse, Director, American Council on Education; Former Staff Member of the U. S. House of Representatives Committee on Education and Labor.

Russell Thackrey, Executive Secretary and Treasurer of Association of State Universities and Land Grant Colleges.

Peter Muirhead, Assistant Commissioner of Education, Office of Education, Washington, D.C.

Philip H. Coombs, Director, International Institute for Educational Planning; Former U. S. Assistant Secretary of State for Educational and Cultural Affairs.

David Riesman, Henry Ford II Professor of Social Science, Harvard University.

Francis A. J. Ianni, Chief of the Cooperative Research Program, U. S. Office of Education.

Jerome S. Bruner, Professor of Psychology, Harvard University.

F. Taylor Jones, Executive Secretary, Commission on Institutions of Higher Education, Middle States Association of Colleges and Secondary Schools.

William K. Selden, Executive Director, National Commission on Accrediting.

Owen B. Kiernan, Commissioner of Education, Commonwealth of Massachusetts.

Frank Bowles, Educational Program Director, Ford Foundation; Former President, College Entrance Examination Board.

Joseph A. Kershaw, Professor of Economics and Provost, Williams College.

Seymour E. Harris, Littauer Professor, Political Economy, Harvard University.

E. Gil Boyer, Assistant Commissioner of Education for the State of Rhode Island.

Harold B. Gores, President, Educational Facilities Laboratories, Inc.

Sidney G. Tickton, Program Associate, The Fund for the Advancement of Education (now Sec-Treas., Academy for Educational Development).

James S. Coles, President, Bowdoin College.

John C. Esty, Jr., Associate Dean, Amherst College.

Harold Goldthorpe, Specialist for Student Financial Assistance Higher Education, Administration Branch, U. S. Office of Education.

Michaél S. March, Assistant to Chief (Legislative and Program Analysis), Labor and Welfare Division, U. S. Bureau of the Budget.

Senator John E. Powers, President of the Senate, General Court, Commonwealth of Massachusetts.

Kermit Morrissey, Chairman, Massachusetts Community College Board; Assistant to the President, Brandeis University.

Howard Rosen, Assistant Director for Manpower, Automation and Research, Office of Manpower, Automation and Training, Department of Labor.

John Dunlop, Professor of Economics, Harvard University.

Edward F. Denison, Economist, Committee for Economic Development and Brookings Institution.

Robert M. Solow, Professor of Economics, Massachusetts Institute of Technology.

Otto Eckstein, Professor of Economics, Harvard University; Member President's Council of Economic Advisers.

Contents

	Page
Introduction by Seymour E. Harris	1

PART I: POLITICAL ISSUES

1. Who Controls the Schools?
   - Neal Gross 19
   - James Q. Wilson 29
   - Discussion 31

2. Political and Religious Issues of Federal Aid
   - Mark DeWolfe Howe 39
   - Gerald A. Berlin 44
   - Monsignor Francis J. Lally 47
   - Discussion 51

3. The Federal Government and Higher Education
   - Logan Wilson 59
   - Vernon Alden 68
   - General James McCormack 71
   - Discussion 74

4. Federal Aid to Students in Higher Education
   - John F. Morse 81
   - Discussion
     - Russell Thackrey and Peter Muirhead 88

5. Educational Planning—Its Goals and Its Dangers
   - Philip H. Coombs 99
   - David Riesman 108
   - Discussion 113

PART II: QUALITATIVE ISSUES

6. Research in Education
   - Francis A. J. Ianni 123
   - Jerome S. Bruner 137
   - Discussion 140

7. Accreditation: The Quality of Institutions
F. Taylor Jones 147
William K. Selden 153
David Riesman 156
Owen B. Kiernan 159
Discussion 161

8. College Admissions: The Qualifications of Students
Frank Bowles 167
Discussion 178

PART III: ECONOMIC ISSUES: THE COST OF EDUCATION

9. Productivity in Schools and Colleges
Joseph A. Kershaw 185
Seymour E. Harris 192
Discussion 194

10. Economics of School Management
E. Gil Boyer 199
Harold B. Gores 206
Discussion 213

11. Planning for Institutions of Higher Learning
Sidney G. Tickton 221
Owen Kiernan 240
James S. Coles 242
Discussion 248

12. Forms and Functions of Student Aid
John C. Esty, Jr. 253
Harold Goldthorpe 262
Discussion 276

PART IV: ECONOMIC ISSUES: GOVERMENT AND EDUCATION

13. Allocation of Resources to Education
Michael S. March 283
Senator John E. Powers 287
Kermit Morrissey 292
Discussion 297

Page

14. Training Manpower in Relation to Needs
    Howard Rosen 301
    John Dunlop 306
    Discussion 308

15. Womanpower and Education
    Discussion 317

16. Education and Economic Productivity
    Editor's Preface 327
    Edward F. Denison 328
    Robert M. Solow 337
    Otto Eckstein 340
    Discussion 342

Introduction

By Seymour E. Harris*

1. *Who Controls the Schools?* is the subject of the first paper by Gross who admirably examines the locations of power. The school superintendent is not generally the source of power though he is the intermediary. The School Board is more likely to be the repository of influence. But many other elements exercise control within the Board or through other channels: finance men, other business leaders, purveyors of commodities and services for the school, state educational Commissioners or Boards, ordinary politicians seeking influence or contracts, taxpayer leagues, the Catholic Church, the teachers, ordinary citizens inclusive of Parent-Teacher Associations all share this control. The distribution of power varies from place to place and from state to state.

But there is no unanimity on the sources of power or on the possibility of measuring influence. The Catholic Church is an example of the disagreements that prevail. In Massachusetts, a state with a large Catholic population, the view is widely held that the Church exercises great influence in the choice of administrators, teachers and the determination of educational policies. But one expert could find no evidence of church influence as an entity in New Haven, a town with a heavy Catholic population. Of this we may be sure: when parochial school populations are large, interest in public schools tends to suffer. The relative decline of Massachusetts schools may not be unrelated to this factor. But Wilson pointed out that Pittsburgh with a record parochial school population nevertheless has one of the best school boards in the country.

2. From Control, the first subject treated in Part I on *Political Issues,* we move on to *Political and Religious Issues of Federal Aid,* with contributions by a Harvard Professor of Law, a Monsignor of the Catholic Church and editor of *The Pilot,* and an Assistant Attorney General of the Commonwealth of Massachusetts.

---

*This introduction is largely a brief summary with occasional comment and updating.

In recent years the Federal Government has supported aid to denominational Institutions of Higher Learning (IHL) but not to parochial schools. Howe raises the question whether this kind of discrimination is supportable on the grounds that higher education is voluntary and lower education is compulsory. Howe also protests against the excessive practice of trying to treat fundamental problems, e.g. federal aid to education, by raising constitutional issues.

A crucial issue is the extent to which religious teaching is involved in the instruction of secular subject matters, that is, if aid is made available for secular subjects, is religious education increased? As Howe expresses it, "instead of adding up three apples and one orange to make four pieces of fruit, they add up three bishops and a cardinal to get a hierarchy of some kind." But the Monsignor denies this—there is no Catholic Mathematics or Catholic French —and seems even prepared to accept standards and rules determined by the government as the price of federal aid. Howe in turn wonders whether the Catholic Church should accept this degree of control.

In 1965 President Johnson proposed limited help to parochial schools in a manner to skirt the constitutional issues, and in so doing earned the approval of the Catholic groups. In particular the criterion established was level of income, not whether the schools were public or private. This may indeed be the entering wedge which Berlin and others feared at our seminar.

Undoubtedly, the Catholic bishops' increasing determination to seek federal aid is based on the premise that the issue is an educational, not a religious or constitutional, one. Increasing costs of Catholic education related to both the dwindling supply of teachers available at bargain prices and the rise of numbers to be educated at ever mounting costs help explain the growing pressure from the parochial schools for federal aid. Monsignor Lally points out that the Catholics finance 13 per cent of the students at a cost of $1.8 billion. But this is a mistaken estimate or else reveals shockingly low costs and standards, for 13 per cent on national standards should cost today about $5 billion.

3. *Federal Government and Higher Education* is the theme to which Logan Wilson, Vern Alden and James McCormack addressed themselves.

On the need of federal aid for higher education there was little disagreement. Higher education has a special claim both because the national interest is served by higher education in a special way, and yet there are serious lacunae of financial resources for higher education.

But it is not necessary to enlist aid for all IHL or for all curricula. As Logan Wilson says, the Harvard House Plan, however desirable, is not a fit subject for federal aid, nor, in his view is Fine Arts, nor is every IHL offering a second-rate curriculum and close to bankruptcy to be salvaged by the Federal Government.

Much can be done by IHL to divert resources to the Humanities and Social Sciences, even as the Federal Government helps the Sciences. Professors of Mathematics are not generally paid more in major universities than Professors of History just because federal programs greatly increase the demand for their services.

Among the criteria which Wilson lists for obtaining Federal aid are: serving the national interest, contribution to resource development, help on the basis of priority, complementarity (not a monopoly by the Federal Government), merit (why concentrate aid for graduate school fellowships largely on the non-prestige IHL?), and coordination. By the last, he would like to exclude much duplication and other wastes.

President Kennedy had asked that Federal participation be "selective, stimulative and transitional", a wise description in the political context of the early 1960's. It is of interest that President Johnson's educational program of 1965 meets these tests, and especially that of selectivity. Instead of massive general programs that would be costly and unacceptable to the Congress, he seeks help in special areas, e.g. low income places and special programs, e.g. scholarships for the impecunious and outstanding, financing of plant and equipment where it is especially needed.

Our participants raise many other vital issues. Higher education should speak with one voice not with many as in 1961. (Wilson's American Council on Education is alerting the Government of the position of higher education generally.) They raise questions on the excessive fragmentation of aid; on the need of assistance for *programs* of the University; on fair compensation on research contracts and allowances for depreciation of science buildings; on the need of not yielding to political pressures for universalizing federal research aid.

Many have recently stressed the high costs to teaching of large research programs. Alden, however, reminds us of the large gains to educational standards of Federal Aid programs.

4. Morse, Muirhead and Thackrey discuss *Federal Aid to Students in Higher Education*.

A crucial issue is the choice between a large scholarship program as against substantial subsidies to IHL, Morse favoring the former though not excluding the latter, and Thackrey reflecting the views of public universities seeking subsidies. Thackrey is fearful that a large scholarship program is not workable. Many supporters of public higher education are distrustful of large scholarship stipends because they stimulate the migration of students to the Northeast and the loss of talent by the West and South to the profit of the affluent East, and also provide special windfalls to private IHL.

Morse is eloquent on the failure to achieve an adequate scholarship program in 1961. The House was adamant in its refusal to support a scholarship program; but the Senate favored it. The House wanted grants for buildings, the Senate was less willing. Difficulties with the hostile Rules Committee, the unwillingness of the House to compromise in conference on scholarships, the emergence of the old issues, such as fear of federal control, the hostility to welfare expenditures, the constitutional issues related to separation of Church and State—these and other matters killed the educational bill. It was not until 1965 that the President found it feasible to suggest a scholarship program.

Under the National Defense Education Act, the government provided a substantial grant to IHL for each additional fellowship financed by the Federal Government. Morse shows how this procedure spread to other federal departments; and yet was one of the obstacles to passage of the 1961 Act.

I am not sure that the institutional grant is to be preferred to student aid. The argument of those favoring this type of expenditure is that the grant thus makes possible reduced costs and reduced tuition. But there is waste involved, for all students profit, irrespective of need, whereas student aid can be allocated on the basis of need and ability.

That student aid is inadequate, that much of the aid money is squandered because of the methods of distribution, that students in the sciences are favored excessively and that a substantial aid program would cut dropouts and raise the number of able students going to College—on these matters there was wide agreement.*

---

*For a full discussion of many of these issues, see my *Higher Education: Resources and Finance*, Parts 2-4, McGraw Hill, 1962.

5. Riesman and Coombs debate the issues of *Educational Planning*. Admitting large gains of numbers (a doubling of enrollment in 12 years), of finance, of schools, of equipment, improvements in curricula, rising interest in the problems of underdeveloped countries, adaption of rate of advance to the capacities of the individuals to move ahead, Coombs nevertheless is impressed by the inadequacies of American education. We have no general survey which would tell us where we have been, where we are and where we are going. The funds spent for research and evaluation of our educational system costing $35 million a year are tragically small. We waste manpower as many of our best students do not acquire the education they should have, we fail to mobilize men and women of ability for the teaching profession, and once we find our teachers, we squander their time and energy in menial tasks. Coombs, attracted by the technique of the Economic Report of the Council of Economic Advisors, which each year indicates the state of our economy, the economic gaps and the means of treating them, would introduce similar techniques in education, with an annual report on the status of education by a Council of Educational Advisors, with hearings by a Joint Congressional Committee on Education and a Report on necessary action by the Government. In short, the problems require general, not fragmentary, treatment.

Riesman is not as enthusiastic as Coombs is in supporting educational planning. He is troubled by the prospect of students choosing schools and colleges on the basis of studies of manpower needs. Much to be preferred is the student deciding what he wants to be, rather than being enslaved by manpower surveys. He cites the example of the German chemists of the 19th Century who, multiplying by the thousands without the help of any general plan, nevertheless created openings for themselves by dint of their quality and achievements. The Robbins Report on higher education in Great Britain, appearing since Riesman spoke at our seminar, has taken a similar position: let us turn out vast numbers of scientists; we need no manpower survey for they will create openings for themselves.

6. Ianni and Bruner consider *Research in Education*.

Almost everyone would agree that expenditures on educational research are woefully inadequate, whether the correct figure is 0.1 per cent of total educational expenditures or even 0.2 per cent. The Government spends less on educational research than on research for Fish and Wild Life Service, and a negligible sum compared to

the $15 billion disbursed in all by the Federal Government for re-
search and development.

For the meager sums disbursed and their effective use, Ianni has
had a large part of the responsibility and to me seems to have performed remarkably well. ". . . Educational research has failed to
catch the political and public imagination because it has been unimaginative. . . ." But Ianni rightfully warns us that additional research
money is not the whole cure, for "we must broaden the frontier
of experimentation in education and create a pervasive professional
mood which not only accepts innovation, but seeks and welcomes
it."

Ianni lists important gains made recently as a result of educational research in his office. It is now possible to increase at least fourfold the rate of listening comprehension of blind children thru the
application of compressed speech; it has been found that presumably
retarded children are often only retarded in the sense that they are
handicapped by non-stimulative environments at home; thru instruction in basic mathematical ideas in the first grade, children can learn
twice as much.

But Ianni is rightly troubled by the long lag between an advance
in educational theory and its application in the real world. Hence
he concludes that effective work means 4 steps—basic research, field
testing, demonstration and dissemination. One estimate put the entire
gestation period of a researchable idea and its dissemination as a
usable tool at 60 years.

Bruner suggested that educational research "is involved in any
research that concerns itself with the transmission of information or
knowledge." The mastery of technology by the individual is a source
of great bursts of intellectual growth. Bruner also urges that educational research and development should be focused on the nature
of the educational process itself and thus be related to the curriculum.

7. The Views of F. Taylor Jones, Selden, Riesman and Kiernan
on *Accreditation; The Quality of Institutions.*

Regional accreditation was the first issue under discussion. What
is the institution trying to do? How does it mature its students? The
regional accreditation agency, originally formed to encourage exchange of ideas, under the pressure of rising enrollment, new IHL
and curricula, soon found itself accrediting institutions. The accreditors watch objective tests, e.g. enrollment, endowment, faculty, and
then form a subjective judgment of the institution as a whole, not
its constituent parts. One objective of the accreditors is to raise stand-

ards of the IHL seeking entry and to protect the community against low-quality education. The top IHL gain from any general improvement of standards. But, as Kiernan shows, the State protects the people against the crooked and shoddy institutions that escape the accrediting net.

In concentrating on what the institution does to the student, the experts might have discussed the problem that today so concerns many, namely, the rising emphasis on research and instruction of graduate students in the modern university, and the neglect of the undergraduate. In other words, the accrediting association in concentrating on teaching may be neglecting the issues of teaching vs. research. Has the Association, for example, threatened de-accreditation to any university that has grossly neglected its undergraduates?

Riesman is concerned about another problem. Accreditation tends to make for conformity. The low-quality institution tends to be excluded and the non-conformist may also suffer exclusion, though Jones claims that each institution is encouraged to express its individuality.

Licensure of the individual is to be distinguished from accreditation of the institution. Licensure is the responsibility of the state, a responsibility largely transferred to professional associations interested in maintaining standards. A condition for professional practice is generally approval of the institution giving the relevant degree. Hence the professional association is likely to have considerable control over the curriculum. Now there are some 20 national professional associations.

Riesman suggests a less formal way of appraising IHL than that used by the accrediting associations; he also wonders about the deterioration of quality in the unorganized groups, and the discouragement of excellence by accreditation.

The system may encourage monopolistic practices, e.g. inflate standards and educational requirements as a means of restricting supply and raising rewards.

Clearly Jones's and Selden's able papers suggest an accreditation operation that is much more sophisticated than the stereotype so often viewed, e.g. accreditation based on the number of books, the number of Ph.D.'s and the faculty-student ratio.

8. Frank Bowles on *College Admissions*: *The Qualifications of Students.*

Bowles's essay on college admissions the world over is a gold nugget. Nowhere in the confines of a single essay are the admission policies as well as the structure of education the world over so brilliantly presented. He compares admission requirements in America, Europe, USSR, Asia and Africa. He probes the methods by which the authorities keep the numbers entering higher education from escalating, and yet shows where and to what extent barriers are being broken down, and especially in Britain. He comments on the lack of education of primary school teachers in Europe and the resultant unfortunate repercussions on attitudes towards higher education. In contrast to the United States where a single type of secondary school leads to many choices in curricula of higher education, in Europe higher education provides primarily technical and professional education. Bowles reveals many of the wastes of the current methods, not only the failure to enter of many deserving students, but also the cruel and costly manner of keeping students out. In Brazil, with 5,000 medical students only 1 per cent graduate in a year, the explanation being the large clusters of students repeating the first year's curriculum.

I can add very little to Bowles's essay. In a study for the *Organization or Economic Cooperation and Development of Economic Aspects of Higher Education*, 1964 (S. E. Harris, Editor and Rapporteur), I present the numbers achieving different levels of education. These statistics underline the extent of difference. Here are some figures for several countries.*

	Completing Secondary Education % Relevant Age Group		All Students, Higher Education % Relevant Age Group		All First Degrees % Relevant Age Group	
	1959	1970 (Anticipated)	1959	1970 (Anticipated)	1959	1970 (Anticipated)
U. S.	65	79	37	41	16.9	20.1
France	11	19	5.4	10	3.4	8.3
U. K.	7	9	4.1	5.0	3.4	—
Germany	5	8	3.1	5.3	2.7	—
Italy	6.5	12.5	3.6	6.3	2.6	5.4

Differences are substantial, and even among major European countries. The Robbins Report on higher education (1963) throws further light on the British situation (see especially *Report*, Chs. 2-5 and Appendix 5, which compare numbers elsewhere). Inciden-

Ibid, p. 84.

tally I would stress more than Bowles the importance of availability of aid, a subject which Bowles studied exhaustively for U.N.E.S.C.O.

9. Kershaw and Harris on *Productivity in Schools and Colleges.*

It is not easy to measure productivity in the schools, that is, the output in relation to a given input of teachers, administrators and capital. An accurate measure would require that we take into account the input, e.g. the quality of the student as well as the changes effected by the educational process. The difficulties are great. For example, one measure of productivity is held to be the greater lifetime income of the educated than of the non-educated or of Ivy League graduates than of all college graduates. But the ultimate product is a function of the initial intelligence and motivation as well as environmental factors. Neither the Aga Khan nor David Rockefeller has an income of many millions because he went to Harvard. A student once suggested we ought to examine what Harvard would do for the graduates of Dubious College whose average students have an I.Q. of 90 (100 = average) as against Harvard's students whose average aptitude test put them in the top 2 per cent in the nation. Obviously the contributions of the classroom must be put against so many other factors such as home influence, discussions outside the classroom, the student's native ability, and so on. Moreover, we have to consider the changing objectives of our educational system.

From all of this I do not mean that education makes no contribution. Aside from its cultural output, education contributes towards economic advances, a point suggested by comparisons over time of income and educational achievements, and over space by comparison of income and amount of education.

Kershaw is aware of the difficulties of measuring the productivity of our schools and colleges. He is also aware, as I am, of the many wastes in education. With current costs about $35 billion, it is important that education achieve its objectives at minimum costs. Even if we cannot measure productivity, we know that we can increase it by reducing wastes: we can treat the proliferation of courses, eliminate small classes that are not justified by special considerations, adjust pay scales to merit and market conditions (a subject effectively presented by Kershaw), experiment with modern teaching methods, avoid wasteful admission policies, allocate educational resources with some attention to the quality of the students, increase planning and research in education—thus productivity might be increased.

10. Boyer and Gores ` Consider the *Economics of School Management.*

Boyer sees the need of mass education; but the educational process should be directed towards the individuals, not to the masses. He wants more pre-school education, he wants less dropouts and more adult education. The last is needed because in a rapidly changing world, periodic adjustments are required. In his Education Message of January, 1965, President Johnson announced a $150 million pre-school program which he supported on the grounds that children from the slums fall 1 year behind by age 5 and as much as 3 years by age 8.

In Boyer's view we should exploit the new technology in the schools, e.g. programmed instruction, which adjusts to the capability of the individual. But in education we use capital and technology inadequately. The impoversihed school district, harassed by lack of funds will spend 90 per cent of its budget on teachers' salaries and neglect the joint inputs of education such as plant, whereas the affluent district will allocate only 50 per cent of its budget to teachers' salaries.

Physical aspects of education are of great importance. Gores is not pleased that 27 per cent of the school budget goes for "containing education." Whereas in industry, the shell accounts for 25 per cent of the budget and tools 75 per cent, in the school 75 per cent goes for the shell and only 25 per cent for the tools of education. Gores is not happy that the physical characteristics of the schools are determined by codes and statutes. The plumbers will "disassemble the fixture [a pre-assembled plumbing facility] on the site and then reassemble it."

Gores is pleased that the "design of schools is changing towards malleable space that can be shaped and reshaped constantly; that schools increasingly are being built to reflect needs of the future as well as those of today" (it is culturally arrogant to build as though only today mattered), and that we are beginning to move the schools to the children instead of always moving the child.

Both of these experts underline the failure to build and teach in the most productive manner. The rising level of educational costs reflects these mistakes, but we cannot measure too well the resultant reduction of the educational product.

11. Tickton, Kiernan, and Coles on *Planning for Institutions of Higher Education.*

No one in the field of education has shown greater skill in the numbers game, and has with greater effectiveness prodded administrators of IHL to plan for the future than Sidney Tickton. Hence Tickton's projections for the next generation of total population, school- and college-age population, of enrollments, of costs of education to the student and to the IHL, and of the changing pattern of financing education must be taken seriously. Tickton is well aware that projections for 20 years from now are subject to all kinds of errors. But he is also aware that these projections can periodically be changed in response to current developments.

To some the projections will seem too high, e.g. a rise of enrollment in IHL of 200 per cent by 1980. But it is well to remember that in the past most projections have been proved to be too low. Even Tickton in the last year on a study for the Consultant to the New York State Legislature has second guessed himself and raised his estimates of enrollment for New York State of but 4 years ago for 1980 by around 20 per cent. Incidentally, I think that Tickton overemphasizes the relevance of automation for the rise in enrollment.

On many issues Tickton's contributions are most welcome. No one has said more effectively that under the rising pressure of higher costs, the liberal arts college, despite its determination to stay small, must increase its enrollment from 100, 200, 300, 500 to at least a 1000. This is the price for survival. No one has shown more effectively the need of reducing unit costs through elimination of small units and recourse to modern technology.

But I do not agree with all that Tickton suggests. I agree more with Coles than with Tickton on the issue of loans for college buildings. College dormitories are viable as a rule only if the capital costs are not financed at the expense of students. Financing academic buildings from fees is far from practical. Though I have argued in the past that IHL can rely more on tuition fees, I would not move as far as Tickton towards higher tuition. Here Kiernan's emphasis on the many who cannot pay high tuition is relevant. On the issue of the optimum size of the liberal arts college, Coles offers a solution proposed for his college that meets Tickton's tests and provides additional gains.

12. Esty and Goldthorpe Analyze *Forms and Functions of Student Aid*.

One of the most controversial aspects of the problem of student aid is the relevance of low economic status against other factors, and especially motivation in discouraging entry of good students. Esty seems to belong more to the motivation than to the economics school. Basing himself in part on his experience at Amherst, Esty reveals several interesting trends: the loss of talent is related to a complex of psychological and sociological factors, for many who should go to college never really get on the escalator. The motivation is lacking; or they are frightened by high costs, or they go to the wrong schools. An interesting point is that the scholarship students record is no better than the non-scholarship students at Amherst. Apparently they are in greater need and receive aid not because they are better students. Esty also makes another interesting point, namely that after 3 substantial increases in tuition, the stipend required for scholarship holders did not rise. I suggest this may be explained by the lag in tuition in relation to per capita income in the postwar period. Per capita disposable income rose by almost 300 per cent from 1940 to 1964. There had been no such rises of tuitions in these years. Another striking point made by Esty is that the relative sources of finance at Amherst with a student cost of $2600 roughly corresponded to that of the nation, with an average cost of $1550.

What especially concerns Goldthorpe are the economic barriers to higher education, though he is clearly aware as is Esty, of the non-economic issues. In the presentation of his paper, Goldthorpe offers some valuable statistical series: the average incomes of families that borrow under the National Defense Student loan program and those of the national sample; average scholarship stipends; factors in several states accounting for failure of all students to enter college; the sources of income of students in 1953 and 1962, and comparison of prices, personal income and tuition trends. On the last I believe Goldthorpe may be on the pessimistic side. He does not allow for the larger rise of incomes than of tuition since 1940.

13. March, Powers and Morrissey Analyze the *Allocation of Resources to Education.*

From this meeting of the seminar, one can draw one clear-cut conclusion: the division of responsibility for obtaining educational funds and allocating them both at the Federal and the State levels means lack of adequate planning, excessive political influences, far from optimum allocations among levels of government, or among objectives of public spending. Even the simple facts of how much is spent on education are not really available. At the Federal level, the responsibility for educational planning and appropriating is divided among numerous departments, and is not well integrated even in the Office of Education—though there have been improvements under Commissioner Keppel since these papers were written. Responsibility is divided even in the Bureau of the Budget, and once the President pares the estimates, the authority in the Congress is allocated among many committees. The fact is that crucial decisions on such matters as how much to spend on education and on what programs are not made in any rational manner.

At the state level, we had an interesting exchange between Senator John Powers, head of the Commonwealth's Senate for many years and Kermit Morrissey who wore 3 hats—an ex-Budget Commissioner for the state, Chairman of the Community College Board and Assistant to the President at Brandeis University. Powers explains clearly the process of providing funds for education in Massachusetts, repositories of power, the obstacles to spending more and the achievements in recent years for a state which has been losing ground. He also is eloquent on the excessive authority of rural legislators and the provision of funds to growing suburban areas that build many new schools, and the neglect of the old urban areas that renovate primarily, for which outlays they receive little help from the Commonwealth. Finally he stresses the political repercussion of granting autonomy to the State University.

Morrissey is not fearful that inadequate funds will be made available for higher education in Massachusetts. The political pressures reflecting the current vogue for higher education are decisive. What concerns him are the malallocations because of the lack of planning and the conflicts among the 6 relevant Boards. The Legislature would like to force them to cut up the higher-education pie.

14. *Training Manpower in Relation to Needs* is the subject under consideration by Rosen and Dunlop.

The former presents well the origins of the Manpower Development and Training Act: large amounts of long term unemployment; heavy concentration in certain groups, e.g. Negroes, young, old, unskilled, those residing in depressed areas, those in factories and the illiterate.

There is wide agreement that workers should be retained so that they can obtain available but unfilled jobs. Often the worker is in the wrong place or the wrong occupation or has an obsolete skill. It is the task of the government under the new legislature to train the worker for a job that is likely to be available.

But there are many problems in pushing thru an adequate program, as Dunlop in particular shows: the illiteracy of the workers greatly in need of training; the small numbers being trained in relation to the numbers unemployed for long periods; the lack of interest of many who should have the training; the reduction of net gains in so far as this program cuts into apprentice training or training in the plant.

We need above all a census of unfilled vacancies. How many are there? Where are they located? What specifically are the vacancies? The British provide us with this kind of material. Why should we not have this information in the United States? The participants in the seminar listed many of the obstacles. For example, an unfilled vacancy depends in part upon the price at which a worker is to be had or on the expected business of a corporation.

In recent years the emphasis has been shifting to retraining workers as a means of solving our unemployment problems. But the possibilities may be exaggerated. When unemployment rises to 5-6 per cent, the unfilled vacancies tend to be small. Moreover, the vacancies may be in skills, e.g. professional or in places, e.g. in California, that contain the numbers that can be converted into jobs. Yet I have estimated that providing a job through retraining may cost only one-fifth as much as increasing jobs through deficit financing. Unfortunately the area of operation of retraining programs is limited to the unfilled vacancies that can be filled.

15. Assistant Secretary of Labor Esther Peterson, President Mary Bunting, Joan Burstyn, Julian Hill (Dupont), John Riley (Equitable Life Assurance Company) and Mrs. Matilda Riley discussed *Womanpower and Education.*

Women account for an increasing part of the working force. They marry earlier and compress their childbearing period in a shorter span than in the past. The increasing recourse to part-time employment, the exodus from the farms, the mechanization of the kitchen, the changing attitudes towards women in the labor market, the shortage of many skills, the reduced death rates in the middle ages, the increased importance of the white collar employees where women are especially effective—these and other factors help explain the revolutionary changes of the last generation and the impending changes.

An interesting conclusion drawn by some was that work is correlated inversely with the family income but the more educated the woman the more likely she will seek fulfillment in work. High incomes discourage work; much education has the opposite effect. One survey of able high school seniors revealed that only 20 per cent of the girls not anticipating college wanted a working career but 75 per cent of those looking forward to graduate work anticipated a career.

16. *Education and Economic Productivity* was the subject for Messrs. Denison, Solow and Eckstein to study.

For many years economists have been puzzled by the greater rise of output than of input of labor, capital and management. This residual increasingly has been associated with education. Denison, more than anyone else, has given some precision to the contribution of education to this residual. His final estimate for the period 1929-1957 is that education accounts for 23 per cent of the growth of national income and 42 per cent of the growth rate of the national income per person employed, the latter a rough measure of the gains of productivity. By examining numerous factors that might account for the rise of output vis-à-vis that of input, Denison then explains the part of the residual which should be ascribed to education. His analysis rests upon the increase of days of education in turn adjusted to the varying value of a day of education at different levels of education, and also to the improved quality of education. For larger contributions of education in the future he would depend especially on the latter.

Solow raises some interesting points. First, we should not exclude the gains of consumption, e.g. more culture and enjoyment of life. Decisions on greater investments in education should be related to this consideration, as well as attitudes towards present and future consumption. Second, we should have a better idea of what education contributes to income than Denison gives us, for he arbitrarily divides the gains to income between education and other factors such as intelligence and environmental factors. Solow proposes a study of school children based on their ability at age 6-8 and schooling, in relation to their achievements over the years. Third, we need more information on the return on investment in education against that of alternative investments.

Denison's emphasis on the number of days of education as the determinant of quantity of education and the pessimistic view of future gains from this source were subject to some criticism. Solow wondered if the product could not be greatly improved not only by increasing the number of days but also by reallocating the days among different subjects and activities in school and college. Eckstein envisages much greater possibilities of increasing the quantity of education.

Eckstein raises another important question. One might explain the residual in another way. Concentrate on research and development (R and D). One might easily discover then that R and D, more than education, is the highly productive factor.

Part I:
Political Issues

1. Who Controls the Schools?

Neal Gross
Professor of Education, Harvard University

It does not take much reflection to realize that the snappy question "Who controls our schools?" is, in fact, very slippery. A systematic and rigorous examination involves us not in one question but in a host of questions. To borrow a phrase from the anthropologists, we have before us not a nuclear but a gross-familia question, which involves a great number of questions of various types.

There are, for instance, comparative questions: Are there major differences in the basic patterns of formal and informal control over educational systems in different societies? What about the control of the schools in America as opposed to, say, France or Iran? And are there basic differences in the patterns of formal and informal control of the school systems in different states, in cities of different sizes, in different types of communities? Specifically, what about cities versus suburbs?

There are also general questions on the sources of control and influence: What types of individuals and groups outside the profession attempt to—or do in fact—influence the schools? Do some agencies exert a greater influence than others; for example, businessmen versus politicians, or churches versus politicians? Does the influence of churches and of politicians vary predictably, as by region or by size of city?

What control is exerted by key functionaries within the school system? What role does the school board play? Who controls the school board, or does anyone? To what extent is the superintendent in control? What influence is wielded by the principals and the teachers?

In what ways do professional groups outside the school system —the National Education Association, the U. S. Office of Education and the schools of education, among others—influence what goes on in the schools? And what is the impact of individuals on the national scene, such as James B. Conant, Admiral Hyman G. Rickover and

John Fischer? To what extent does their wisdom, their advice and their involvement in key decisions influence the local school system?

Other general questions focus on *what* is controlled: Who controls the budget? the educational philosophy? the curriculum? the selection of personnel? Who controls what takes place in the classroom?

All these and many other questions must be asked, and they lead to an immensely complex analysis. So we must also ask: Are there any systematic patterns of variability? If so, of what factors are they functions—the organizational structure of the school system, or the system's policy toward involving parents in school affairs, or what?

Our topic, then, involves us in a myriad of questions, each of which has complexities that warrant a full monograph. Little solid information is available, however, and even that little is very hard to uncover. So if monographs were prepared, they would consist largely of common-sense generalizations, based on case studies of relatively few single school systems among the 24,000 in the nation. Every social scientist knows that it is dangerous to generalize and that what passes for common sense is frequently nonsense. Anyone who is foolish enough to agree to discuss the question "Who controls the schools?" must, therefore, focus on a few elements—and hope for the best.

I propose to talk primarily about one of my own research studies that bears on a few of the questions I have mentioned. Then I shall try to assert some *tentative* propositions which are suggested by this work.

My data will be drawn from the School Executive Studies' project on power, which focused on the power agents who operate over the decisions of school superintendents. These data were elicited in very intensive, eight-hour interviews with school superintendents, half of them in Massachusetts. The data were not taped until the sixth hour of the interview, when we had achieved good rapport and could talk at bedrock. The data were collected in 1952-53, but I have rechecked some of them in recent years with the superintendents who had not changed jobs, and my impression is that most of what I am saying still holds true.

It is very important, when we talk about power and control, to have a sound conceptual scheme. A lot of nonsense has been written about this subject. In my judgment, Harold D. Laswell's work is perhaps the most incisive in examining several aspects of the problem of analyzing power systems.

For our inquiry, we required a conceptual scheme that would be both theoretically and empirically useful in helping us to answer the following kinds of questions: To what extent are the school superintendents' important decisions actually affected by power agents? Is there evidence of a single, overriding power system or a multiple power system affecting the decisions made by school superintendents? And does the differential social structure of a community (for example, its political structure or its economic base) result in more or less power phenomenon—or different types of power phenomenon—operating on the school superintendent's work?

We were very anxious to avoid two critical pitfalls. We wished to be on guard against the fallacy of misplaced concreteness, the danger that our techniques would force the emergence of apparent power relationships or a power system when, in reality, there was none. And we wanted to be sure that our conceptual scheme would not simplify the variety and the complexity of the power-phenomenon operation. We did not wish to emerge with a misleading single-power system if, in actuality, various power phenomena were affecting the superintendent's decision making.

This led us to emphasize the major, concrete decisions that had been made in the community in regard to the schools during the previous year or two, decisions in which the superintendent was the central figure, and then to attempt to isolate the power phenomena that had influenced him in making those decisions.

Let me present now some case material from which I shall draw certain propositions:

Case 1: This is a fairly wealthy Massachusetts community within fifty miles of Boston. For all decisions regarding major financial expenditures, the superintendent was clearly influenced by a few power agents whose combined influence may be designated a system of social power. These power phenomena were described by the superintendent as a baseball game in which he must participate. The game is played in the following manner:

In making any major financial decision, the superintendent must initially contact the local newspaper publisher. This individual is on the board of directors of all major financial institutions in the community. He can and will apply sanctions to the superintendent unless his views as to the course of action to be taken are followed.

In the superintendent's words "If Tom says, 'I don't think you should ask for a $100,000 increase in the school budget,' I just don't ask for such an increase because I know I can't get it. If Tom says no, that is all there is to it, and I don't proceed any further. [But] if Tom says 'Okay' or 'I think I would ask for a maximum of $75,000,' then I have cleared first base." He knows then that he can move ahead, at least for the $75,000.

Tom, in short, is a representative of and the key person in the power structure of the town. His judgment is respecved by all the important people. The community will not go ahead on anything unless Tom gives the nod.

"The second baseman is Ed. He is a prominent young lawyer connected with the law firm that represents all the major industries in town. When I see Ed, he says 'What did Tom say?' If I can report that Tom gave me the green light, then Ed will listen to me. If I have to report that Tom said 'No dice,' then Ed says, 'What's the point of talking?'

"Ed usually wants a week or so to think about the matter. If the amount involved is relatively small—say, $50,000 or so—Ed pretty much makes up his own mind without consulting anyone else, except for a few of his cronies. If it is a relatively large amount, however—that is, over $50,000—he talks the matter over with the top people in the big firms in town. After all, the tax rate is involved." If Ed then says no, "I know I am through. If he says 'Okay,' then and only then are we in business. Ed will handle the short stop and the third baseman—that is, he will secure the support of the Rotary Club and pass the word on to the town finance committee that the budgetary increase should be passed.

"Only after this process do I bring the matter up to the school committee and, of course, it automatically goes through. If I don't clear with Tom or Ed, I am a dead duck, and so is any budgetary increase."

Here is a clear-cut case of power operating over budgetary decisions. The action of the superintendent is clearly determined by other social actors. Two sanctions are involved: the superintendent will secure no support for his program unless a course of action desired by Tom and Ed is followed, and if the superintendent should attempt to by-pass these men or take the matter to the general public, it is clearly implied that he might have to look elsewhere for a job. However, Tom and Ed are apparently highly respected in the community because of their family backgrounds and their contribution to the community's welfare in terms of time, interest and philanthropy. The superintendent does not perceive their influence or his relationship with them as nefarious. As he puts it, "This is the way the world goes around."

Case 2: This is a town with high socio-economic status, in which all personnel decisions are made by the school board on the basis of the superintendent's recommendation. This man has not had one personnel decision turned down during his five years as superintendent. All curriculum decisions are made by the school board, again on the basis of the superintendent's recommendations. He only has to convince them each time that the particular curriculum reform "will help our kids get into college."

To prepare the way for any major change which the superintendent wants but which he believes the school board would tend to oppose—for example, a big, new guidance program (a lot of people in this school system are worried about the psychological stuff) —he calls his power agents into action. These happen to be the members of the League of Women Voters. They sell their husbands, and the husbands sell the school board.

There are, by the way, other communities in Massachusetts where the superintendents warn you, "To have the League of Women Voters on your side is the kiss of death. If they are for you, the conservative Republicans will be against you, and they control the town finance committee. So you say to these women, 'For gosh sakes, give me your informal support. But don't shout, or you'll kill what I want.' "

Case 3: This is a religiously split community in which there is great tension between Catholics and Protestants. The population is divided roughly in half. Each group runs its own slate of candidates, and everyone knows it: you vote for the Catholic group, or you vote for the Protestants. Any issue remotely bearing on religion must be worked out, must be negotiated.

Here is a riotous example. It is against the law in Massachusetts, as in most states, to ask about a person's religion when you are considering him for employment. But the members of this six-man board —three Protestants, three Catholics—have run to see that their own people are hired, that nothing is put over on them.

There was an opening for a new principal. The previous time, a Catholic had been brought before the board, and the Protestants had said, "No, this has to be a Protestant." So this time, when the superintendent brought up a Protestant, the Catholics said, "No, this has to be our appointment." For the next nine months there was an acting principal, and nothing happened. Finally a compromise was reached: the principal will be a Catholic, but the coach is going to resign, and his replacement will be a Protestant. It is a deal.

The superintendent, therefore, went to one of the local universities (not Harvard) and searched for a good young man. He could not ask his religion, and so, to take no chances, he picked a Mr. Maloney. Mr. Maloney was appointed. Everything was fine. But three months later, there was an explosion. The town had suddenly discovered that Mr. Maloney was a Protestant!

Some superintendents are major heroes, in my judgment, fighting a real battle for public education. I don't see how they take it.

Case 4: This is a community in which the jobs that the school board controls are political plums. Everything is tied to the political structure of the community, and the politics are rough. The school-board members insist upon their quota of appointments, teachers as well a custodians. Every major appointment in the hierarchy of the system must go to one of their boys. They insist on getting their share of contracts—for oil, for new furniture, for cement. This is the community.

The superintendent, during his first year on the job, worked with architects for six months, day and night, trying to design a new, streamlined school, taking out all the extras. He wanted to be able to say to his school board, "Look, I can give you a good school, and let's use that extra money for teachers' salaries." When the design was ready, he recalled, "I bring this in to my school committee, and they laugh. And they say, 'Where is the cement? Where are the trimmings? Where is the graft?' "

These school-board members have constituents; they have to take care of their people. And when someone is in trouble, they are going to handle the case. This is another instance, too, in which the Church happens to be involved in the political structure, for major issues are cleared with the Church.

How can the superintendent, a moral man, stay in such a job? "Well," he explains, "it is very uncomfortable, but what would you do? You are fifty-five. You have two kids in college. If you leave, the school board will give you the business. They will blast you in the press. You will never get another job. What would you do?"

In the superintendency business, particularly at certain levels, there is what is called the stigma. The career of school superintendents is largely in the hands of layman school boards, who do the selecting. When a school board wants a superintendent, it has to consult the candidate's previous school board. If he has been in trouble—and people with exciting ideas, new ideas, get in trouble frequently in an area like public education—he has the stigma. He is through. That is why so many school superintendents are, more or less, double talkers. You listen, and you are not sure what they are saying, because they have learned to cover their words with a certain protective coating.

How isolated is this case, in which raw political power operates over the decisions? In a later research study, covering forty-one cities across America, we asked the principals, "To what extent do you feel that your school boards really are dominated by local politicians or free of them?" Over half of the principals responded that there is major political domination in regard to appointments, contracts and other important decisions.

Case 5: This is a big city where, in the words of the superintendent, "the Church is the silent power. Anything that it wants to veto, it can; and when it wants to, it does. My job is to hold the line as best I can." The Church has ideas about its building program, and this intensifies the whole question of double taxation. The superintendent, who is himself a Catholic, must contend with this type of power operating over the system.

Case 6: This community, which is not in Massachusetts, is an illustration of state control. The power of levying school taxes is in the hands of the state legislature. The superintendent can do little because the taxing power is out of his hands. He has to work through the state politicians, and in doing so, he has become quite a politician himself.

From these very elliptical summaries of six concrete cases, I want to draw some tentative propositions about who controls our schools:

First, it seems apparent that the patterns of control of school affairs vary considerably among American communities. They vary, for example, in the extent to which school boards, who have legal responsibility to control the schools, use their formal position in the authority structure. Some school boards know that they have the formal authority and use it and do not get especially pressured; they make the basic policies and see that these are carried out. Other school boards are rubber stamps for the superintendent. Still others are representatives of special-interest groups. And many school boards operate on their own but, in hot issues, yield to local pressures.

Second, the school-board member's job frequently has latent as well as manifest functions. As Robert Merton's studies have shown, people who seek membership on a school board do not always have pure motives. One out of every five school-board members in Massachusetts in 1952-53, according to their superintendents, ran for the board primarily because they were interested in political matters, political careers. And one out of five superintendents said (they may be wrong, but these are their words) that their school boards constituted a major obstacle to their carrying out their jobs in a professional manner.

Third, external power agents frequently attempt to influence basic school decisions—especially on budget, personnel and curriculum—and they frequently succeed. In many communities in Massachusetts, the superintendent holds an informal discussion with the town finance committee about the school budget before it is ever formally submitted to the school board. Legally the finance committee has nothing to do with the budget, but without its approval the budget does not go through. Similarly, a number of superintendents review the first draft of the budget with the executive secretary of the taxpayers' association. And if the taxpayers' association says, "We are going to raise holy hell over this item," it goes back to the school board for further reconsideration.

Who are these external power agents? They include economic groups, such as the taxpayers' association and the chamber of commerce. They very often include economically influential individuals. (This is especially true in small communities. If you own the only factory in town and decide to leave, the community will be in trouble.) They include the local politicians, of course, because the school takes so much of the tax dollar. They frequently include religious groups; and local universities may also be represented in the educational power structure. Pressure may also be felt from groups outside the community, such as the National Association for the Advancement of Colored People. Superintendents in the big cities are quite concerned about the political pressure such groups can bring to bear.

Fourth, one of the major sources of pressure, particularly in the big cities, is internal. We tend to think of power being exerted from outside, but the teachers are extremely important in the power structure. Our research supports this quite clearly.

Fifth, schools are often exposed to crosscurrents of pressure. Half the superintendents we interviewed, for instance, were getting strong pressure to keep the tax rate down and, at the same time, strong pressure to increase it and improve the school program. These counter-pressures frequently have a positive value, depending on how skill-fully the superintendent plays off one against another.

Sixth, There are strategies available to superintendents to cope with these pressures and these influence agents. Some superintendents have a sounding board—for example, the League of Women Voters—and they enlist its support before they press for a major change. Of course, if the superintendent is really good and has a strong reputa-tion, a simple threat to quit may be enough to neutralize the pressure.

Some superintendents, in fact, are the key power agents in their schools, although officially they are only the executive officers of the board. A shrewd superintendent, that is, can be so persuasive and can so magnetize his board that he becomes, in effect, the decision maker.

The most determining factor in the whole structure, it seems to me, is the school board. The board is crucial in determining the extent to which outside influences control the schools. This in turn means that the community is crucial, because the community elects the school board.

What are some of the variables that may account for the different power systems we find in different communities?

The first is the formal organizational structure itself. One of the major differences between the American and European systems of education is that ours is highly decentralized. It is, I think, unique in the world in the amount of local control it permits. Each school system is locally anchored, so that a citizen can easily reach the super-intendent and the school board. At the same time, the other functions of our society are being increasingly administered at the state and Federal level. If a citizen wants to exert his influence directly, one of the few chances he has left is in the schools.

Three other, closely related factors interact within each power system: (1) The quality of the school board. This is largely a matter, in my judgment, of their motivation for wanting to join the board in the first place. (2) The guts of the superintendent. There are superintendents who take a stand early and say, "Look, if you try to pull this, you are going to get blasted in the papers," or who lay out the ground rules early, or who say, "I will quit if—" This takes real moral courage because they have careers at stake and fam-ilies to support. If the superintendent has this sort of courage, there is a major force dealing with pressure. And (3) the interest of the community. If the community is interested and concerned and wants good schools, it will not tolerate nefarious pressures.

Another factor is the economic structure of the community. A one-industry town is very dependent on the man who runs that one industry. If he is really interested in civic welfare, a lot can be accomplished. But if all he wants is to keep the tax rate down—particularly if he lives elsewhere and simply takes his profit from the industry—then it gets rough. Under the corporate structure, America is getting more and more of this type of outside control.

The political structure is also important. Tell me the nature of the politics of a community, how much graft is going on, how votes are obtained, and I think I can tell you something about the kind and quality of power operating in the schools. The religious structure of the community may, of course, be closely related to this.

Finally, a factor which I think is quite important—and which we too often overlook—is the quality of the state department of education. In New York State, for example, when a school board gets out of hand, the commissioner of education has the right to oust that board, and he exercises that right. A weak state department of education, however, which does not use the power, may allow much nonsense to go on.

These, then, are some speculations and hypotheses about factors that seem to be related to different types of power arrangements. What this list of variables suggests above all is the need for more intensive research.

Now let me make a few summary comments. First, we must be thoroughly aware of the complexity of this problem. There are many facets and many angles, all of which can be dealt with at many levels, so we must be very careful.

We must understand the local anchoring, the local context, which is the essence of the American educational system. And we must understand the network of interpersonal relationships and social systems in which the schools are embedded. We must see how the schools are tied up with the economic structure of the community, with the tax rate, with the political structure. We must realize that, in many small communities, the schools are the biggest employer in town and have the best contracts to offer. We must take into account that, in certain systems, jobs are given on a pro rata basis: now it is time for a Negro, now it is time for a Catholic, now it is time for a Jew

We must be very, very sure to understand that pressures are not automatically bad. On the contrary, they can have wholly beneficial effects. In a series of interviews with principals in schools across the country, we asked, among other things, "Do you feel that these pressures are harmful or beneficial to the schools in the long run?" In eighteen out of twenty-one pressure areas—curriculum reform, guidance, and so on—the majority of the principals said, "These pressures are basically beneficial." They even saw some value in selfish pressures notably to put students in particular classes, because these at least show parental interest.

Finally, it is my judgment—and I could be quite wrong—that there are two key areas of pressure: finances, especially control of the budget, and personnel. The individuals who control these areas can control, for the most part, what goes on in the schools. Here, above all, is where we must protect the schools from nefarious influences.

The control is ultimately, of course, in the hands of the people. If they really want it, they can have it any time, since it is they, after all, who elect the school boards.

COMMENT BY . . . *James Q. Wilson*
Professor of Government, Harvard University

These few comments are not criticisms or evaluations of what Mr. Gross had to say. They are, rather, a couple of items which deserve to be added to his initial list of complexities. That was certainly comprehensive enough, but I want to make it even more comprehensive and perhaps even more complicated.

I have had practically no experience in studying the power structures of schools. My concern is with the study of urban institutions generally. But I have been concerned with the problems of studying power, and since this is directly to this point, let me make two observations.

First of all, in a study of this kind, as in a study of almost any other kind of local institutions, the essential problem is to define and compare power. This is relatively easy to do—at least, it is relatively easy to arrive at moral certainties, although perhaps not statistical certainties—when you are dealing with a relatively homogeneous community, perhaps one such as Mr. Gross described in which the baseball game takes place. There are only one or two key actors, and the presence or absence of their veto is unambiguously determinable, at least for the superintendent and whomever he chooses to confide in. But when the city is any larger or any more complicated, a variety of power agents are operating (to use Mr. Gross's terminology), and the question becomes: how do you assess the relative power of each?

Robert Dahl, professor of political science at Yale, wrote a book called *Who Governs?* in which he addressed himself in a sophisticated and elegant fashion to this very problem. He tried to describe the politics of New Haven, Connecticut, including the schools, and his conclusion was that no one can explain who governs. He provides several hundred pages worth of well-documented reasons and speculation as to why the question cannot be answered for a city of any given size.

The difficulty of assessing power is that one must take into account, not only the ends sought by the various actors, but also the costs which they attach to the efforts required to attain those ends. For power is limited, and each use of power entails the expenditure of one opportunity to use it. Moreover, power is used to achieve a variety of ends through a variety of persons, who are susceptible to power in varying degrees. Thus the question of comparing power agents, of deciding who is most strongly influencing the schools' finances or curriculum or teacher hiring, becomes extremely difficult in a heterogeneous city. Even though the individual actor—say, the school superintendent—may have a very clear mental map of the power distribution, it is very difficult to reduce that map to writing in such a way that it will be intelligible to people who do not have direct access to the superintendent's mind.

The second problem is more fundamental: power for what? What difference does it make whether the community is run by a baseball game consisting of a newspaper publisher and a key lawyer, or by the omnipotent ladies of the League, or by a small group of monsignori and archbishops, or by a patronage-fed political machine, or by individual politicians with personal and selfish aspirations?

It seems to me that, regardless of the combination of these factors, the matter ought not to be prejudged. This holds true even when the urban politics are corrupt. There are certain cities—Boston is an excellent example—in which a good deal of individualistic bargaining occurs in the corrupt political marketplace, characterized by a concern for one's own interests and a good deal of freedom in the choice of means to realize those interests, and this seems to have a profound effect on the character of public education, although we have yet to explore this in great detail. Yet in another city—say,

Chicago—where the total value of corrupt exchanges is about the same, corruption may be differently organized, and education may not suffer at all. Indeed, education may be protected because if the man who heads the essentially corrupt political machine is correctly motivated—and it is an open question whether he will be or not—he may be able to take the heat off the school board. When pressures are applied, he can act as intermediary; and depending on his motivation, he can either back up his personal choices or insist that the choices be made a nonpolitical matter. There is no way a priori to determine which way he will act. There have been politicians in Chicago who have intervened seriously in the operations of the Chicago schools, and there have been politicians in Chicago who have not.

The same can be said for economic bosses in a one-industry or multi-industry town. Are they enlightened or unenlightened? Or, to put the question in more rigorous terms, to what ends are they acting, and do they consider education relevant to their ends? These questions must be asked about every power agent, including the League of Women Voters, the NAACP and the school board itself.

I agree with Mr. Gross that the quality of the school board is extremely important in determining the quality of education. But the quality of the school board cannot be inferred from the motives of the members. A school board could, at least logically, consist of persons whose motives are entirely personalistic—who are on the board to advance their careers, or to get ahead in political office, or simply to become well-known in the community, or to be able to rub elbows with the social elite or the newspaper publisher or the key lawyers in the community—and yet who serve those personalistic ends by actions which are objectively healthy for the schools and the community. Of course, selfish motives may also lead to actions which are deeply detrimental to the school system; but we cannot automatically assume this. We must ask the question anew, empirically, in every case.

Let me stress again that I know Mr. Gross is deeply aware of these questions. I am citing them only to introduce further complications into the minds of those who might once have felt that the study of who runs our schools is a simple matter.

SUMMARY OF THE DISCUSSION

The general discussion concentrated on four topics:

Internal power systems: The interaction of power within a school system was examined from the top down, beginning with the school board. Mr. Gross declared that in fact, if not in pure logic, there is a very close correlation between the school-board members' motivations and their behavior. All his research on the subject demonstrates this convincingly. No correlations were found between behavior and such objective characteristics as education, occupation or income; but members with respectable motivations tend to act in accordance with "professional standards." Asked what these standards are, he explained, "It means accepting professional recommendations for employees; it means representing the whole community rather than certain constituents; and so on. Everybody agrees on how a good school-board member should behave."

There are exceptions, however. "I know some superintendents who say, 'I would rather have one or two crafty politicians on my board who know their way around. Let them steal a little bit, as long as they get me the money I need to accomplish what I want to accomplish.' "

Two other characteristics of school-board members were also mentioned. (1) It makes no difference, so far as behavior is concerned, whether a board is elected or appointed. "You can *elect* lousy or good people," said Mr. Gross, "and you can *appoint* lousy or good people." True, an individual running for election needs political support, but in general the same pressures operate either way. (2) "Our research shows that school board members who send their children to private schools tend to have a *noblesee oblige* orientation and to maintain high professional standards."

The next lower level of power is the superintendent, who is subject to roughly the same pressures as the board, though he should react to them in quite a different way. "A superintendent," said Mr. Gross, "should have educational ideas, should know what he stands for, but he should also be a strategist, and this means that he is involved in political structures." If he is not an effective political operator, no matter how sound his ideas are, he is not likely to accomplish much. "One very prominent superintendent says that 'a superintendent is a political enemy.' By that, he means that he must understand the power forces; he must be able to operate informally, use pressure groups and deal with the realities of political life. Every successful superintendent I know in the country is of this type."

It follows that the superintendents who run the best systems concentrate on external relations. They pay some attention to what is happening in the schools, but they do not waste time visiting classrooms. Mr. Gross quoted a shrewd superintendent as explaining: "My job is to go out and sell the community on the importance of education, sell it on the importance of what we are trying to do, get it to ante up the money, so that I can hire the best principals to direct the curriculum and guidance, and pay the salaries that will attract the best teachers. All I do is lay out the premises for the decision making."

One discussant asked, "In towns where the superintendent is not good but just mediocre or worse, who runs the schools?" No one answered, and the question was not pressed.

The next lower level of power is the principals and—in the big-city systems—the associate and assistant superintendents and other "higher administrators." Mr. Gross referred to a research study then in progress which sought to trace the impact of the school board and the superintendent on the higher administrators, principals and staff; he termed this chain of impact the "spill-over effect." The hypothesis was that "the leadership climate should affect what goes on below," but preliminary data was not wholly confirming this. New York City was mentioned as an example of a system with a consistently excellent and dedicated professional staff, regardless of the erratic quality of the school board.

One informal observation that may be of considerable importance, however, was that the higher administrators—those between the superintendent and the principals—are not young men. "They are in their late fifties and early sixties," Mr. Gross reported. "It takes a long time to get up there. And when you talk with these men, you get a curious feeling of inertia. You throw out an idea, and the reaction is 'It can't be done' or 'Oh, we heard about that years ago.' The man on top may want to make changes in the schools but he has to work through this structure, and it may be very difficult."

The power exerted by teachers was discussed solely in relation to salary demands. Mr. Gross observed that there were many variations among communities, depending on such factors as the existing salary scale, the per captia income of the state or region, the proportion of married women on the staff and the presence or absence of an aggressive union. But these are variations in degree; there are pressures for higher salaries everywhere. One discussant asked whether the salary scale affected the extent to which teachers exerted pressure generally, but the question was not answered.

External pressure groups: Fundamental to any study of external pressures, Mr. Gross observed, is the fact that they are not the superintendents' major obstacle. On the contrary, the real obstacle is public apathy. Except in rare instances, the vast majority of citizens do not become involved in school affairs. This is especially true of upper-class families which send their children to private schools, but even the parents of public-school students take surprisingly little interest. Most superintendents would welcome far more pressure of the right kind— pressure for improvements in curriculum, guidance programs and other services, rather than on personnel selection and pupil placement.

A corollary is that pressures must be interpreted in terms of the community. If a special-interest group claims to speak for the whole community, the superintendent can test this claim through a formal or informal public-opinion poll, or the school board can hold meetings in various parts of the community to seek a consensus among interested citizens. But once these distortions are corrected, the pressures must be taken as valid in the sense that they represent basic conflicts within the community as a whole. Mr. Gross emphasized that "the schools are practically the only institution where latent community conflicts—of religion, of race, of social strata—can come into force."

One discussant (an unidentified student in the audience) commented on this point: "I assume that every community has recognized pressure groups with some strength and longevity, but I also have an idea that people can shift their membership from one group to another. Also, nearly everybody, at some time, gets heated about a controversy and becomes almost automatically a member of some pressure group; but it becomes a pressure group only if it has the leadership to exert the pressure."

External pressures show up most consistently in relation to the school budget, especially in communities which rely less on state aid than on local real estate taxes. Budgets are cleared in advance, more often than not, with town finance committees and taxpayers' associations—a procedure which may involve extremely sophisticated timing and strategy. This clearance does not necessarily depress the level of expenditure, however; some Massachusetts communities with the highest per captia expenditure do the most assiduous checking. Pressures may also be exerted in the selection of textbooks; this can be extraordinarily damaging, but fortunately it is quite infrequent. Mr. Gross discovered such pressure in only 3 or 4 per cent of the communities he studied.

How can school boards and superintendents cope with undesirable pressures? One way is to confront them openly, to present their case directly to the public and seek its support. A concomitant way is to mobilize counterpressures. Labor unions, for example, are major supporters of educational reform when their support is requested. "In my judgment," said Mr. Gross, "this is one of the great untapped resources. Most school boards tend to have upper-class members, and it simply never occurs to them to talk with the unions. But the unions have great power, which can be used for the benefit of the schools."

Another possible way to cope with undesirable pressures, said one discussant, would be to form strong professional organizations and economic-research groups with sufficient authority to command attention within a community as well as on the national scene. The National Education Association, in Mr. Gross's judgment, does not meet this need. It is too big and clumsy, and some superintendents insist that "it does not keep up with the basic problems." The NEA's power at the local level "is essentially in the suburban systems and a few of the big-city systems." The American Association of School Administrators and the Association for Supervision and Curriculum Development are, he said, equally limited.

Religious pressures: Discussion of religious pressures on the schools was concerned almost exclusively with Roman Catholics and the Roman Catholic Church. The question was raised whether the Church itself, when it is strong in a community, exerts pressure on the public schools, either directly or through political intermediaries. There was unanimous agreement that the Church sometimes does and sometimes does not. Mr. Gross said that he "can cite case after case in Massachusetts communities where the Catholic superintendent will tell you precisely how the Church has entered in. On the other hand, I can cite many cases where the Catholics in a community have been very great supporters of the schools. It is a very complex area."

Mr. Wilson recalled that Robert Dahl, in his study of who governs New Haven, "was unable to document a single substantial case in which the Church, as an organized entity, attempted to influence the public schools. In fact, the contrary is the case. All the superintendents, all the assistant superintendents, all the principals and about seventy-five per cent of the teachers are Catholic. They have an enormous personal stake in the public schools and would be the last to attempt to place the schools at any disadvantage."

(The discussion of the relationship between the parochial-school system and state aid to public schools is dealt with separately in the fourth and last part of this summary.)

At the school-board level, Roman Catholic pressures are equally variable. "Some school-board members who are among the strongest fighters for the public schools are Catholics," Mr. Gross noted. "On the other hand, it frequently happens in Massachusetts that a board which has a majority of Catholics will name a Catholic superintendent. In other communities where the boards are becoming fully Catholic, the superintendents report that they are beginning to feel pressure. But there is no fixed pattern, and we must be very careful about generalizations." Mr. Wilson recalled that Pittsburgh, which "has a larger percentage of its children in parochial schools than any other American city with a population of over 100,000," has one of the most highly respected school boards in the nation.

In his depth research of principals, however, Mr. Gross was uncovering data which left him "scared." Value tests were administered to each principal in the study, and these showed "striking differences" between Catholic and non-Catholic principals with regard to acceptance of authority. The data were being subjected to intensive analysis; if this bears out the apparent correlation, the finding will have a "major impact" on public education.

With regard to the hiring of teachers, trouble can arise if a Catholic superintendent seems to be hiring an undue proportion of Catholic teachers. Mr. Gross described a predominantly Protestant community in Massachusetts in which the school board had hired a Catholic principal. The board found him excellent, but he incurred such wrath in the community that the board feared "an explosion" if they gave him a raise. "One of the rumors was that he was loading the schools with Catholics." An impartial investigation revealed that three-fourths of his appointments had indeed been Catholics, and the reason was simply that three-fourths of the graduates of Massachusetts state colleges (formerly teachers colleges) are Catholics. "This is the route of mobility of the ethnic groups which cannot send their children to Harvard or MIT." The superintendent had offended the community because he had not been discriminating *against* Catholic applicants. "He had no bias, He was a very tolerant man."

The possibility of religious pressure by Protestants or Protestant churches was not raised at any time throughout the discussion. Jews were mentioned once, and Mr. Gross commented: "If there is a relatively high proportion of Jews in a community, there will very likely be strong support for the schools. Most superintendents say this automatically. There will be trouble about the Christmas-Hanukah celebrations, but they are willing to tolerate that because Jews will stand by the schools. I have talked with superintendents at really gut level, and they feel strongly about this. They talk about the Jewish and non-Jewish school-board members, and they say, 'When the chips are down and you need something, the non-Jew will frequently go with the political boys, but the Jews have the guts to stick by education.' "

Religion and state aid to schools: A recurrent topic of discussion was the relationship between the Roman Catholic parochial-school system and state taxation to support public schools. A general impression was reported—states with low Roman Catholic populations tend to have higher levels of state aid, and vice versa—and the discussion searched into possible explanations. Double taxation was mentioned, as was simple disinterest: "Those who send their children to parochial schools look on the public schools largely as an area where jobs are available." The fact was noted that parochial schools fill up very rapidly and that the significant figure might be the percentage of Catholic children in the public schools. At last, one discussant questioned the original assumption, citing a recent book, *Schoolmen and Politics,* to the effect that "there does not seem to be any significant negative influence by the Church on state aid to public education." No rebuttal was offered, and the discussion of this topic then ceased.

In the course of the discussion, two other factors affecting the level of state aid had been adduced. One was economic affluence or depression. The other, proposed by Mr. Gross, was the extent of reliance on private institutions of higher learning. "My own belief is that the pinnacle of a system has much to do with what goes on below. In Massachusetts, with Harvard and MIT dominating the educational scene, people generally had the impression that education within the state was good. The influence of the best institutions colored public thinking about all levels of education. If there is trouble in the schools, they felt, Harvard will take care of it. We had no Horace Manns in this century creating pressure groups and real interest. And so we have a tremendous lag.

"In the Midwest, all the great institutions are essentially land-grant universities, which have much closer liaison with the public schools at the state level. The schools and the public university form one big educational package. As a result, the level of state aid to the schools is considerably higher than it is here."

2. Political and Religious Issues of Federal Aid

Mark DeWolfe Howe
Professor of Law, Harvard University

It seems to me that I may be helpful if I outline two of the conflicting statements that have been presented by responsible bodies with respect to the issues of Federal aid to education, specifically as it applies to religiously affiliated schools and colleges. The two statements that I have in mind are (1) the memorandum prepared by the Department of Health, Education and Welfare in support of President Kennedy's affirmative suggestions and his negative pronouncements, and (2) the memorandum issued by the National Catholic Welfare Conference, which was, in a sense, designed to answer the HEW memorandum.

One cannot, of course, avoid the political backgrounds of this controversy, and I think it is by no means unrealistic, though it may be unlawyerlike, to take some of those considerations into account. Senator Kennedy, as a candidate, found himself virtually compelled to take certain positions with respect to the kind of aid he would support for religiously affiliated schools and colleges. He found it politically necessary—and I think he was quite right, in the situation in which he found himself— to take what seems to be an excessively restricted view as to the powers of the Federal Government. He said very specifically during the campaign that it would be unconstitutional for the Federal Government to finance parochial-school programs in any way. He stood firmly on this position as a *constitutional* requirement; and I take it that he emphasized this for the very good reason that he was then stating not a personal decision but a decision which he felt compelled to reach.

Given this political background, it was not surprising that the program of aid which was offered by the incoming administration did entirely exclude any aid to parochial schools. This was the Government's official position, and this negative aspect of the program was one of the elements to which the HEW memorandum was directed. The memorandum, in this negative aspect, simply reiterated certain constitutional assumptions which the President had made, assumptions built out of certain decisions of the Supreme Court and certain dicta of the justices of the Supreme Court, which do, on the face of it, seem to thoroughly support the President.

If it really be true (as Justice Black, speaking for a majority of the Court, had said) that the Government cannot provide any aid to one religion or any aid to all religions; and if it be further true (as the Court had indicated in the Everson case) that though the state may help children to travel to and from parochial schools by paying for public transportation, it cannot aid the school in providing an education, whether that education be secular or religious—if these assertions be accepted, then I suppose the President and HEW were right in saying that any form of aid to parochial schools is unconstitutional.

I had some doubts—and I think the Catholic Conference had some doubts—whether these statements of the Court should really be taken at face value. But that is another phase of the problem, and I shall say a little about it later on.

On the affirmative side of the program, I think it was not so easy for the HEW lawyers to give, as they sought to, a persuasive defense of some other aspects of the administration's program. It was proposed that Federal aid in one form or another—perhaps by loan, perhaps by grant—need not be limited to public schools and state universities, but that it is also permissible to provide public aid to private colleges and universities, and that denominational affiliation does not bar these institutions from receiving aid, at least for the secular aspects of their educational programs. I am not sure of the analysis which the HEW memorandum produces to explain this distinction, but, in essence, it seems to draw a constitutional differentiation between schools, on the one hand, and colleges and universities, on the other, in their relationships to the Government. This is built partly, I take it, on the fact that school attendance is normally compulsory.

It was proposed, in short—and the Department of Health, Education and Welfare supported the proposal—that aid should be given, by loan or grant, to denominationally affiliated colleges and universities for their programs that are nonreligious in essence. But if we take with complete seriousness the pronouncements of the Supreme Court about the unconstitiutionality of *any* aid to religious institutions, how can this be justified? How can you justify putting public money into the hands of, say, Holy Cross, even for a program in physics or for a new gymnasium, if such aid enables the college to expand its religious program? Is there any real constitutional difference between aiding the physics laboratories in a Catholic high school and aiding the physics laboratories at Holy Cross? Does the Constitution draw this line?

One may find good reasons to draw the line as a matter of policy, and it can, I suppose, be argued with some force that religion necessarily plays a bigger and more permeating part in all phases of instruction at the earlier stages of education than it does at the college level. I do not know enough about the actualities of education in parochial schools to be sure, but I suspect that there is more of a religious atmosphere, at least, if not more religious instruction, in physics courses in parochial schools than in the physics courses at, say, Fordham University. But these differences, in my judgment, do not amount to constitutional differences. And the fact that the Kennedy administration was favoring this kind of aid to higher education, while asserting that the Constitution forbids it to give similar aid to parochial schools, did, I think, considerably weaken its position.

If it had stood on the absolute principle that any religiously affiliated educational institution, whether a school or a college, must be excluded from the program, that would have been a logically defensible position; it might also have been defensible in policy. But once the administration began to draw this somewhat narrow line between schools and colleges, I think their position was weak.

The National Catholic Welfare Conference replied to the HEW memorandum largely in these terms. Its answer insists, in the first place, that the Court's barriers to aid are not as absolute as the President assumed them to be. It emphasizes—with some justification, it seems to me—as a matter of equity that if the Federal Government can put money into a secular private school for a new gymnasium or a new physics laboratory, it can put money into a parochial high school for equivalent new facilities. Since we assure all citizens that they have religious liberty and that the Government will protect every parent's right to send his children to parochial or private schools, is it fair to exclude the Catholic school from the benefits that are granted to the secular private school?

It is not, then, simply a problem of discriminating between Catholic schools and public schools. The problem is also discrimination between the religiously affiliated private school and the secular private school. If it is appropriate for the Federal Government to put money into secular private schools, what justification is there for excluding religious private schools from similar aid in their nonreligious instruction? Furthermore, if the Government concedes, as it had conceded, that it can provide aid to denominational colleges, how can it insist on a distinction between parochial schools and Catholic colleges? Is there a constitutional difference between the school, which has behind it the compulsion of the state, and the college or university, in which education is not compulsory?

So the Conference memorandum, building upon only slightly different presuppositions from those accepted by the Department of Health, Education and Welfare, came out in favor of limited aid to parochial schools as well as to denominational colleges.

One of the presuppositions that is of fundamental importance to the persuasiveness of the Catholic memorandum (and this is a question of fact on which I cannot speak with any authority) is that in parochial schools and Catholic colleges, there is no significant religious element in the instruction in secular subject matters. Many critics have questioned this assumption and have produced a good deal of evidence that the instructional materials used in denominational schools, even in the sciences and mathematics, are full of religious elements. Instead of adding up three apples and one orange to make four pieces of fruit, they add up three bishops and one cardinal to get a hierarchy of some kind. So apparently there are theological overtones in these textbooks, even in subjects that are presumably secular.

If it is a fact that all instruction in parochial schools, whatever the denomination, is religious instruction, new strength is added to the view that the Government should not provide any aid to any aspect of their program. But if this is not a fact—if some subjects are taught just as they are in public schools—there seems to be a good deal of equity, at least, in the claim of the denominational schools that they should not be discriminated against. Furthermore, those who have been most fearful of giving public aid to denominational schools and colleges have not, I think, been sufficiently sensitive to the problem of discrimination that follows if aid is given to secular private schools and denied to denominational schools. It does seem an odd fact that the religious liberty secured by the First Amendment is somehow rendered ineffective by a discrimination which denies to religious schools benefits which are granted to secular private schools.

A close examination of this dilemma leads inevitably to the ugly fact, as I see it, that there are really two inconsistent principles in the First Amendment—the principle that Congress shall adopt no law respecting an establishment of religion, and the rule that Congress shall adopt no law abridging religious liberty. The fact is, as Justice Jackson and others have pointed out, that when the Government protects religious liberty, it is very often, in fact, giving aid to religion. If it tells the Jehovah's Witness that he is entitled to use a public park to preach his faith, it is saying, "You can use public property. To that extent, the state must aid you." But can we have it both ways? Can we have a rule that forbids the Government to give any aid to religion and, at the same time, requires it to defend religious liberty? And how can we make effective the Court's assurance that not only the individual but also the churches have rights under the guarantee of religious liberty?

There are also deep problems of policy on which churches should speak and not I. One is whether they are wise in seeking Federal aid. Suppose that all the textbooks in a great many parochial schools do, in fact, have a religious slant; and suppose that if they retain that slant, they become, as I think they should become, ineligible to receive public aid. Is it then desirable for the church to say, "Well, we shall give up the kind of textbooks that we prefer to use, and we shall surrender the right to use this subject matter for religious instruction. We shall accept the same textbooks that are used in the public schools." Should the Catholic Church submit to this temptation—this bribery, if you will—of getting public aid at the expense of giving up its right of self-government?

This and similar problems pose, I think, significant dangers. They are not, as I say, dangers which should bother me particularly. But I think they should be of concern, perhaps more than they have been, to the churches that are anxious to get public aid.

There are, then, many aspects to this issue. There are problems of what price the government pays and what price each citizen pays in allowing new kinds of support to be given. But there are also, I think, very important problems from the standpoint of the churches: what price must they pay if they become the beneficiaries of public largess?

Gerald A. Berlin
Assistant Attorney General, Commonwealth of Massachusetts

Let me, at the outset, issue a disclaimer for the record. I most certainly do not speak for the Commonwealth of Massachusetts, but perhaps that will become more apparent in a few minutes.

It is my feeling that the Health, Education and Welfare memorandum was not excessively restrictive; on the contrary, it went much too far, and the distance between the memorandum and the bishops' [Conference] response was very narrow.

It seems to me that the HEW memorandum sought to introduce a rather new idea into the concept of separation as it has heretofore been interpreted by the courts and as it is understood by a vast proportion of our population. This new idea is that there is somehow a distinction between aid to schools and aid to higher education. The memorandum argues, for instance, that because a child is compelled up to a certain age to attend school, no aid should be given to that child. I don't understand the meaning of this argument, for it seems to me that such an argument can run as easily, or more easily, the other way—that it is a real interference with a child's religious freedom to deny him aid through an institution which he *must* attend.

The memorandum then cites the older precedents, including the G. I. Bill of 1944, the Korean G. I. Bill of 1952 and the National Defense Education Act of 1958. Those precedents, however, were never challenged, largely because of the technical difficulties in achieving standing, a problem on which I shall comment later. If they had been challenged, considering the drift of the interpretations of the establishment clause by the Supreme Court over the last fifteen years, I find it difficult to believe that they would have been held constitutional in all their dimensions.

As a practical matter, we cannot really make such distinctions between denominational schools and denominational colleges. Because of this inability to make meaningful distinctions, all that can be done, both as a matter of constitutional interpretation and as a matter of policy, is to draw a line making no distinctions, in the full knowledge that those who follow their religious beliefs to the extent of attending sectarian institutions will have to pay a price for living in our type of society.

The American Civil Liberties Union, which has been regarded as virtually absolutist on the notion of separation, has nevertheless proposed a middle course. It suggests that the question of whether an institution is eligible for aid should depend on three criteria: (1) whether the students and faculty are required to be adherents of the religious groups with which the institution is linked, (2) whether indoctrination in the tenets of the particular faith is a required part of the curriculum, and (3) whether the determination of the instructional program is committed to the hands of those charged with educational or with religious responsibilities. (These criteria, incidentally, are wholly absent from the HEW memorandum.)

This approach troubles me. First of all, it would require a rather close initial examination by the Government into the affairs of each sectarian institution; and once aid is granted, it would require a continuing oversight to see that the criteria are always fulfilled. This returns us to Mr. Howe's question whether, as a matter of wisdom, a religious body should subject itself to that type of scrutiny. It also raises a hard-boiled, practical question—whether, in fact, the secular officials in many communities can provide the kind of inspection and oversight that would be necessary. I do not believe that, even with complete good will on both sides, such an inspection of a large and well-founded parochial-school system could ever be accomplished. On the national level, I do not believe that the commissioner of education, a public appointee, would really want to exercise the power, if he could; and I doubt that a church could or would let him in.

Another problem which concerns me—and which I think is not susceptible of solution—is how to determine whether the allocation of funds for a gymnasium, say, or for textbooks, or for laboratory materials, will not indirectly benefit the religious purpose of a sectarian institution. The religious body undoubtedly has a fixed amount of money to expend for its educational institutions; and any money that is supplied for secular functions will release money for the clearly religious function of the institution. This is indirect aid to religion, and the fact that it is indirect does not stop it from being aid.

The HEW memorandum also dealt with the question of scholarships to deserving students, citing the precedent of the G.I. Bill. I believe that the memorandum talked about $350 scholarships to deserving students. I am inclined to believe that, in this respect, no constitutional question is involved, although nobody seriously doubted that the G.I. Bill grants had an unconstitutional flavor. It seems to me that the HEW proposal did not enter into either constitutional or ideological no man's lands; but there are persons, more absolutist about these matters than I am, who sharply disagree.

The response of the National Catholic Welfare Conference raised a very, very old question of constitutional interpretation. It really, I think, rests on the assumption that the establishment clause means that there shall be no preferential treatment of religion and that it does not demand nontreatment of religion altogether. Edward S. Corwin and other specialized students of the Constitution support this view with considerable cogency. But the opposite view, to the effect that there shall be no support of any religion (as set out in the Everson case and almost all subsequent cases), is equally cogently put forth.

I do not believe that, in either case, an antiquarian examination of constitutional antecedents ought to be the basis on which these matters are decided. We decide what we want ideologically, and we then use history to dress up our opinion. The Constitution always bends to the prevailing ideology. This raises a serious question: should we even attempt to approach this issue as a matter of constitutional interpretation.

Let us remember the histories of previous attempts to pass aid-to-education bills since about the end of World War I: the "Bad" bill, the Black bill and the Bardon bill. The acrimony and dissension which ensued at the introduction of each of these bills must concern any sober student of our society. They point, I think, to the wisdom of a position which resolves the issue by leaving the church entirely to itself and the state entirely to itself.

Let us note a troubling, postwar phenomenon in European countries: the rise of religiously oriented political parties, particularly Roman Catholic political parties, as in France, Italy, Belgium and Germany. And this is not necessarily a European phenomenon. We have recently seen for the first time in our own hemisphere—indeed, in our own protectorate, Puerto Rico—the rise of a political party which is largely religious in orientation, the Citizens for Educational Freedom. In New York City, in 1961, when an election was held to fill the seat of a deceased representative in the borough of Queens, a Republican ran on an aid-to-parochial-schools program and very nearly defeated a Democrat who had been assumed to have a commanding lead.

We dare not, then, say placidly that European history is different from ours and that the terribly divisive conflicts that have arisen in Holland, Belgium and France on this very issue of state aid to religions can never happen here.

Flexibility is the glory of our Constitution, but if we once breach the wall of separation, we will tend inevitably to make the breach wider and wider because there is no logical cut-off point. Anybody who argues for a further change in the constitutional concept will invariably cite this as a precedent and argue that, as a matter of due process or of appropriate exercise of police power, the next breach is justified. Therefore I would reject the position of the HEW memorandum virtually in its entirety, except for the provision allowing individual grants-in-aid to deserving students.

One final word: the problem of achieving standing in the courts, which is important to all of us who would like a clear test of practices in this area, could be met, it seems to me, by allowing the states themselves to make the determinations about aid to denominational institutions. Every one of the fifty states has a clause in its constitution prohibiting grants to an established religion. If a state were unable to withstand the pressures of religious groups and decided to authorize a grant in defiance of its constitution, a challenger would be able for the first time to go into the Federal courts and seek a clear determination of the meaning of the establishment clause in relation to the issues raised in the HEW memorandum.

Monsignor Francis J. Lally
Editor, *The Pilot* (Archdiocese of Boston)

I would like to point up some of the matters already discussed and perhaps introduce some new ones. Certainly, as with Mr. Berlin, I have to make it plain that I do not speak for the Catholic Church but for one small member out of 400,000,000. For all of that, I probably have a few people who share the views that I present.

We ought first to emphasize what Mr. Howe has emphasized very clearly—that this is not a religious issue. In point of fact, the division of opinion in the United States on this topic is not along religious lines. Those who have testified in favor of Federal aid to religious schools include Orthodox Jews and certain Protestant groups—small, to be sure, but large enough to have schools in various parts of the country which feel that they are entitled to Government assistance.

So it seems to me important that we do not draw a spurious line between an imaginary "Catholic position" and "Protestant position." It is not that kind of issue, although a large number of Catho-

lics certainly are on one side of this issue and a large number of
Protestants on the other. Orthodox Jews are, I would say, on the
side of the larger body of Catholics, while Reform and Conservative
Jews are aligned with the larger Protestant group. There is no theological problem involved, and after hearing Mr. Howe analyze the issue,
I am inclined to believe that there is not much of a constitutional
question either. But I am not competent to do more than react to
that.

There is, of course, a very serious question of public policy regarding education: should nonpublic schools be considered part of
the American educational system and so receive some Government
benefits? This is the major question to which we should address our
attention, and we might begin by asking: what is the basis for the
claims of all these nonpublic schools, religious and nonreligious, to
some sort of Government assistance?

First, let us recall that the religious school antedates the public
school in the United States and that, in many ways, the public school
grew out of it. It is common knowledge that during the nineteenth
century, the American public school was almost always distinctly Protestant. Indeed, in the Midwest and the South, the public school is still
easily identified as a Protestant school run under public auspices.

Religion, then, has always had a place in American education,
though perhaps not always the place it should have had; and the
schools of religious origin, some of which later became independent
schools, are part of the American educational structure. If the Government turns its attention to the education of its citizens, it cannot
leave out this numerically large and historically important group of
educational institutions.

Second, the major claim advanced by the nonpublic school is
the fact that it provides a secular education, which has to be described
as a public service. To be sure, the parochial school also supplies
a religious education, but it primarily supplies the regular, compulsory secular education of the American youngster.

The educational crisis in teachers and in classrooms—the crisis
to which President Kennedy made such strong reference when he
submitted his bill and about which educators have been worrying
for a long time—is a threat to the whole population. It is not a
crisis for just the public schools; it is an educational emergency (assuming that it is in fact an emergency) for the whole nation. President
Kennedy summarized it as a need for the pursuit of general excellence,
for "the maximum development of every young American's capacity."

This is everybody's need, not just the need of those who happen to be attending public schools.

Catholics, to mention the largest group attending nonpublic schools, are presently educating almost 13 per cent of the total school population in the United States. (This figure includes higher education.) If, in the pursuit of the maximum development of every young American's capacity, the Government immediately excludes a significant percentage of these young Americans, it seems to me that it is merely sabotaging the very point it is trying to develop.

In parochial schools, religion is taught in addition to the secular subjects that are taught in the regular public schools. Catholics plainly have a philosophy of education; they feel that religious principles and religious ideals permeate not only a course in Christian doctrine, or liturgy, or theology, or whatever title you may choose to give it, but permeate the student's whole existence and should be the background against which even secular subjects are taught. However, I myself cannot understand how a school could have, for example, a Catholic language program. There is not a Catholic French and a French French, a Catholic German and a German German.

In the same way, there is not a Catholic mathematics and a secular mathematics. The addition problem which Mr. Howe mentioned strikes me as a matter of the school's bad taste and, perhaps, bad education, rather than a matter of religion. If you add up three bishops and a cardinal, what you are likely to get is an argument because you probably cannot find three or four that get along together on anything.

I think that the students who are exposed to this kind of instruction are exposed to a good deal of ineffective indoctrination in vocabulary, but I would not call it religion. And I am inclined to believe that parochial-school instruction in all of the courses that the Government now supports—science, languages, physical education and so on—is specifically secular and that no efforts by any of us could possibly turn it into sectarian presentations.

Third, there is the fact that a vast number of schools for "exceptional" children are run under Catholic auspices. This includes schools for handicapped children, deaf and dumb children and youngsters with cerebral palsy. We feel that these schools provide a significant public service and deserve some assistance.

Fourth and last, it is worth considering, as a matter of the public welfare, that Catholic schools and institutions of higher learning involve a very large annual expenditure; in 1961 the total was approximately $1.8-billion. It is not important, so far as principle is concerned, whether the figure was $1 million or $1.8 billion, but I think it is very important to realize the size of the contribution that Catholic schools are making to the educational effort in America. All the resources of our country should be used to keep all our schools advancing, consonant with our pluralistic traditions.

In this connection we might consider as another parallel effort—hospital aids. The Federal Government supplies a good deal of funds for private hospitals. Catholics do not operate the majority of the sectarian hospitals in the United States; most are under Protestant auspices. And the Government does supply a vast amount of funds, both for building and for maintaining these hospitals. Ironically, some of this legislation was passed at the request of the Baptists, who are the strongest advocates of the separation of church and state. It seems to me that if it is possible to distinguish between the secular and religious functions of a hospital—to be sure that public funds are not going, for example, to the chapel or to provide statues in the corridors—it should also be possible to make this distinction in a school operation. Catholics have been accepting hospital-aid funds on this basis from the Federal Government for a great many years, and so have an assortment of twenty or more Protestant sects.

Catholic schools and institutions of higher learning are already sharing Federal aid under several programs. The HEW report mentioned forty-one religious institutions that are now receiving Federal loans. Catholic institutions are being aided through scholarships, tuition payments and tax benefits. They participate in the College Housing Act, the Surplus Property Act, the National Defense Education Act and so on. As a general rule, so far as the secular aspects—the so-called neutral items—are concerned, church-related schools are receiving funds for substantially the same purposes as public schools. The corollary to this, which I think is mentioned in the bishops' [Conference] memorandum, is that the Government should never be asked to bear—and should never bear—the complete cost of maintaining nonpublic schools. It should contribute only to those operations that can be determined as secular.

I want to say one last word about the position held by the majority of Catholics. They have experienced what they call an evolution, but what others might call an about-face, in regard to Federal aid. When I was young, Federal aid was considered a very bad thing; Catholics were sure that they would not accept it under any circumstances. They took for granted that control of the purse means control of policy. However, this concept has evolved in the minds of some members of the hierarchy, and these men now seem willing to accept certain auxiliary aids—the most familiar of which, I suppose, are the school-lunch program and bus transportation.

At the present time, the official presentation of the Catholic Church to the Congress is summed up in this tenet: if education is to be assisted by the Federal Government, all children should be included. It would be a grave mistake to think that this represents the position of all the bishops, many of whom have taken pains to point out that it does not. Cardinal Cushing of Boston, for example, has said that he would never, under any circumstances, accept loans of any kind for building schools or for paying teachers' salaries; the most he would ever accept would be certain auxiliary aids. Cardinal Ritter of St. Louis has said that he believes no Federal aid of any kind should be given, since the Federal Government does not belong in the educational picture; education, he believes, should be left to the states. Certain other bishops also have their own points of view. But the bishops have agreed to present to the Congress, through their spokesmen, the proposition that if the Federal Government is entering into this field, it should do so in a manner which would assist all the children in the United States.

Let me conclude with four propositions which I have stolen from somebody else—I think it might be the bishops' memorandum—which seem to me to sum up the consensus of most Catholics on this issue. *First,* a parent may choose to have his child educated under religious auspices or in public schools, according to his disposition, as long as the schools selected are state-approved, having fulfilled the requirements of the state education laws. *Second,* the Government cannot impose a single school system upon the country. There must always be room for private endeavor in this regard. *Third,* education is a public function, whether it is carried on in church-related or in public schools. And *finally,* schools can be aided to the extent—and only to the extent—that they perform a public function.

SUMMARY OF THE DISCUSSION

The tone of the general discussion was characterized by Mr. Harris in a remark at the close of the session: "This has been very interesting—and certainly most unheated, considering the issues at stake." Within this atmosphere of controlled but insistent controversy, questions of deep-reaching importance were examined, though not resolved.

Public policy or constitutional law? Mr. Howe initiated the discussion by deploring Americans' "tendency to turn every question of public policy into a question of constitutional law." The implication of his protest, though he did not spell it out, was that policy can and should remain flexible; it loses this flexibility if each separate policy decision must be made rigid and binding as a definitive interpretation of the Constitution. Certainly there are issues which demand such interpretation, but other issues do not. On federal aid, for example, he would generally agree with Monsignor Lally on the question of law and with Mr. Berlin on the question of public policy. "The perplexing problem is to determine the point at which an argument of policy should be translated into an argument of constitutional law."

The prevailing opinion, he noted, in American life and in the present Supreme Court, is that "if one feels strongly about a policy, one should put his position in constitutional terms. The reasoning is that constitutional law is made by turning important contemporary policy into rules of law. I still gag a little over this attitude toward constitutional questions. It may be politically accurate, and this is in fact what Americans do. I just wish they did not do it."

One of the difficulties in constitutional law in the area of Federal aid is the apparent self-contradiction in the First Amendment, which Mr. Howe had illuminated. Another participant returned to this problem: "The amendment says, on the one hand, that the Government must ignore the fact that the religious group exists. On the other hand, it says that the Government must recognize that the religious group exists and must clearly separate the activities of the group from those of the state." (The relevant part of the First Amendment reads: "Congress shall make no law respecting an establishment of religion, or prohibiting the free exercise thereof.")

Another difficulty to be kept in mind, said Mr. Berlin, is "the danger of the thin edge of the wedge. Once Federal aid is admitted under constitutional law, there is no end. No fixed line can be drawn; it will always be redrawn. I do not know where this will come to rest except in the sort of dissention that has resulted in France and Holland. I do not want to see the day when that happens in America."

To this Monsignor Lally responded: "Redrawing lines is part of democratic life; but we can at least draw a line for this moment in time, and we can build-in safety catches so that it cannot be moved until we change our minds. As for the stresses in some European countries, a vast number of factors totally unrelated to education have gone into their making. Moreover, the so-called Christian Democratic movement which was felt so strongly in Europe after the war was not a sectarian expression; it was an expression of a Christian ideal, which was not specifically Catholic. Many Catholics are involved in these parties, but membership in the Church is not required. The parties are not sectarian in any sense."

Two examples of the difficulty of drawing a fixed line were mentioned briefly. (1) Some observers argue that there is a constitutional difference between grants and loans to religious schools, reasoning that since loans are repaid, they do not constitute an outright aid to religion. Mr. Howe described this as "a rather shady line." (2) The HEW memorandum was conditioned by the fact that denominational colleges and universities were already sharing Federal aid under a number of programs. "Not only in education but in many other areas," said Mr. Howe, "we find aid being given to religion in ways that we tolerate and permit. Some people, including Justice Douglas, would say that all these aids must go. But they are not politically likely to go; and while they continue, it is hard to pretend that there are absolute barriers to any kind of aid."

While some persons find the First Amendment too easily breached, others find it too restrictive. The Supreme Court's decision in the school-prayer case of 1962, said Mr. Berlin, evoked serious attempts to amend the establishment clause in order to lower permanently the wall of separation. He cited in particular the efforts of Bishop James A. Pike of the Protestant Episcopal Church and Cardinal Spellman of the Roman Catholic Church.

Turning from constitutional law to congressional legislation, Monsignor Lally noted that "although the bishops have taken a position before the Congress on the issue of Federal aid, some bishops have said publicly that Catholics should not attempt to exert massive pressure on legislators in order to circumvent an unwilling public. The policy should depend on the American climate, on the way Americans want their school systems to be run. Catholics, as part of the American scene, should do all they can to persuade their neighbors of the validity of their position. If they fail now, they should keep trying and not use political pressure until it comes spontaneously from the people."

One of the immediate difficulties, he agreed, is to persuade the non-Catholic community that, despite the philosophy of education of the church, there is a clear and definable difference in instruction between the secular and nonsecular subjects. This might be achieved, said Monsignor Lally, in two ways: by using the same textbooks as local public schools for secular subjects and/or by accepting the conditions proposed by the American Civil Liberties Union, which Mr. Berlin had cited. "Those conditions seem to me a bother, perhaps, but no more; certainly not an affliction. As for the kind of childish indoctrination which some Catholic educators have allowed themselves, I think there are ways of making it plain that this is not part of the philosophy of Catholic education at all. It merely represents certain mannerisms—and, I would say, mannerisms in bad taste—that have crept into the situation."

Questioned about the role of Catholics in the defeat of recent Federal-aid-to-education bills, he answered that a general impression to this effect is inaccurate. "Catholics had no such power, either numerically or in their influence on the Congress. The 1961 bill, for example, was defeated by a combination of groups which—in combination, if not individually—are considerably more persuasive in those halls than the Catholic Church. These included the National Association of Manufacturers, the U. S. Chamber of Commerce, a strong coalition of Southern senators and congressmen, and a large number of conservative members of Congress. This combination, along with the Catholic spokesmen, defeated the bills."

Reminded that there were eighty Catholic congressmen in 1961, he replied: "Yes, and some voted differently from the Church on this matter and have publicly taken a position different from that of the hierarchy."

The need for greater public discussion was emphasized by another participant, who called for a mature, two-sided conversation between Protestants and Catholics on the broad question of religious education. The fact that there is no such conversation at present, he said, reveals "our basic lack of maturity." To this Monsignor Lally assented: "I think we have a long way to go toward that ideal of a mature conversation."

Proposed solutions: Three possible solutions to the immediate problem of Federal aid were suggested. The first, which was championed by Edward C. Banfield, professor of government at Harvard University, was that the government—local, state or Federal—provide direct scholarships to every student, rather than invest the money in free public schools. The public authorities, under this plan, would continue to set minimum standards for all schools, including such matters as curriculum and teacher qualification. Nonpublic schools are already, of course, under such regulation. The public authorities would also decide how much of public funds should be invested in education per student. This amount—say, $500 a year—would be made available as a credit to the parents, who would then be free to enroll the student in any school of their choice.

Theoretically, parents might decide to use their credits to maintain the public schools, but this is quite unlikely. Most discussants took it for granted the plan would result in the creation of many new and varied private schools, both secular and religious. In economic terms, this would replace government, allocation of resources with a free-market approach designed to maximize consumer satisfaction. An incidental benefit of the plan is that it would probably increase the total amount of national resources devoted to education, since many parents would probably decide to supplement the government credit out of their own income in order to provide a finer quality of schooling for their children.

"As far as I can tell," said one discussant, "this plan offers no policy or legal difficulties. And it seems to me that the relationship between church and state does not enter into this plan at all." He turned out to be quite wrong.

Three major objections to the plan were expressed. *First,* "The American people," said Monsignor Lally, "have a healthy concern for the public school as an institution in American life and for the contribution that it makes to the democratic way of living." Evidence of this is the fact, adduced by Mr. Harris, that while up to 10 per cent of non-Catholic families with incomes over $10,000 can afford to send their children to private schools, even while paying local school taxes, only 1 or 2 per cent actually do so. (Approximately half of all Catholic children in America go to parochial schools.)

Mr. Banfield pointed out, however, that "a homogeneous upper-class community insures, through the instrumentality of its local government, that the public schools will provide the kind of service which it would get from private schools."

Second, one participant questioned the assumption that it is more democratic to be able to choose one's own school. The actual effect might well be antidemocratic, since the class strata would be defined and isolated at a much earlier age. Today class distinctions tend to become rigid as students enter college, largely because different colleges feed their graduates into the economy at different levels of status and income. If the public schools are weakened or eliminated, these distinctions will be made at much younger ages, before the children have any wider experience. Scholarships might boost a few talented children over these class lines, but the problem would remain for the society as a whole.

Third, the constitutional objection can still be raised that the scholarships would constitute indirect aid to religion, since they would release funds that the churches had earmarked for educational uses. Monsignor Lally suggested that this argument is specious, since in practice, churches spend their money first on their religious needs and then use what remains for the secular aspects of their educational programs. The scholarships would strengthen the language and science courses; the chapels would be built anyway. He noted that exemption from taxation might also be considered unconstitutional aid, if the same objection is logically applied, "but in my judgment that goes beyond the bounds of common sense."

Two other possible solutions to the problem of Federal aid were also discussed. (1) Federal funds might be given to the states, who would then disburse the aid to public and nonpublic schools. This would interpose a barrier between the Federal Government and the schools, but the effect would simply be to raise the same question at the state level. Most states, said Mr. Howe, have stricter constitutional prohibitions on aid to religion than is implied by the First Amendment, so aid might well be blocked rather than facilitated under this plan. Mr. Berlin indicated that it might at least cure the problem of standing; Mr. Howe suggested that simpler means have already been found, such as writing provisions for standing into the aid-to-education bills.

"In any case," said Mr. Howe, "members of Congress who do not want aid given to religious schools would want to know, before appropriating funds, whether any given state planned to release Federal funds to parochial schools. They are not going to vote an appropriation and look the other way."

(2) Public and nonpublic institutions might be formally affiliated so that a student could take secular courses in one and religious training, if he wishes, in the other. In higher education, this plan has been established at the University of Toronto, which is an affiliation of four colleges, three religious and one public. The degree each student earns from the university thus represents his education in the public college and often in one or more of the religious colleges. "If we can multiply something like this at the college level," said one discussant, "where it would be simplest to operate, where the need for courses in religion is very strongly felt and where parental

opposition would be minimal, we might be able to use it for leverage in secondary schools."

Other objections to Federal aid: The proposed solutions, then, evoked a number of objections to Federal aid to religious schools. Three additional objections were raised independently. *First,* such aid would inevitably break up the public school system. To this Monsignor Lally replied in two, apparently conflicting, ways. He first said, "I think that the American public school is so solid that good public schools will attract students, no matter how many private schools we have. They are that much of an American institution." Later, however, a discussant asked him directly, "Can we legitimately use public funds to fractionalize public education?" He then replied, "We do not have a monolithic school system; we have a pluralistic school system—private, religiously affiliated and public. Since it is already very much divided, we have nothing to break up."

Second, Federal aid to parochial schools would often be an economic waste. Even today, in many smaller communities, the youngsters enrolled in parochial schools could easily be absorbed into the public schools. The very existence of two parallel systems in these communities entails a duplication of resources, which Federal aid would only make worse. Monsignor Lally acknowledged the problem but laid the blame on lack of communication. "In many cities the public schools and the parochial schools do their planning quite separately, with the result that a great deal of space in public school is wasted." As for Federal aid in building parochial schools, he said, "there would have to be some sort of population formula to determine the point where a new school would be economically viable, where it would pay for itself."

Third, a discussant stated his general impression that educational standards are significantly lower in parochial schools than in public schools. When, as often happens, the parochial schools have more applicants than they can accept, they take the best and shunt the less able back to the public schools. This seems to assure the community that many of its most promising youngsters will receive the worst education. Does it make sense to use Federal aid to reinforce such a practice?

Monsignor Lally dissented from both assumptions. In choosing students, "it is inevitable that school administrators and school teachers, in their less idealistic moments, prefer bright youngsters to those who are not quite so bright. But the Church tries to be cautious in this regard. It is interested in the education of students at all

levels of ability, since each is a human soul in the eyes of the Church."
As for the quality of parochial education, his own experience suggests
that it is about on a par with that in public schools.

He pointed out, however, that if both assumptions in the objection were correct—if parochial-school education were inferior and
if the brightest students were attending parochial schools—that would
seem to indicate that Federal aid is needed urgently to improve the
secular education given in parochial schools.

Two barriers to Federal aid in general, apart from the religious
issues, were mentioned very hastily. Mr. Harris noted "the antispend-
ing attitude of the Congress, which was very important in defeating
the aid-to-education bills. It probably influenced many more congressmen than did the constitutional questions." And Mr. Howe called
attention to the impact Federal aid would have on America's race
problem. "To the extent that we give Federal aid to private schools,
we will encourage the creation of racially segregated private schools,
especially in the South. This will undermine our efforts to desegregate
public schools; it will provide a line of defense for Southern resistance.
For that reason, among others, I would be hesitant about giving
strong support now to Federal aid."

3. The Federal Government and Higher Education

Logan Wilson
President, American Council on Education

More than five generations have passed since the Federal Government first concerned itself with education. During that period Federal involvement has become established beyond any question. It is thus absurd to ask (as many people are asking) whether the Federal Government should become involved in education. There is nothing absurd, however, about the need to reexamine continually the nature and extent of the involvement.

At the level of higher education, this need is urgent, for the interdependence of the Federal Government and higher education is both inevitable and accelerating. In 1776 there were only nine institutions of higher learning in America; today there are more than 2,000. Our history attests the vital role which colleges and universities have played in assuring the nation's security and progress, and our present circumstances magnify rather than diminish that role. Since the final responsibility for our collective security and welfare can reside only in the Federal Government, a close partnership between the Government and higher education is essential. Our present task, it seems to me, is to make this partnership as effective as possible.

Noting one aspect of this relationship, President Eisenhower's Science Advisory Committee stated in 1960: "The partnership is a fact. It has done much more good than harm. It seems certain to grow in importance unless the American people decide to accept a second-rate standing in terms of power, of comfort, of knowledge." The committee's report then set forth some guidelines for the advancement of science: it urged the nation to give Federal support for excellence, to increase the number of first-rate teaching and research centers, to attract more talented students into science, to encourage the study of new fields of knowledge and so on. Fortunately, many of these guidelines for the development of science are now being followed extensively.

Unfortunately, the need for comparable guiding principles for Federal participation in the development of higher education as a whole has not been widely recognized. In some quarters there is still a strong sentiment that our colleges and universities should function strictly as local, state and private enterprises. Those who hold this view are often unaware that the Federal Government already has a heavy commitment in certain sectors of higher education. Even in Washington—as the piecemeal, *ad hoc* pattern of Federal programs suggests—there is reluctance to face up to the implications of this permanent and growing partnership.

Congress has, to be sure, evidenced specific concerns. The keen legislative interest in what medical-school research can do for the bodies of the elderly is an obvious example. (There is apparently less interest in what liberal-arts colleges can do for the minds of the young.) Various Federal agencies have also been explicit about the missions or tasks which they have wanted colleges and universities to perform for them. And this interest in narrow projects works both ways: various segments of higher education have worked energetically to promote Federal aid for their particular objectives. As a result, Federal participation in higher education is badly fragmented.

The most pressing need today, therefore, is for a comprehensive view of the partnership and a unified approach toward its future growth. President Kennedy's proposals on education reached in this direction. Their goals were to expand individual opportunities, to improve quality on all levels and to strengthen vocational, special and continuing education. President Kennedy did not advocate that the Federal Government take over local responsibilities; but he did contend that state, local and private efforts no longer suffice. The main principle which he laid down regarding Federal participation was that it "should be selective, stimulative and, where possible, transitional." Although these proposals may for now be politically inexpedient and may not be quickly translated into law, there can be no question about the wisdom of this attempt to view comprehensively the needs of our entire educational system.

Before we can decide how the Federal Government shall act most appropriately and effectively in this area, we must agree upon basic principles and establish clear guidelines for action. This is a task for Congress, the Administration, leading educators and other national spokesmen. However, acknowledging my temerity, I shall take the liberty of venturing my own tentative views in the form of six basic principles. These are drawn mainly from my experience with the American Council on Education, which frequently mediates between the Federal Government, on the one hand, and higher education, on the other. These principles reflect my own observations; they do not necessarily represent the council's position. I offer them, not in the expectation that they will be immediately and widely endorsed, but in the hope that they may help the educational community to reach more quickly its own consensus.

The first principle: the national interest. In assisting higher education, the Federal Government should make the national interest, rather than local or special interests, paramount. To fulfill its responsibilities, the Federal Government must seek to extend educational opportunity, promote economic growth, upgrade manpower, undergird our security and advance our collective well-being. It must insure that individuals are educated for useful citizenship, as well as for the furtherance of their private goals. Colleges and universities are essential to the achievement of all these objectives, as well as their own special and distinctive ends.

It would be a mistake, however, to assume that all institutions of higher learning and all educational objectives are equally important to the national welfare and hence equally deserving of Federal support. It is undoubtedly important to increase the number and geographic spread of first-rate teaching and research centers, but it would be preposterous to withhold Federal research and development funds from our present first-rate institutions and to spread those funds thinly among a large number of other institutions whose aspirations often exceed their capabilities. The wastage entailed in such an indiscriminate, across-the-board doling out of Federal money would be appalling.

On the other hand, even our greatest institutions, which are truly national and even international in their service, render services to special constituencies which seem to me inappropriate for Federal support. The house system at Harvard, for example, provides a fine environment for undergraduate learning, but the expense entailed is certainly beyond what the Federal Government should be expected to underwrite. Similarly, there are many subjects in addition to theology which have no valid claim to Federal support.

Few, if any, of our colleges and universities were founded with the national interest primarily in view. (The military academies at

West Point and Annapolis are the only long-standing institutions having this original purpose.) However, in a society as mobile and interdependent as ours, the Federal Government must promote the national interest by assisting educational endeavors of national importance—regardless of their original purpose—for which local, state or private support is either lacking or insufficient. This may mean placing an expensive scientific installation, such as a particle accelerator, on the campus of a single university which already possesses great human and material resources. It also may mean special assistance to poor states whose inadequate schools depress the level of our national manpower resources.

Federal aid should not be offered to any segment of the population merely to ease the burden of carrying local or special obligations. When the national interest is not being adequately served, however, I believe that there is no substitute for Federal concern and support.

The second principle: resource development. Federal assistance should be conceived not as a form of benevolence to institutions and individuals but as an investment in a national resource. Colleges, universities and students should not be aided merely because they are needy; Federal support is warranted only by their potential contribution to our collective achievement as a people.

According to one analysis, which President Kennedy reported to the Congress, some 40 per cent of the nation's growth in economic productivity in recent years can be attributed to education. He dramatized the cost of inadequate education by pointing out that one year's income lost as a result of unemployment is more than the total cost of twelve years of education through high school. Other studies have demonstrated convincingly the greater earning power and productivity of the college-trained.

A brochure by the American Council on Education, *Higher Education as a National Resource,* states this case for Federal concern: "American higher education is a priceless asset fundamental to the national purpose. It cannot be spoken of simply in terms of the value of buildings and equipment, the total number of persons served, the teachers involved, or the research performed. The nation's colleges and junior colleges, universities, research institutes, and professional schools are all of these things, but something more. Broadly conceived, higher education constitutes a precious national resource essential to the achievement of great national goals and to the achievement of worthy aspirations of individual citizens. It is a resource also in the sense that, given favorable conditions, it is as capable of self-renewal as is a properly conserved forest."

In view of the growing pressures on higher education—the pressures of enrollment increases and new knowledge—and in view of the tax-revenue limitations of localities and states, together with the declining proportion of total support from private sources, how can one escape the conclusion that the Federal Government must assume a larger role in the conservation and improvement of higher education?

Furthermore, while all regions of our country have great potential human resources, the means to develop those resources through higher education are very unevenly distributed. Financial stringency makes it especially difficult for institutions in some states and regions to give adequate support to graduate and professional education, and the problem is complicated further by the siphoning-off of talent to more prosperous sections. The result is a tragic and perhaps dangerous waste of human capabilities.

The expansion and improvement of higher education are too vital to our future to be left entirely in the hands of local and private enterprise. Adequate financial support for colleges and universities must be regarded as a funding operation rather than a relief measure, and the cost must be treated as an investment in human capital rather than an ordinary expenditure. The investment required is indeed a heavy one, but not nearly so heavy as the penalties we and oncoming generations will have to pay if we fail to conserve and strengthen this critical national resource.

The third principle: priority planning. If the Federal Government is not to assume the whole burden of support for higher education, its allocations must be based on clear priorities. But priorities are not universally desired. Although colleges and universities are accustomed to getting their state and private moneys with strings attached, some of them are impatient for substantial Federal grants which they can spend as they please. Other parties, eager to spread decision making, would prefer to have Congress apportion funds to the fifty states for internal allocations. Still others would have the Federal Government resort to simple formulas for spreading funds everywhere.

In my judgment, these schemes are neither practicable nor desirable. These are Federal funds, and the priorities—by levels, institutions, programs and projects—must be set at the Federal level. However, a more suitable pattern can surely be found than the one now resulting from our piecemeal approach. The first requisite is a meeting of minds between Government and education about priorities of importance and urgency.

For example, it seems to me that Federal aid is more necessary for higher education than for elementary and secondary schools. This is not to say that higher education is more directly related to the national interest or that its needs are more urgent. Admittedly, more dollars are needed to bolster primary and secondary education. At those levels, however, local concern, understanding and support are strongest; we pride ourselves on the fact that our public schools are community-centered enterprises.

Our colleges and universities, on the other hand, have always had a different structure of support and control. Their constituencies are more widely dispersed; political and geographical boundary lines are less relevant to the services they perform; and their policies are much less susceptible to uniformization. Furthermore, lesser sums of money are required in higher education to produce stimulative or multiplier effects in response to changing national needs. While Federal support is needed at all levels of education, it seems apparent that colleges and universities should have priority.

Priorities are also needed among the academic disciplines. Art and philosophy may be more essential to a liberal education than astronomy and engineering, but is this a valid reason for expecting the Federal Government to support all aspects of the curriculum? In my opinion, it is the responsibility of individual institutions to maintain balance in education and to resist or countervail influences to the contrary. But it is equally true that institutions cannot maintain this balance successfully unless the Government underwrites the full costs of Federal projects in high-priority disciplines. At present the Government is not only falling short of meeting institutional indirect costs on research projects; it is also not reimbursing out-of-pocket local costs for ROTC, international education programs and various other services which institutions are preforming for Federal agencies.

Working through voluntary associations such as the American Council on Education, colleges and universities are trying to define their own priorities of importance and urgency. But we are still a long way from a consensus among all concerned as to which investments will be of maximum benefit to both the Federal Government and higher education.

The fourth principle: complementarity. Federal aid should strengthen diversity of support and control, and it should complement rather than supplant local effort. The American system of higher education has great strengths which should be proudly maintained. The dualism of public and private institutions, for instance, reinforces the pluralism of our culture; and the diversity of sources of financial support protects higher education as a whole from the domination of extraneous influences. The tradition of autonomous governance of colleges and universities and the wide variation in their aims and scope foster a free competition in the advancement of knowledge which is of inestimable value to a dynamic society.

Federal aid has been opposed on the grounds that it weakens this diversity of support and control. It seems to me that quite the opposite is true. Wisely and fairly distributed, Federal funds add another element to the mixed pattern of support which is beneficial to all institutions, public and private. This can be insured in most situations by linking Federal aid to incentives for increased local and private support. (I am cognizant of the difficulties inherent in matching requirements, and I do favor outright grants for certain kinds of aid.)

Politics and education are becoming inseparable, and it is up to us to make the most of this fact of modern life. Past experience alone should remove any fear that Federal support necessarily carries with it Federal control. My own dealings with state legislatures, private donors and the Federal Government confirm McGeorge Bundy's observation that Federal support has been and can continue to be "a reinforcement of the freedom of the higher learning." Our task is to see that Federal aid offsets the shortcomings of the American system of higher education and builds upon its strengths.

The fifth principle: merit. Although Federal assistance will be needed to increase the availability of higher education, it will be needed even more to improve quality. In the long run, quantity and quality are not conflicting objectives; but in the short run there is no doubt that advocates of expansion and of improvement will compete strenuously for whatever funds are available. Since egalitarian sentiments—and the heaviest local pressure—will probably tip the scale toward expansion at the expense of improvement, only a discriminating use of Federal allocations can assure that standards are maintained and strengthened. All things considered, Government money will produce the best results if it is concentrated primarily on institutions which have demonstrated merit.

How is merit to be determined? Despite occasional charges of bias and favoritism against Government agencies which use panels of experts to help them allocate funds, that procedure seems to me the only appropriate one in many cases. The National Science Foundation, for example, utilizes advisory panels drawn from the academic community itself, and its procedures closely approximate those used on most college and university campuses to allocate institutional funds.

Conversely, Federal funds will not produce the best results if they are given as subsidies for budget-balancing purposes to institutions perennially on the verge of bankruptcy or to institutions with overly ambitious ventures. As a current example, Title IV of the National Defense Education Act seems to me misconceived in providing support only for new and expanded graduate programs. It is, in effect, an encouragement to vertical and horizontal expansion, with no incentive for strengthening existing programs.

Too many states are already suffering the unfortunate consequences of the so-called university syndrome—the insatiable desire of junior colleges to become senior colleges and of four-year institutions to become universities. There is nothing wrong per se with such aspirations, but in the process of change, some institutions are transmogrified rather than transmuted. The nation has no need for more second- and third-rate institutions at any level, but it does have a desperate need for more first-rate centers at all levels. We cannot afford to value quantity above quality in higher education.

The sixth principle: coordination. Federal assistance should be guided by a long-range plan for the most logical development of the American system of higher education as an entity. There is now too much unplanned diversification among our colleges and universities. We really have no system of higher education in the strict sense of the term; we have merely a congeries of institutions. Some regions have too many institutions, often indiscriminately established and inadequately maintained, while in other regions there is a dearth of colleges and universities. The presence of "diploma mills" in many states demonstrates the ease with which almost anybody can get into the business of higher education.

Decentralization has its virtues—and its defects. Our heralded "rich diversity" of higher education is at times a poor divisiveness.

Disparate educational endeavors do not produce the total endeavor required to meet our national needs, and the unevenness of educational opportunity limits the entire nation's manpower potential. Just as we can no longer afford to behave as a mere federation of states in international affairs, so can we ill afford to continue fragmented educational policies and practices in an era of increased interdependence within the nation. The costs of unilateral action have become too high and the penalties of wasteful competition too great.

In view of our changed circumstances, we should not expect the Federal Government merely to underwrite the status quo in higher education. Both our institutions and our Government must aim for higher and better things. There must be more institutional cooperation and unity of effort, and these must be guided by a sense of common purpose. We are fortunate in being one of the few modern nations whose educational establishment is not controlled by a government ministry. Lacking this central direction of enterprise, however, we must demonstrate that cooperation, no less than coercion, can bring us together and accomplish national objectives. Organizations concerned with state, regional and national cooperation have already emerged, and some states and regions now have long-range plans. It remains for us to develop some plan for the nation as a whole.

The American Council on Education is moving in this direction. Through our Commission on Federal Relations and our Commission on Plans and Objectives for Higher Education, we are addressing ourselves to the kinds of questions which must be answered, and we are calling upon the most knowledgeable persons we can bring together to promote a better partnership between the Federal Government and higher education. As the major organization of colleges, universities and other associations in the field of higher education, we are making every effort to formulate proper guidelines and get widespread acceptance of them.

We are moving ahead as promptly as we can, in the full knowledge that the actions of Congress and of more than four Federal agencies are already making national policies and setting directions which affect the future of American higher education. In our view, there is no longer an option in educational circles between institutional laissez faire and coordinated enterprise. Each institution should have its own sense of public mission, of course, but the educational community as a whole has a right and a responsibility to share with the Government in the determination of policies and directions that will, as much as any other factors, shape our whole future.

COMMENT BY . . . *Vernon Alden*

> President, Ohio University; Former Associate
> Dean, Harvard University Business School, and
> Associate Director, School for College Presidents

Let me begin by observing that my first year or so as a college president has been very instructive. For years I've sat in Mr. Harris' seminars—and even helped to plan some—in which we talked about the problems of Federal aid. We talked about the same problems in our various seminars for new college presidents and academic deans and trustees. I assure you that it is quite different being actually on the firing line in an institution that is growing very, very rapidly.

In the next ten years, Ohio University will have to admit as many students as it has admitted in the last 159 years of its history. This is one of the things that keeps me awake at night—worrying about where we are going to get the funds, the physical facilities and especially the new faculty members to support this rapid expansion. These problems are the same, of course, for all the other public institutions in this country. There is, though, one personal difference: I am one of the few state university presidents who are young enough to have to live with our own decisions for the next fifteen years. When I talk about 1980, I have to be sure that my forecasts are reasonably accurate and that the decisions I make today are fairly sound, because I will hopefully be around and responsible then.

I would like to offer just three comments on the question at hand. First, I think that Federal aid to higher education—and certainly Federal *concern* about higher education—may help institutions of higher learning across the country in important ways, apart from providing the money we need. Those who work at Harvard and Radcliffe and certain other institutions in the Northeast tend to take for granted some things that cannot be taken for granted elsewhere. For example, at some institutions around the country, institutions which have fairly good reputations, people do not really believe fully in academic freedom. They do not really believe in having faculty members take responsibility for educational planning at the institution. They do not have sufficient courage to allow controversial speakers to come onto the campus and say what they wish. I have been involved in some of these problems, and I find that a number of university presidents really do not share my point of view on these issues.

One reason may be that there is fear, in some public institutions, of the reactions of provincial legislators or of people in the local community. If we bring a national point of view to bear on some of these problems, I think we can set these local pressures in perspective. We may be able to strengthen some of the administrators and trustees and others who are responsible for substantial institutions of higher learning—people who are now afraid to make some of these fundamental decisions in the direction of academic freedom. Federal concern about higher education may thus help to build into these institutions some qualities that we take for granted in the Ivy League institutions.

The second point I wish to make concerns the fear that Federal aid will mean Federal control over higher education. This danger has been discussed so intensively for so long that, in my judgment, legislators and administrators in Washington, as well as other thoughtful people around the country, share our concern. They are just as fearful of Federal control over higher education as faculty members and college administrators are.

Furthermore, having worked as president of a public institution, I find that some of my own fears—about control by the legislative body, pressure from rural legislators and pressure from strong editors of metropolitan newspapers—are not as well-founded as I had thought. I have encountered no more pressure from legislators at Ohio than I had from alumni and business corporations when I worked at Brown, Northwestern and the Harvard Business School. Public institutions have the same ability and, I think, the same responsibility to rebuff efforts at control by those offering gifts with strings attached.

My third and last point is that Federal aid to higher education will come eventually. It is already overdue. Many of us administrators have had to sneak Federal aid in through the back door in order to secure some of the funds we need to prepare for the enrollment bulge we shall be facing during the next ten years. Few people in legislative bodies recognize, for example, that to recruit able faculty members requires a long lead time. We talk about the population bulge of 1965, and legislators say, "All right, in 1965 we'll provide the money you need." They do not realize that we need to hire the faculty members a few years in advance. And they do not recognize that such things as sabbatical leaves and opportunities for research are important even in a state university.

During my first year at Ohio, I used Federal money to try to build up the faculty that we need for 1965. I did this by embarking on some new overseas programs with Federal funds. In 1958 my predecessor, John Baker, opened a teacher-training program in Nigeria sponsored by Ohio University with AID funds. This program had been so successful that I felt that we could undertake additional programs. So we expanded very substantially our existing AID-sponsored programs in Nigeria; and we moved into Northern Nigeria, where there are 18 million people with a literacy rate of 9 per cent. We also moved into Southeast Asia with a big program to help the universities in Vietnam with curriculum development and with economical construction of physical facilities. We have also been involved in building an engineering school in Pnom-Penh, Cambodia.

We are in these programs because we want to be helpful to these developing nations, but we have some personal reasons as well. From now through about 1970, we shall have roughly $20 million in AID contracts. With this Federal money, it has been possible for me to give quasi-sabbatical leaves to some of the faculty members who have taught for many, many years at the undergraduate level and have not done the research they should have been doing. (Ohio does not give sabbatical leaves.) Granted, they will be doing some teaching on these AID projects, but it is a different kind of teaching, and they will have a very different kind of experience. They will come back—this has already been demonstrated—enriched by their experience, and this cannot help but rub off in the classroom.

So a great many of our first-rate faculty members are now in Southeast Asia or in Africa, and I have recruited some very able young people to take their places. By the time our veteran faculty members return, two or three or four years from now, we will have state appropriations to sustain this larger faculty. We will also have a larger student body generating more tuition money. By using Federal money, we have given ourselves lead time to get ready. Without this Federal aid, we could not possibly have the faculty that we shall need then; the state has simply not granted us the money soon enough.

I think some other institutions are also sneaking in Federal aid through the back door to strengthen their faculty ranks, and I know that many are looking forward to Federal money to help us meet the desperate need for physical facilities. I am quite sure that there is a general agreement among educators on the desirability of Federal aid. Now we have the massive task of educating the American public and legislators; it will be no mean task to persuade people all around the country to support this idea. I suspect that a massive newspaper campaign will have to be launched. Above all, I think that we must demonstrate to the public the very close link between the country's economic development and its investment in higher education.

COMMENT BY . . . *General James McCormack*
                                    Vice President, Massachusetts Institute of
                                    Technology

My remarks can be most usefully aimed, I think, at the somewhat narrow concern of Federal programs in research in universities, particularly those in the physical sciences and engineering. On this front, the difficult thing to realize is the scale effect—or what I have sometimes called the size effect—of these funds in their impact on higher education. Higher education in science and engineering would really be flat on its back without massive Federal support. I am not passing judgment on whether the present level is exactly right or too much or too little, but massive Federal support is an absolute essential.

In 1940, Federal support of university research amounted to some $15 million annually, practically all of which went to the agricultural experiment stations. Today it is something like $700 million, which is almost exactly three quarters of the total amount spent on academic research on campus. I am not including here the operation of major laboratories; I am speaking only of the money that goes to professors and academic departments to support research, primarily by graduate students.

Obviously, this Federal support determines, to a large extent, our programs in science and engineering. In the areas enjoying Government support, there is a real possibility of doing good teaching. It is, however, much more difficult to maintain a degree of excellence in an area not enjoying Government support. With this in mind, President Eisenhower remarked with some concern that the large flow of Federal dollars into the educational system may have a distorting effect on the general framework of the curricula across the country. Well, the support is with us, and it is here to stay. I agree totally with Mr. Wilson that the Government should not support all the areas of higher education. We must simply learn to live with this fact of life.

At MIT, for example—excluding the large defense laboratories, which are, in essence, operated for the Government—about 78 or 79 per cent of our research effort in the physical and life sciences and engineering is supported by Government funds, as against the national average of 85 per cent. This makes it all the more incumbent upon us to maintain our own balance by raising funds to back research in the areas which the Government does not support—in some instances, areas which have not yet been opened up to the point where officers of the Government can see the possibilities that would justify support. Above all, it is our responsibility to maintain the very best sort of teaching we can in all the areas not receiving Government support—areas which, by and large, we would not like to see supported by the Government.

But the more painful distorting factor, by far, was one which President Eisenhower did not mention. (I am not sure that his staff ever briefed him on it.) This factor is the short fall in the Government's reimbursement to the universities of the costs of the Government research programs. The costs which the universities pay and which the Government fails to reimburse run to approximately $35 million to $40 million a year. These are very precious funds, considering that the total research funds available to all universities, including their state and local governmental appropriations, is little more than $200 million, a part from Federal funds. Thus a rather large fraction of the universities' free funds are actually pre-empted by the Federal projects. I suppose one could say that if this short fall has created distortions, the institutions have mainly themselves to blame, because they can always say no to the proffer of Government assistance; but this is not an easy thing for all the struggling schools across the country to do.

One of the finest things that could happen to us is for the Congress to remove this fundamentally nonsensical restriction on Government payment of the full cost of its program. The main trouble lies in the failure to realize the scale effect of these funds. Certainly it is true that requiring the university to pay some part of its own bill helps to keep the projects honest. But when this means taking away a very large fraction of the available university support for other areas—areas which are often just as important to the universities but which the Government is not supporting—a painful distortion is inevitable.

A major improvement could also be made in the administrative concept of Federal research support. I suppose, offhand, that there must be at least twenty thousand federally supported research projects on the campuses of the nation's universities and colleges. It seems to me clear that the Government and the universities could both benefit from a wider use of support by broad program, as opposed to support by narrow project. There would be enormous administrative savings; but far more precious than that—especially with carefully selected, somewhat larger programs—would be the intimate management which the universities are in a better position to supply, in most instances, than are the officers of the Government. But universities want to supply this management within an over-all institutional framework, so that they can maintain balance among their programs.

Programmatic support would also tend to assure continuity of support of individual projects, which today, all too often, are subject to the whim of a project officer—or, especially in the military services, the differing whims of two project officers, one of whom succeeds the other unexpectedly just as the money is about to be sent out.

Let me comment, finally, on the question of facilities for research and development used on Government programs. Our current plight is the result of some of our own sins, as well as those that may have been committed by properly appointed officers of the Government.

Back when the rules were first being written for the use of facilities on Government programs, industry took a completely practical approach. It set up schedules; and the Government then set up schedules for industry to write off its facilities, generally on bases that accord with the normal rate of obsolescence in scientific and engineering research today. The universities, on the other hand, were caught in a rut. To a professor and even to a university administrator, in those ingenuous days of 1946, a building was sort of a monument, being outside the tax picture which industry, of course, lives with all the time. (Probably no building on any university campus in the country is carried on the books at any valuation other than initial cost plus the cost of major modifications.)

Well, buildings do not serve forever as research laboratories. The present Government practice of allowing a 2 per cent annual building-use charge, rather than some realistic write-off figure, assumes that a laboratory is good for fifty years. What research being done today in any of these Government programs bears any resemblance at all to any research that was being done fifty years ago? This practice is simply nonsensical.

Equipment, if it comes through the contract route rather than through the grant route, suffers from the same flaw. It is a financial burden on the universities. We are wearing out our university research facilities. New facilities, hard as they are to come by, are being helped along with matching grants; and in our recent fund-raising campaign at MIT, we have found a fairly sympathetic public response to the construction of new laboratories. But the fundamental problem remains: how does a university set up reserves for the eventual replacement of these buildings, without Government support, when three-quarters of all current research is on the Government account? This is, needless to say, a very tangled problem.

SUMMARY OF THE DISCUSSION

The general discussion was focused on three closely related issues:

The national interest and education: All participants in the session agreed that the Federal Government has a valid interest in education at all levels, in large measure because of the undeniable link between education and economic productivity. This link, however, has not yet been measured precisely. Mr. Wilson had quoted President Kennedy as attributing to education "some forty per cent of the nation's growth in economic productivity in recent years." Mr. Harris noted that "nobody really knows how much education contributes to growth or productivity, although some economists have said they know. An argument can be built for 20 per cent, or 30, or 40, or 50. Certainly it makes an important contribution, but we do not know yet how important. The same is true for the impact of education on individual earning." (His explanation drew on reasoning which is presented in detail in Chapter 9 and which need not be repeated here.)

Mr. Wilson rejoined that "forty per cent is a nice round figure to use to impress people. I suspect I will continue to use a figure like that to put this point across to the public at large, even though we are not sure just what the precise percentage is." He added that "our abysmal ignorance" on this point is a challenge to economists: "it is about time we quit being rhetorical and started to be more precise, because education is big and important business."

Reinforcing this general argument for Federal aid is the need to compensate for inequalities in state and local support of education at all levels. "It is true," said Mr. Harris, "that in the last decade, state and local governments have increased their total spending from $20 to $50 billion a year. This suggests that large resources remain to be tapped at these levels. But there are great differences in the proportion of those resources that can be made available for education; and the more impoverished the state or locality, the greater the effort relative to income and the less the achievement.

"Education, particularly higher education, is a very expensive matter in low-income states. Regardless of the cost in dollars, the average cost of an education in relation to per-capita income is much higher than in high-income states. One explanation, of course, is that prices are set on national markets. Professors, for example, are in a national market, and the impoverished states have to pay the same high prices for their services, financing the cost out of their low incomes."

Two important limitations to Federal involvement in education were carefully identified. *First,* Mr. Harris pointed out that in the United States, unlike France and the Netherlands and Sweden, there is strong opposition to centralized planning of the national economy. As a result, there is no over-all economic plan to which educational planning can be geared.

Second, Mr. Wilson emphasized that the Federal Government is validly concerned with only certain desciplines of higher education, not with the entire curriculum. "Maybe I am old-fashioned and conservative, but I think there are a lot of spheres that are none of the business of the Federal Government. I would not want it to become too involved in the fine arts and other cultural areas. To me this would be quite different from Federal aid for, say, engineering or ballistics.

"I think it is the job of a faculty and an administration to decide what constitutes a balanced education—to determine what goes into the making of a well-educated man or woman. This is the most important decision a faculty makes. The answer will vary, of course, from one institution to another, as is necessary in a pluralistic culture. Otherwise we will move toward an authoritarian society in which every concern is a governmental concern. And that is dangerous."

Practical problems of Federal aid: General McCormack's appeal for research support by program, rather than by project, encountered two pragmatic questions: what sort of programs might be established, and how might they be administered? Rather than answer these questions, he emphasized that he advocated the use of both projects and programs, not just programs alone. "Except for certain very large projects, such as building a radar astronomy installation in West Virginia, the research effort has been increasingly fractionalized as the budgets have climbed." It is time to reverse the trend.

Repeating his belief that "institutional management—selected, presumably, with prudence and care—will get the Government many things it otherwise has no way of getting," he offered as an example

the Center for International Studies at MIT. "This grew out of a
project to see what might be done about overcoming the Russian
jamming of the Voice of America broadcasts. Fortunately, those who
designed the project realized that the outcome of research often is
not predictable. This project was defined broadly enough to let the
researchers use their heads and look not only at the problems of
our transmitters but also at alternative means of communication.
Technically this was a project; I would call it a program. Well, this
project or program certainly paid off. It produced a whole new field
of technique as well as technology—the scatter communications system
which really makes world-wide communications possible."

Two arguments were adduced, however, in favor of the project
approach. *First*, the cumbersome red tape associated with narrow projects does provide closer supervision by the Federal agencies and Congress. This has advantages as long as gross instances of incompetence
or worse occur, however rarely, in the administration on campus of
Federal research funds. Rather than lobby against red tape, the academic community might be wiser to make it unnecessary by an effective
self-policing.

Second, projects are normally screened and defined by committees
and panels of authorities from outside the Government. Programmatic
aid—with large sums handed over to institutions to administer, free
of detailed instructions—is likely to be a direct transaction between
the Government and the institutions. "And I shudder to think what
will happen," said Mr. Wilson, "if we throw this into politics. We
can have a pork barrel in education just as we do in rivers and
harbors, maybe not immediately but in ten or twenty years. Once
the decisions become political, the key factor is no longer the quality
of the institution but its political contacts. It becomes purely a matter
of who has the votes."

The merit principle, which Mr. Wilson had suggested as a practical criterion for allocating Federal support, was endorsed enthusiastically by some discussants and questioned by others. There was unanimous agreement, however, that the problem of maintaining quality
throughout higher education is acute. Mr. Harris reported a study
of the economic indices of quality (such as the dollar investment per
student) which "gives a very distinct impression that the average student today is graduated from a college inferior in quality to those of
twenty-five or fifty years ago." Others noted that the eagerness of
institutions to take on new research, add new departments and start
new graduate schools—enterprises for which they are often not really

qualified—is tending to disperse the resources and lower the over-all level of higher education.

To sprinkle Federal funds indiscriminately among all colleges and universities would, in the view of several discussants, aggravate this decline. General McCormack, speaking particularly of curriculum research, made the point forcefully: "No one knows the answers in this area, so the funds must be given with rather broad authority. The Government has to select people who know how to do the job and then turn them loose. If an institution isn't good enough to be given the nod, it should be prevented from getting the money and wasting it."

Mr. Alden, on the other hand, pointed to the crucial difficulty of the merit principle. "In merit rating," he asked, "who will be making the judgments, and how can we be sure that the judgments are not too highly subjective and parochial? What body in America is well enough informed on educational developments throughout the country to be able to make these judgments responsibly now?"

Mr. Wilson, in reply, offered two possibilities. *First,* "I think I could gather a group of twelve people who would show a surprising degree of consensus" in identifying the two dozen universities with the best potential for developing into "great centers of graduate education." (He did not say what might happen if someone else picked the jury, nor did he hint at the criteria on which the twelve would be chosen.) He proposed that Federal funds be given to more than this number of institutions, allowing some room for competition. "Up to a point, competition is very beneficial, since a monopoly in education, like a monopoly anywhere else, makes for overconservatism." But it would be wasteful to make no discriminations whatsoever.

Second, merit judgments might be made on the basis of careful analysis by "economists, political scientists and others" of "the tax base, population growth and all sorts of other things. These analyses could not be precise; they could not define an exact cut-off point. But they could certainly separate the sheep from the goats."

Some discussion also occurred on the various possible forms of aid to students in higher education. Loans were praised as both effective and more economical than scholarships. Tax relief to parents was criticized on three counts: it erodes the tax base, goes to many parents who do not need it, and does not help the parents who need it most. Scholarships were endorsed as extremely important. "We have increased our scholarships by about $100 million since before the war," Mr. Harris pointed out, "and this has made it possible to increase tuitions by something like $1 billion with no serious change in the structure of the student body. To keep this leverage, we need some Federal cash for scholarships, as well as help for buildings and facilities."

Mr. Wilson offered a caveat: "This question is not quite as simple as it first appears. It is hard to devise a Federal program that will reach the students who most need it; the state scholarship programs really haven't accomplished this either. Federal scholarships are not worthwhile if they merely increase the range of choice for students already planning to enter college—so that instead of choosing among three scholarships, they can choose among four. The people we must reach are those who never consider the possibility of attending college, largely for economic reasons, though they can handle college-level work. Somehow we must reach these students and induce them to go."

The voice of the academic community: Among the most serious obstacles to an intelligent expansion of Federal aid, in the view of most discussants, is "the cacophony of voices" with which the academic community speaks to the Federal Government. There are significant differences of interest among institutions of various types—prestige and nonprestige, public and private, independent and church-related, two-year and four-year. Some institutions feel themselves vitally affected by Federal aid; others see the connection as quite remote, except perhaps on the issue of scholarships. If higher education is to get the sort of help it needs, the discussants agreed, it must resolve its differences and learn to "speak with a single voice."

Actually, the discussants agreed, Federal aid is directly important to every institution. Recent bills drawn up by the Kennedy and Johnson administrations call for help not only to graduate schools and large, research-oriented universities but also to small liberal-arts colleges—in such forms as library assistance and aid for science instruction. Moreover, each type of institution has a personal stake in the improvement of all types, since all are interdependent. The major institutions draw many of their graduate students from the small colleges, and the colleges find their teachers in the graduate schools. A weakness in any type of institution weakens them all.

"The entire academic community must work together," Mr. Wilson asserted, "to coordinate the development of higher education. At the same time, each institution should make sure that its own interests are not being represented in Washington by different voices speaking without faculty or administrative authorization." To the extent that apparent conflicts of interest can be resolved within each campus and within higher education as a whole, the academic community can seek a unified Federal approach to its problems.

In Washington, the discussants reported, higher education normally is heard sympathetically by the executive agencies, including even such fiscal watchdogs as the Bureau of the Budget. In the agencies, said Franklin L. Ford, dean of the Faculty of Arts and Sciences at Harvard University, "many people have university backgrounds, and they understand what we mean on the issue of institutional help. In the Congress, however, the lack of comprehension is at times almost total. The battle line of Federal aid is really drawn between the Congressional committees on one side and the agencies and the academic community on the other. And one of the hardest problems for higher education is to formulate the kind of aid we can give to intelligent, sophisticated agency heads when they are presenting their case —and ours—to Congress."

On the other hand, General McCormack observed that there is "a real yearning, in the congressmen I know, to hear from the grass roots on educational programs." They want to hear directly from the academic community, not only from the administrative agencies concerned. Mr. Wilson concurred: "That is where the best lobbying is done—at the grass roots. But we must recognize that the individual congressman is likely to be more influenced by the president of the college in this home town, regardless of its size and quality and influence, than by the president of any institution outside his district. The *entire* academic community is in politics; and the sooner it realizes this and gets mobilized for action, the better."

With regard to the Federal agencies, Mr. Wilson remarked, a greater unity of approach may or may not be desirable. "The authority to allocate funds to colleges and universities is now scattered among at least forty agencies—the National Institutes of Health, the National Science Foundation, the Office of Education and so on. Many educators, prefer it this way. They are wary of the idea of a single bureaucracy which would control all the funds for higher education. They believe that there are advantages to education in keeping this authority spread, since it minimizes bureaucratic control over the funds.

"On the other hand, there have been various proposals for ways to bring greater unity and coherence into Federal thinking and planning about higher education. One possibility is to form a Presidential advisory committee. Another is to improve and strengthen the Office of Education, making the commissioner a cabinet-level officer. My own feeling is that our immediate task is to bring more coherence and unity into our own thinking within the educational community. If we can do this, I think we will be listened to."

Finally, the discussants agreed that the academic community must alert the general public, as quickly as possible, to the meaning and importance of the needs of higher education. "We must understand," said Dean Ford, "that we are not just arguing with Congress. Our task is to educate the American public and win its support."

4. Federal Aid to Students in Higher Education

John F. Morse
Director, American Council on Education; Former Staff Member of the U. S. House of Representatives Committee on Education and Labor

To speak of the Federal Government's involvement in—or its attitude toward—student aid is to invite confusion. It is quite misleading to assume that the Federal Government is an entity in its relationship to higher education, any more than higher education itself is an entity. There are many Federal Governments, in both the executive and legislative branches, involved in one way or another in education. But with a few exceptions—the Office of Education, the two congressional committees and possibly the National Science Foundation—none of these Governments is concerned with education as such. Each is seeking to achieve a mission, and its programs are tailored to help fulfill that mission. What happens to students or to educational insitutions seems at times incidental, or at least of secondary concern.

At present, Government assistance to students is heavily concentrated in a limited area: providing full support to full-time graduate students for study at the postbaccalaureate, predoctoral level. With very few exceptions, this support is limited to the physical and life sciences and to engineering, although lesser amounts of money are going to such fields as the rare foreign languages, nursing, vocational rehabilitation and such specialized fields as the teaching of the deaf and the mentally retarded.

It is fairly easy to determine why this should be so. These fields have at one time or another been identified as areas of grave national concern and acute shortage. The death of a prominent figure from some dread disease almost automatically increases the number of fellowships available for graduate study in that area of medical research. The launching of Sputnik was probably the single most important factor in the sharp increase in the National Science Foundation's

81

budget and in the passage of the National Defense Education Act. The race for the moon brought into being an entirely new fellowship program which was scheduled to support 4,000 graduate students of space-related science and technology in some 150 universities. In short, in a crisis the typical response of a congressional committee or a Federal agency has been to appropriate more money for research and to send more students to graduate school.

Over the years, however, an interesting corollary has developed. When these fellowship programs began, the stipends were barely adequate to provide the graduate student with the minimum necessities of life and to pay the regular tuition and fees to the institution in which he elected to study. This policy gave little recognition to the enormous expense incurred by the institutions in educating graduate students. It was particularly hard on the public institutions, which rely heavily on state tax support to keep tuition charges—even for graduate and out-of-state students—at a very low level.

During the 1950's various Government agencies, in an effort to relieve the institutions of some of this burden, began adding a cost-of-education grant of a few hundred dollars to whatever they paid in tuition and fees. These grants provided some relief, but they did not solve the inequality between payments made to public institutions and those made to private institutions, where tuition fees cover a larger percentage of the cost of education.

Title IV of the National Defense Education Act of 1958 includes a provision that payments to institutions are to cover the *full cost* of educating each fellow, up to a maximum of $2500 per year. This provision, it seems to me, launched one agency of the Government into a new method of providing direct Federal subsidy of educational programs, in public and private institutions alike, using students as a means of transmission. If this concept had been limited solely to NDEA fellowships, it would probably have had little impact on the educational system. Since 1958, however, the National Insititutes of Health, the National Science Foundation and the Atomic Energy Commission have adopted the policy of paying a flat sum of $2500 per fellow to the institutions in which their fellow recipients are enrolled. The Space Agency went even further: it removed the $2500 ceiling and is paying all attributable costs for its fellows, ranging as high as $4000 in one institution.

I do not wish to dwell overlong on this development, but it seems worthwhile to point out that what began as a program to increase—almost on a crash basis—the number of highly trained professionals in certain academic disciplines is now serving as a useful device to provide financial support to educational institutions. Furthermore, a number of agencies, having found this device useful, are moving toward still broader support in the form of training grants awarded to individual institutions. These grants may be used not only to support students but also to buy equipment, pay faculty salaries and cover some of the institutions' indirect costs. They take Government agencies out of the difficult and expensive business of selecting fellows, and they provide considerably more flexibility in the use of funds.

This new policy is by no means universal throughout the Government. The Department of Defense, for example, expends more for the education of its personnel in civilian academic institutions than do all the fellowship programs of the Government put together, and with very few exceptions it pays only tuition and fees. The same is true of the State Department exchange programs and of most of the far larger operations conducted by the Agency for International Development. Nevertheless, a pattern is established; and it has been my experience that once a pattern is established, it tends to grow and spread automatically.

These large fellowship programs are important: in 1961-62 they supported approximately 14,000 graduate students at a cost of $60 million. Yet so far as I know, neither the Congress nor any executive agency has specifically determined that it is a matter of Federal policy to support students in their effort to acquire an education. The programs which I have described are designed to produce men who have certain skills that the nation needs, just as the three service academies are designed to produce officers for the Armed Forces. The two G.I. bills, which as of 1963-64 are providing negligible support, were enacted primarily to ease the veterans' transition from military to civilian life. The enactment of the National Defense Student Loan Program did indicate Government recognition that some provision must be established to enable very needy students to help themselves. But this program provides very little in the way of subsidy.

Perhaps I can best illustrate the diversity within the Federal Government's present attitude toward higher education by citing briefly the history of efforts, beginning in 1961, to enact a Federal scholarship program. As originally proposed by the Kennedy Administration, scholarships ranging up to a maximum stipend of $1,000 per year would have been provided through state commissions to promising and needy students who might not otherwise be able to attend college.

This proposal represented almost the first major effort on the part of the Government to fulfill the American dream of providing our ablest youngsters, regardless of their economic circumstances, an opportunity to go as far in their education as their talents would take them. Efforts were made in the legislation to avoid heavy reliance on objective tests, which were presumed to be biased toward youngsters in the higher socio-economic levels; and stipends were to be paid only to those students who could, on the basis of a fairly stringent means test, demonstrate need for them. In keeping with the established pattern in fellowship programs, a cost-of-education grant of $350 per year was to be paid to each institution for each stipend-recipient enrolled.

It was clear from the start that the Administration proposal had strong bipartisan support in the Senate, and it was eventually accepted by that body without amendments. I believe that any other financial-aid proposal—so long as it has Administration backing, provides assistance to needy students and does not lay too much stress on academic excellence as opposed to need—will also receive favorable action in the Senate.

The story was far different in the House, however. There the bill ran immediately into heavy weather. The arguments against it were so numerous and so varied that it is difficult to separate those which were advanced in a genuine effort to improve the bill from those which were advanced to kill it.

The cost-of-education proposal came under particularly heavy fire; colleges and universities were envisioned as scrambling for scholarship recipients in order to capture the $350 bonus, while discriminating against students who could bring with them no such nugget. State commissions were viewed with skepticism; it was suggested that only the individual colleges and universities could discover talent. Not unreasonable fears were voiced that objective tests, despite efforts in the legislation to minimize their use, would be helped to increase their hold on the American educational system. Doubts were also expressed that there are indeed young people in this country who are financially unable to seek a higher education. Admittedly, statistics relating to the number who are thus deprived are soft, but common sense tells us that it must be large.

Eventually a scholarship bill did emerge from the House Education and Labor Committee, but it bore so little resemblance to the original bill as to be scarcely recognizable. So far as I can tell, none of its provisions had ever before been proposed in a bill, or by an educational association, or by any administration. None of its provisions had been discussed in public hearings by knowledgeable witnesses. Rather, it seemed to spring, like Venus, full-blown from the committee. Unlike Venus, it saw the light of day only briefly before disappearing forever into the murky depths of the Rules Committee.

For a variety of reasons, this scholarship proposal had been tied to a bill which would have provided major assistance to educational institutions for the construction of academic facilities. There is widespread agreement, both in the educational world and in Congress, that the provision of facilities is of first importance if we are to meet the challenge of numbers. Since the scholarship proposal was felt to be something of an albatross to that bill, the House, under the leadership of Representative Edith Green of Oregon, voted by an overwhelming majority a bill for academic facilities with no provision for scholarships.

This bill was forwarded to the Senate, which immediately amended it to include the original scholarship bill, which had been proposed by the Administration and which had fared so badly in the House Education and Labor Committee. Thus amended, the bill passed the Senate with a large majority. The stage was set presumably for a resolution of the problem in conference.

Unanimous consent is, of course, required for the appointment of House conferees to iron out differences in bills passed by the House and Senate. In this case, a lone dissent barred the appointment and sent the bill back to the Rules Committee. Unquestionably, the scholarship issue caused this dissent. There was widespread feeling, perhaps concentrated on the Republican side, that the House had never had an opportunity to debate the question of a scholarship program and that the Labor and Education Committee had already rejected out of hand the one now contained in the Senate bill. Through the long winter, spring and early summer, the bill sat in the Rules Committee, where it was joined from time to time by other pieces of legislation which had also been reported favorably by the Committee on Education and Labor.

At last, in July, the Rules Committee permitted the bill to go back to the floor of the House and to conference. There was apparently a tacit understanding that this would be the one piece of educational legislation to be given a rule. Furthermore, the committee extracted a firm commitment from both Chairman Adam Clayton

Powell and Mrs. Green that, in conference with the Senate, they would under no circumstances agree to a scholarship bill.

As a rank amateur in the field of congressional maneuvering, it is perhaps presumptuous of me to express any opinion, but it seemed to me then and it seems to me now that it was virtually impossible for the House conferees to discover a satisfactory compromise. The Senate bill for academic facilities contained only a provision for loans; the House, throughout its earlier debates, had made it clear that a bill which did not also include grants would be considered of little use to higher education and would win little House support. The House was also adamantly opposed to other features in the Senate bill on which the Senate was expected to yield if a compromise was to be found. The Rules Committee, by forbidding any concession by the House conferees toward a student-aid bill, left room not for compromise but only for capitulation by the Senate.

Through the late summer and early fall, beset by difficulties of all kinds—among them the unrelated but upsetting Supreme Court school-prayer decision, the warfare between the House and Senate Appropriations Committees and the onrush of days toward the upcoming congressional elections—the conferees worked patiently to find some acceptable solution. Weeks passed when no conferences were held, but there was genuine feeling in both parties and in both Houses that this was vital legislation and that there must be a way out.

What finally emerged is, I believe, worthy of serious study by those who are interested in possible future student-aid legislation. In a sense it was born of desperation. It in no way represented modifications of earlier scholarship proposals; and possibly because the bill failed to pass, this provision has not since received the attention I personally feel it merits.

Out of the conference came a phrase which should live long in the wild lexicon of Washingtonese: "the nonreimbursable loan." I am not, I assure you, prepared to defend the phrase; it was difficult even for its inventors to pronounce it with a straight face. Nevertheless, the concept it embodied might well win the support of experienced financial-aid officers all over the country. Basically, the compromise bill provided a large increase in the funds available to colleges and to universities for student loans, and it stipulated that 20 per cent of the allocation to any university might be used, at the university's discretion, to provide a unique sort of loan for particularly needy students—those whose financial situation is such that they cannot attend any college without a large amount of assistance. The unique characteristic of these loans was that they need not be repaid.

This was getting close to the heart of a problem with which I, as a financial-aid officer, used to struggle. I have never seen any reason why students should not borrow to get a college education. I have always been worried, however, that those from our lowest income groups must, if they are to rely on loans alone, assume an undue burden of debt. I have been reluctant to authorize loans as large as these youngsters needed, for the mere prospect of such indebtedness would too strongly influence the student's decisions about his life after college, including the very real probability that he would not feel free to apply for graduate or professional school.

In short, I have long felt that there should be some means of equalizing the burden of debt carried by financial-aid recipients so that the neediest and those moderately well off would assume approximately the same loads. I even managed, while still on a university campus, to convert the use of one large scholarship fund to provide gift aid to even barely passing students, if their indebtedness had already reached what I considered a dangerous level.

Here, dreamed up in Senate-House conference, was a national program to provide just this kind of assistance. Unfortunately, the bill was lost, and there seems to be a widespread belief that any possibility of a Federal scholarship program was lost with it. This I do not believe.

When the conference report came back to the floor of the House with a one-hour limitation on debate, it was beset by double-team blocking of the kind that every football coach dreams of. An outpouring of telegrams inspired by one educational association raised once again the religious issue over grants for academic facilities. There was far too little time to counteract this pressure by reaffirming and documenting the fact that grants of tax funds are being made by many agencies of the Government to public and private, sectarian and nonsectarian institutions for far broader purposes than were encompassed in the bill. At the same time there was considerable resentment over the fact that the conferees, while technically abiding by their agreement not to accept a scholarship bill, were playing a game of semantics in coming back instead with "nonreimbursable loans."

At the end of a long and wearing session—with tempers frayed, election only a few weeks away and the inevitable rumors (some proving well founded) that legislators with long years of service were in serious trouble back home—the bill could not survive the dual attack. It was sent back to conference to die.

I have perhaps dwelled overlong on the history of this bill, and even so I know that I am guilty of skimming over important details. Nevertheless, I think certain things on the bright side are worthy of note.

Despite all the skepticism, the conference report—with what may be called its scholarship provision—had the support of all but one of the House conferees, including the man whose dissent had earlier sent the bill back to the Rules Committee. It had the support of all but two of the Senate conferees, and their failure to support it had nothing to do with the student-aid provisions. Furthermore, despite all the difficulty the bill encountered, the shift of a mere fifteen votes on the floor of the House would have assured the bill's passage.

Efforts to achieve a viable Federal scholarship program must be continued. We cannot go on endlessly increasing the number of fellowships, particularly in science and engineering, until we increase the size of the pool from which fellowship recipients are drawn. We read daily of the alarming shortage of highly trained people in virtually every profession, and we direct all our efforts toward selected areas of graduate and professional study in an effort to alleviate this shortage. Yet we know that in the late high-school years, in the transition period to college and in college, our loss of talent is acute. The fact that no one can tell the exact size of the loss—or, to put it another way, determine the extent of the untapped pool—does not justify us in ignoring it.

When the nation is faced with an acute shortage of a strategic mineral, it immediately starts exploration for additional sources of ore and is quite prepared to extract and stockpile it, regardless of the expense. I cannot believe that the day is distant when we shall be willing to expend equal amounts to discover and refine our hidden human ore. When we do, I think we shall find our investment far more productive than that in the material stockpiles scattered all over the country.

SUMMARY OF THE DISCUSSION

The following summary is based not only on the general discussion but also on three other brief papers which were presented at this session. For diverse reasons, these papers are not appropriate for publication here. The discussion itself was devoted almost exclusively to the issues and questions raised by Mr. Morse's paper—thus demonstrating, as one discussant observed, "how poignant and dramatic the idea of Federal scholarships has become."

Issues concerning Federal aid to students

The need for Federal aid: The discussants were unanimous and emphatic in asserting the need for action by the Federal Government to make higher education available to every competent student in the nation. Some debate occurred over the precise steps to be taken but not over the urgent need for some action. There appeared also to be full agreement on the reason for this urgency: the critical shortage of persons who possess the skills required for the nation's economic growth and military security. (The desirability of individual fulfillment was mentioned a few times in passing.)

"In the minority groups, in women and in the very poor economic groups," said Mr. Morse, "we are losing talent that we cannot afford to lose." This loss was confirmed by Peter P. Muirhead, assistant commissioner for program and legislative planning of the U. S. Office of Education: "Various studies suggest that about 150,000 high-school graduates of outstanding ability fail each year to continue their education. From 60,000 to 100,000 of these students stop because they cannot surmount the economic hurdle of the cost of higher education. This group of superior students constitutes an untapped reservoir of potential leadership. We must act vigorously and quickly to reduce this talent loss."

Even among students who enter college, the Federal Government is doing almost nothing to avert dropouts among talented students for economic reasons. Despite a false but widespread impression to the contrary, Mr. Morse asserted, the Government is making virtually no effort, except through the Student Loan Program, to conserve and develop our young talent at the undergraduate level. Fellowships are concentrated in graduate studies, and there are no general Federal scholarships at any level except for a few tightly restricted programs, such as those for Indians and for the Naval ROTC. Even accepting the Government's special concern for graduate studies, this neglect of college students is shortsighted, since college education is the base upon which graduate education is built.

A serious loss of talent occurs also at the graduate level, where Federal aid to students is concentrated in the physical and life sciences and in engineering. Virtually no student aid is granted in the social sciences and the humanities. One possible solution, Mr. Morse suggested, is a coordinated approach by all the Federal agencies which award fellowships. "At the present time, roughly 44 per cent of the fellowships under the National Defense Education Act are going into the same disciplines that are being supported by the National Aeronautics and Space Administration, the National Science Foundation and, to a degree, the National Institutes of Health. Why should we not use the opportunity to put the weight of the NDEA program on the neglected sciences and the humanities? This could be regulated by a joint effort of all the agencies, without making any one agency —as some people fear—the sole distributor and awarder of fellowships."

Objections to Federal scholarships: In the face of an apparently clear-cut need, why has no Federal scholarship provision won final approval by Congress? "No one factor ever defeats a bill," Mr. Morse observed, "but a major obstacle has been the refusal of the House Rules Committee to let a sound scholarship bill come to the floor for debate. The Senate has endorsed a scholarship program, and I do not believe that the opposition in the House has been as strong as it appeared. But the House is naturally unwilling to accept any proposal that has never been threshed out on the floor."

Two other factors complicate the situation. *First,* the executive branch has no agency empowered to make a concerted drive for scholarship legislation. "The Department of Health, Education and Welfare," Mr. Morse noted, "has never been given a mandate for the overall educational system comparable to that of the National Science Foundation in its own sphere," and no other executive organ has education as its primary concern. *Second,* the goals and philosophy of a general scholarship program are very difficult to define and quantify. A space-research project can specify that X scientists are needed for Y years to get a man to the moon. General support, especially in the social sciences and humanities, cannot be projected and justified with such apparent precision.

But the failure of efforts thus far to secure passage of a scholarship bill is not due solely to parliamentary barricades and theoretical vagueness. Opponents of such aid have raised a number of definite objections, six of which were mentioned—not always sympathetically—by the discussants: (1) "The idea of working one's way through college is still a romantic concept to many congressmen," Mr. Morse reported. "They feel that it is somehow noble and not really difficult—an impression that has, of course, no realistic reference to typical college

costs today. The scorn with which some members of Congress pronounce the word 'grant' makes one realize how strongly they feel that
a student ought to rely on his own resources."

(2) The talent loss has not been shown to be a *national* problem.
"There is no question that there is a very substantial talent loss,"
said Russell Thackrey, Executive Secretary-treasurer of the Association
of State Universities and Land-Grant Colleges, "but we ought to find
out exactly where it is. Some states have an extremely high percentage
of young people going to college; others do not. It it turns out that
the talent loss is centered in particular states or regions, perhaps
a national scholarship program is not our primary need."

(3) A number of opponents declare that the country simply
cannot afford the expense of a Federal scholarship program. Mr.
Harris, in rebuttal, pointed out that the British economy is able
to support a much heavier program than any proposed for the United
States. "We now give over $100 million in scholarships from all sources
but if the British system were applied to our enrollment, we
would require $1.5 billion. Compared to the scholarship programs
in most European countries, ours is very inadequate."

Mr. Morse offered a further rebuttal. "This would be an investment, not an expenditure—an investment in the development of our
most productive natural resource. And this investment cannot be
shirked. We are going to spend the money eventually, one way or
another. Either we must spend some to develop talent of youngsters
during their school years, or we must spend much more to retrain
them in their later years. The Defense Department, for instance, in order to get a few more engineers, has been forced to send enlisted men
for four years of undergraduate instruction at a cost to the country
of about $5,500 per man."

(4) Spokesmen for public colleges and universities are frequently
cool toward a Federal scholarship program on the ground that it
tends to favor private institutions. A grant paying a student's full
tuition, for example, would bring more dollars to a private than
to a public institution; it would also cover a greater proportion of
the cost of that student's education. In a sense, the state is being
penalized for its willingness to underwrite through taxes a large share
of the cost of education. Supplementary grants, as described by Mr.
Morse in his speech, reduce but do not eliminate the inequity.

(5) "There is a very real and possibly legitimate concern," Mr.
Morse noted, "that a massive scholarship program would simply encourage all institutions, public and private, to increase their fees by

the amount of the scholarships." The scholarships would then offer no real relief to the recipients, and they would make higher education even more expensive for nonrecipients. Such grants would amount to a direct subsidy to private institutions. In the case of public institutions, they would amount to a direct grant to the state governments, whose legislatures would be relieved of the necessity to appropriate that amount out of state revenues.

(6) Occasionally the discussants wondered gingerly (as one put it) "how much the roots of opposition are related to the church-state issue." But there was no discussion of this question.

If a scholarship bill is to be enacted, these and other objections must be answered, not only to congressmen who propound them but also to the general public. "As a nation," said Mr. Muirhead, "we are committed to placing responsibility for education at the state, local and institutional levels. There has been some success in getting public awareness and acceptance of the value of using Federal resources for purposes which are in the national interest and which the state or community or institution cannot be expected to meet alone. Witness the phenomenal success of the rare-languages program and the National Science Foundation. Now we must seek an increased public awareness that Federal resources must be tapped in order to improve the quality of education as a whole."

Student aid vs. institutional aid: The sharpest controversy of the session arose over the relative importance of aid to students (through scholarships, loans and work-study programs) and aid provided direct to institutions for buildings, facilities, faculty salaries and similar needs. The discussants agreed that both forms of aid are necessary; they disagreed on the matter of priorities.

Two broad alternatives were set forth by Mr. Thackrey. The first is for institutions to gain new and essential income by raising tuitions and charges. Each step in this direction places the cost of higher education outside the range of more students; as a corollary, more students need some form of financial aid. Higher education is striding rapidly in this direction: "The average income of the families of scholarship recipients is increasing steadily because it is becoming harder and harder for even relatively affluent families to send their children to college. Eventually, almost every student will need a subsidy. President David Dodds Henry of the University of Illinois has said that we may reach the point where access to higher education will be controlled almost entirely by those who control the scholarship funds."

The other alternative is to provide direct support to institutions so that they can keep tuitions and charges low. Many students who would otherwise need scholarships will then be able to pay for their higher education. "If we get a fairly massive program of institutional support, the scholarship problem will be manageable. If not, we will need hundreds of thousands of scholarships, or else many competent students will find higher education far beyond their reach."

Two possible disadvantages of institutional aid were identified, however. First, such aid often requires matching appropriations by the institution; in any case, it almost never pays the full cost of the activity it encourages. The net result is to take institutional funds that might be used for student aid and earmark them for activities receiving Government support. To this Mr. Thackrey replied, in effect, that the argument assumes that an institution without Government support would not invest in growth. But, in fact, institutions must grow, and those apparently uncommitted funds would have to be earmarked for growth activities in any case. They would merely be tragically inadequate.

A more serious disadvantage was noted by Mr. Harris: institutional aid lacks the flexibility of scholarships in its effect on students. Keeping tuitions low helps all students equally, those who could afford higher tuitions and those who could not. By raising tuitions and providing scholarships as needed, the cost of higher education can be more effectively distributed according to the students' ability to pay. Furthermore, another discussant observed, the scholarships would increase each institution's flexibility in financial aid; they would permit a much more supple and far-reaching use of packages combining scholarships, jobs and long-term loans.

Mr. Thackrey replied that this flexibility would be lost if the scholarship program became unmanageably large, as it must if we miscalculate the balance between student aid and institutional aid. Another discussant added that "if we keep tuitions low, loans and work are a real alternative to the needy student, whereas they may not be if the tuition becomes too steep."

Other issues of Federal aid to higher education

Federal control: Fear that the use of greater Federal resources will lead to Federal control of education was named by Mr. Muirhead as the most important barrier to increased Federal aid. "The question is: will such aid damage our cherished state and local control of schools, and will it damage the independence of our institutions of higher learning? I think that this fear loses much of its validity in the face of the non-Federal-control precedents established by the Land-Grant College program, the National Vocational Education Act, the Federally Affected Areas legislation, the work of the National Science Foundation and the National Defense Education Act. But the argument does continue—and it should continue until the argument is resolved and the issue clearly understood.

"My own position is that it is high time we put to rest the myth of Federal control. Everyone agrees that it would be intolerable, but it can be prevented by paying attention to the proper balance of power and responsibility among the three levels of government. This has been demonstrated time and again, as we have enlisted the resources of the Federal Government to meet urgent problems in the national interest.

"The time has come, it seems to me, for us to recognize that our Federal Government belongs as much to the people as do our local and state governments. We have the right to insist that our national resources be used in the national interest, at the same time protecting the diversity of American education. As Commissioner of Education Francis Keppel has said: 'The basic aim of Federal support must be such that at the end of any program, the institutions—state agencies, schools and colleges—are stronger and freer than they were at the start.' "

Later in the session, this issue was approached again, with a somewhat different conclusion. One discussant, a graduate student at the Harvard University School of Public Administration, had suggested that Federal research grants are, in effect, "a type of control." The following exchange then took place:

MR. MORSE: "Federal programs have had an enormous impact, but I kon't know that I would use the word *control* as synonymous with *impact*. These are free decisions made by free institutions."

STUDENT: "Free decisions of institutions are going to be greatly influenced by the availability of funds. They will freely decide to expand in areas where they can get money."

MR. MORSE: "Yes, but the decisions will also be a measure of the courage of the president, the board of trustees and the dean of the faculty."

MR. THACKREY: "I agree with you in general, but I know of at least one instance in which a 'free decision' was made to accept an NSF grant only because failure to accept it would have meant the loss of an entire physics faculty."

MR. MORSE: "I know this. I am talking theory, and you are talking fact."

Budgetary concern: "Another problem that vitally affects Federal legislation in the area of education," Mr. Muirhead observed, "is that of economics. In the face of the Federal Government's other responsibilities—defense, tax reform and so on—can the Government afford it?" The discussants agreed unanimously that it can.

Mrs. Alice Rivlin, staff member of the Brookings Institute, noted that "in the perspective of the national economy, higher education is not very expensive." Its total cost as of 1970 will be $15 billion at the most, probably very much less. This generous estimate is only 2 per cent of the estimated Gross National Product in 1970. "There should be no trouble finding the money."

Mr. Harris agreed that if present economic trends continue "there will be no problem of getting an adequate supply of money" at the national level. "Furthermore, in the 1950's the state and local governments increased their expenditures from $20 to $50 billion—or from $20 to $40 billion in stable dollars. Obviously there will be a lot of money available for education at the state and local levels."

There was general agreement that higher education must first decide how much money it needs and how the money is to be spent. When the academic community has reached a consensus on a realistic program, Federal support will be forthcoming. An analogy was drawn to the major Federal efforts for defense and for scientific research: once a need has been clearly identified and recognized as a national objective, the Government finds the money to support it. But a vague insistence that some amount ought to be appropriated for something or other to help higher education is unlikely to win much support from either the Government or the general public.

In the long run, Mr. Muirhead concluded, "the Government cannot afford *not* to commit some of its resources to the support of education." He quoted from President Kennedy's message on education of January, 1963: "This Nation is committed to greater investment in economic growth; and recent research has shown that one of the most beneficial of all such investments is education. . . . It is an investment which yields a substantial return in the higher wages and purchasing power of trained workers, in the new products and techniques which come from skilled minds, and in the constant expansion of this Nation's storehouse of useful knowledge."

Geographical distribution of Federal aid: Mr. Muirhead took strong exception to the present, mission-oriented system of channeling

Federal funds to education. He raised two sharp objections. *First,* the funds are being concentrated in relatively few universities, which are presumably already strong in resources and excellent in achievement, at least in the areas with which the missions are concerned. This concentration of funds not only deprives other institutions of an opportunity to realize their potential; it also jeopardizes such excellence as they have attained. The finest faculty members in these institutions, for example, are often bought away by the top universities, where they are paid out of Federal-support funds. Thus "for every step the Government has taken to strengthen the capacity of colleges and universities outside the top twenty or thirty, it has taken two to reduce their relative capacity to compete."

Second, while some institutions outside the top few do secure Federal funds, the basis for these grants is curious, to say the least. Ostensibly the Government is guided by the judgment of supposedly objective panels of experts, one of whose tasks is to identify scientific potential that would justify a Federal grant. "I would note that there seems to be an amazing correlation between the location of this scientific potential and the geographical areas represented by the members of certain of the appropriations and legislative committees of the Congress."

These two weaknesses are significant not only for the harm they do but also for the good they fail to do. "It is generally recognized that in a nation as large in area, population and resources as ours, it is desirable to have high-quality educational opportunity, including centers of strength in graduate education and research, available in many areas. Further, it is highly desirable to stimulate local and regional interest and initiative in attacking research problems.

"A great deal of unrealized potential in colleges and universities in every state, in every region, is not now being used and is not likely to be used under the present system. One way to correct this is to take some of the Federal-support funds—not all of them, perhaps not even a majority of them, but some—and earmark them for geographical distribution to the various regions. In this way we can begin to carry out the national objective of strengthening education and research throughout the country. Moreover, the pressures for political allocation of funds will be alleviated when all regions are assured that they will no longer be completely frozen out of participation in some important Federal programs affecting education."

Three other relevant factors were also mentioned. *First,* Mr. Thackrey noted a direct relationship between the long-continued presence of research activity in a college or university and the career decisions of its students. Where significant research activity exists, a far higher proportion of students in that discipline in that institution tend to continue their education and to earn doctoral degrees.

Second, he emphasized that Federal support must be coordinated with the states' educational plans, if education is to develop rationally rather than haphazardly. "When the Federal Government decides, as it recently did, to locate a major research installation at a small public college in a community which happens also to be the home of one of the most powerful members of Congress—an installation whose nature requires that high-quality graduate education and research programs be locally available to its staff—the impact on the carefully planned structure of public higher education in the state is obvious."

Finally, Mr. Morse pointed out that "industrial development and economic growth seem to be remarkably concentrated around the great centers of higher education." This fact has not gone unnoticed in Congress, and it is giving not a little thrust to the growing concern over geographical distribution of Federal aid to higher education.

5. Educational Planning — Its Goals and Its Dangers

Philip H. Coombs
Director, International Institute for Educational Planning; Former
U. S. Assistant Secretary of State for Educational and Cultural Affairs

America's historic interest and heavy investment in education and in the development of people has been a major factor in this country's impressive economic, social and political development over the past century. It helps to account for the position of world leadership in which the United States finds itself today. This fact is obvious and need not be elaborated here (though some economists and others are busily engaged in documenting it); but two corollaries should be noted. First, if education deserves considerable credit for the past national advancement, then it must also be partly responsible for our present shortcomings in national performance, including our shortcomings in the international field. And second, it follows that the history of the twenty-first century is being partially written right now in the classrooms of our schools and colleges. This is a rather sobering thought.

The revolutionary changes which have swept the world since the close of World War II, with the consequent vast transformation of America's international posture, have imposed upon American education a new crop of important tasks relating to world affairs. Some of these tasks are very broad; others are quite specific. One of the broadest is to overhaul, update and upgrade the entire school and university curriculum in order to turn out a new type of graduate who can live effectively in the modern world, which is drastically different from that contemplated by formal education only a generation ago. Anyone who has ever been on a curriculum committee knows full well the difficulties of such a massive revision, however much it may be required.

The more specific tasks include strengthening the teaching of foreign languages, deepening the nation's knowledge of foreign areas and of international affairs generally, and meeting our urgent new manpower requirements for specialists in the realm of world affairs. In all these respects, American education was seriously ill-prepared at the close of World War II. We have not yet been able to meet adequately the educational needs imposed by our heavy new international responsibilities, so we have not yet been able to utilize fully the powers and opportunities which accompany them.

In addition to meeting these domestic needs, our educational system, particularly higher education, has a multitude of new foreign customers to serve. Our campuses have been stretched to embrace virtually the entire world. In 1961-62 there were 60,000 foreign students in this country—three-quarters of them from Asia, Africa and Latin America—and the number is rising by at least 10 per cent a year. These foreign students require somewhat different treatment than domestic students, and many of them will be strategically important people in their own societies when they return home.

We are also busily engaged in rendering university services overseas, particularly in helping the developing nations to strengthen their educational means for human-resource development. It is hard to get up-to-date statistics, especially on education, from the Agency for International Development; but as of mid-1961, at least 58 universities were involved in development projects in at least 37 countries, under 100 different Government contracts grossing $106 million. Other universities were functioning overseas under various other arrangements, as with private foundations or through sister arrangements with foreign universities.

Another specific task for American education is to meet the skyrocketing demand for instructors who have been trained to teach English as a second language. The correlative task, in view of the acute shortage of such teachers, is to devise new and more effective techniques for teaching second languages well with a more economical use of trained instructors.

All these and other tasks imposed by the world situation have largely obliterated the old distinction between domestic and international education. And there is every reason to expect that these international burdens and impacts on American education will grow at an accelerating pace. Our AID officials and world bankers, for example, have discovered that viable societies cannot be developed without enormous investments in education and in people. As a result, they have made educational development a legitimate object for international loans, and our colleges and universities can expect to be called upon increasingly to render technical assistance overseas.

American education's response to these postwar demands and these convulsive, world-wide changes has been extremely impressive, at least judged by any previous standard. More educational change, expansion and improvement has occurred in the last ten years in the United States, it seems safe to say, than in any previous half-century.

In the secondary schools, for example, the teaching of mathematics, physics, chemistry, biology and foreign languages is being thoroughly revolutionized. The social sciences and humanities are next in line, though things move more slowly there. Improvements in high-school curricula are, in fact, so sweeping that they are forcing the colleges to re-examine their academic requirements for the freshman and sophomore years. Indeed, the entire chronological lockstep has been jarred loose in wholesome fashion by such innovations as the advanced-placement program, early admission to college and flexible programs which allow able students to proceed at their own best pace.

In many colleges the virtue of independent study has been rediscovered, with the result that faculty members are increasingly being used to do those things for which they are uniquely qualified. Students are spending less time listening and more time learning how to learn for themselves—an indispensible preparation for life in a world where a person, to remain educated, must run fast all his life in order to stand still.

Great progress has also been made in harnessing new communications technologies to the service of learning, as with educational television and language laboratories, and in introducing other new techniques to increase the speed and improve the quality of teaching and learning. The profoundly significant technique of programmed learning, whose import has been somewhat obfuscated by its identification with "teaching machines," is making headway in a variety of subject fields.

At the university level, the number of area centers for study of the hitherto dark continents, established both for research and for the training of specialists, has grown from a mere handful ten years ago to more than fifty today. Indeed, no university now can hold its head high, unless it has at least one foreign-area center, preferably enough centers to blanket the world. At the same time, in the schools of education, a profound revolution has been occurring.

The old teachers college is, like the plow horse, rapidly vanishing. Things are decidedly looking up in the quality of teacher preparation.

These and other major improvements of quality, substance and technique have occurred in the face of rapidly mounting enrollments, teacher shortages and financial stringencies, of which the following are indicators: Public-school enrollments doubled in just twelve years, from not quite 20-million in 1950-51 to nearly 40-million in 1962-63. In the same twelve years, total higher-education enrollments rose from about 2.1-million to an estimated 4.6-million. Financial figures for education are always treacherous, but the Office of Education estimates that total expenditures on formal education in the United States, at all levels, public and private, rose from $3.2-billion in 1941-42 to $11.3-billion in 1951-52 and to nearly $30-billion in 1961-62.* This is hardly the record of a nation which is miserly with education, even if at times we might wish that its support were even more generous.

So the postwar era, especially since about 1950, presents an astonishing record of educational accomplishment in the United States, judged by any previous standard. Perhaps the Soviet Union can match it, but I doubt that any other nation can, at any time in history.

Despite these impressive advances, the American educational establishment today, in relation to the obligations and opportunities confronting it, is grossly inadequate and in a state of dangerous disarray. The sad fact is that the accelerated rate of change in American education has been outpaced by an even more accelerated change in the world around it.

We emerged from World War II grossly ill-equipped educationally for the tasks immediately at hand and for those that lay ahead. Furthermore, as Walter Lippman pointed out very cogently in the mid-50's, this serious gap between our educational needs and our educational performance has been growing ominously wider with the rush of events. We have, to be sure, put schoolhouse roofs over the heads of many more students; we have somehow rounded up more teachers and come forth with vastly more money for education. Yet in the important specifics, the educational gap continues to widen.

The curriculum advances to which I referred have thus far touched only a minute fraction of the students and teachers in the country. The curriculum at every level is still loaded with cobwebs, with obso-

---

*Now close to $35 billion.—Ed.

lete and ineffectual material on which students should not be required to waste time. Innovations such as educational television have made rapid strides, yet only the surface of their potential has been scratched. Programmed learning is likewise a mere toddler. Our national competence in foreign languages, in knowledge of other nations and in awareness of foreign affairs generally, though well ahead of where it was in 1945, is grossly inadequate for a nation which carries our responsibilities.

Most serious of all, our knowledge of human beings and human society—how they develop; how they accommodate to technological, political and cultural changes; how they can organize to master the great forces and knowledge that science has placed at mankind's disposal—is still in a primitive state.

A great many questions deserve to be asked about the progress we have made and have not made in education in recent years— questions for which we do not have adequate answers. For example, how much have we really done to attract more of our ablest young people to elementary- and secondary-school teaching, to utilize our best teachers more productively and to stop treating all teachers as if they were identical? What have we done to keep all our teachers abreast of new knowledge and teaching techniques, so that they do not become incurably obsolete?

What progress have we really made in the big cities toward adapting our rigid educational patterns to fit the special needs and circumstances of the millions of culturally handicapped youngsters whose stunted potential represents a tragic waste to themselves and to society?

How much money have we spent on intensive research and development to improve the substance, the quality and the efficiency of education, as compared to what we have spent on research and development in such fields as weaponry, industry and agriculture?

Has the typical college curriculum improved even as much as the high-school curriculum? Why are the colleges today abandoning general education—because the high schools have really improved so much that they can take it over, or because the colleges simply could not figure out how to make general education work?

What sort of example have the graduate schools, the pinnacle of our educational pyramid, set lately? What sort of leadership have they given? And is it any more possible today than it was ten years ago to tell a bright college senior how long it will take him to get a Ph.D in English or history or economics, as he could if he were seeking a law or medical degree? While this remains vague, how can the senior plan his life?

How much stronger are the state departments of education today, relative to their expanding responsibilities? How much more efficient, productive and better organized are they than the Federal agencies which deal with education, research and manpower?

What contributions have the great national educational organizations and professional societies made? How much leadership have they given in recent years to propelling education along the new paths it must travel? Conversely, how much resistance have some of these organizations offered to the unfamiliar but provocative, the untried but promising?

We do not have the answers to these questions. We have our private hunches, but there is no authentic evidence, no progress report on which we can rely. It is nobody's business to monitor progress in American education in an orderly, comprehensive and reliable fashion, This omission is perhaps our most grievous flaw.

Given the fact of this educational gap, what can we do about it? Can the gap be eliminated or, at least, significantly reduced? I have no pat answer, but it might be helpful to examine some recent experiences which perhaps offer us clues.

We might begin by asking: how did we get such change and improvements in education as did occur in recent years, even though it was far from enough? No social scientist, to my knowledge, has ever looked into this, but we can hazard a few guesses. At least four factors seem to be involved:

First, people in education, in government and in the general public became increasingly aware that education was facing very serious problems and needed help. The country got into the mood of feeling that something ought to be done, though most people did not know precisely what. (If they thought they did know, it was apt to be an oversimplified cure-all.) Much of the public discussion and awareness was tied to the numbers game—the problem of rising enrollments, teacher shortages, classroom shortages, double sessions and the like. Most educators, though they knew better, tended to state in public that, in effect, there was nothing wrong with education that more money would not correct. This was, of course, a dangerous half-truth. Then came Sputnik, and the talk turned to much more elusive things, such as "quality" and "excellence."

Second, a factor which I suspect was very important was the succession of significant investigations and reports made from different vantage points by different groups, some governmentally and some privately sponsored. Among these were Dael Wolfe's ground-breaking study, *America's Resources of Specialized Talent,* which incidentally has not been revised; the report of the President's Commission on Scientific and Technical Personnel, which also is now largely obsolete; the report of the President's Committee on Education Beyond the High School; Beardsley Ruml's and Sidney Tickton's study of teaching salaries; Ruml's *Memo to a College Trustee;* and various reports reports issued by the Fund for the Advancement of Education and the Rockefeller Brothers Fund. These and other major statements had a significant impact on people's thinking, on their decision making, and hence on the progress of education.

Third, there was a substantial proliferation of practical experiments, many supported by foundations and encouraged by the popular feeling that something ought to be done. The number of these experiments increased to the point where it became not merely legitimate but almost fashionable to innovate and to challenge the educational status quo—not only the curriculum, where challenge has always been acceptable, but also the structure, the methods and the lockstep, where challenge in the past has been considered educational heresy.

Fourth, many individual communities, colleges and universities —and then whole states—began to *plan* education, trying to see where they had been, where they were, where they should go and how they could best get there. This effort began to bring some semblance of rational order and decision making into education, which until then had been the real bastion of laissez faire in our society.

These and a number of other factors help to explain the rather astonishing advances made by American education in the postwar period. But we must also ask: what limitations and constraints prevented us from advancing quickly enough to close or at least narrow the educational gap?

The popular awareness that education had serious problems and needed help was relatively superficial. Speeches and articles on the subject had a tone of precision and assurance out of proportion to the slim base of facts and analysis on which they rested. There was nowhere to turn—there is nowhere today—for a really competent, authoritative, disinterested diagonsis of the situation. The studies have been, at best, piecemeal and sporadic. Progress has depended much more on accident than on design.

The various expert reports, as helpful as they were, had typically two main defects: each looked at only one sector of the whole problem, and each was uncoordinated with the rest. As a result, when their various recommendations are gathered together, there is no common perspective and no consensus on priorities.

The experiments were likewise random. They occurred wherever there happened to be a maverick willing and able to try something new, but there was no adequate way to appraise the results or even to know what really happened. There was no systematic, reliable way to pass on the news, good or bad, to others who could use it. There was nothing like an over-all strategy of research and experimentation.

Obviously, an important way to close the educational gap is to reinforce those factors which have made our advances possible, while attempting to cure those faults which have slowed the pace of our advance. To the extent that we succeed, educational planning will be less haphazard and certainly far more effective.

Two other postwar experiences may also offer us clues to some means of closing the gap between our needs and our performance. The first of these relevant experiences is our role as counselor in this field to the emerging countries, advising them on ways to develop their educational systems and their human resources. The more sophisticated economists, educators and other advisors have been emphasizing that these countries should have long-range, comprehensive plans for educational development, geared to their manpower requirements and carefully integrated with their over-all plans for economic and social development. This advice seems very sound. Perhaps we should listen to it ourselves.

But how can we plan education on a national scale in our pluralistic society, where we are as jealous of the sovereignty of each school district, college and university as we are of our national sovereignty?

Perhaps part of the answer lies in the second relevant experience—our postwar monitoring of the performance of our economic system (under the Employment Act of 1946) with the aid of those interesting institutional inventions, the Council of Economic Advisers, the President's Annual Economic Report and the Joint Committee of Congress Report on the Economy.

Certainly the Employment Act was no panacea for all our economic ills and imperfections, yet it did provide invaluable help. For the first time in our history, a mechanism was established to assure us of a periodic and comprehensive audit of the national economy—where we are, where we have just been, where we seem to be heading, what problems seem most urgent at the moment, and what steps might be taken, among others, to deal effectively with these problems. The President's Economic Report is primarily influential, I suspect, because it provides a fairly clear and comprehensive framework within which anyone—an individual company, an industry, a state or local government, a Federal agency or the U. S. Congress—can appraise and plan more rationally in his particular sphere.

We have no such diagnostic frame of reference for education, and we ought to have. Who is projecting our national manpower requirements as a basis for our educational development? Who is determining, for example, our retraining needs, our health-manpower needs and our overseas-manpower needs, and who is relating all these needs to our evolving educational enterprise? Who is responsible for telling us how we did last year, how much ground we gained or lost, in relation to these important needs and goals?

This is why I say that American education, both inside and outside government, is in a state of dangerous disarray. We have no bearings, no compass, no log. While we debate endlessly, for instance, the issue of Federal aid to education, the enterprise bungles along, and no one even really knows what the impact of existing Federal aid programs has been on education.

Whose job should it be? Whom can we trust to provide a disinterested, competent, comprehensive frame of reference—an annual review of our progress, problems and prospects in education—which we can take or leave as we please, but which in all likelihood would improve our insights and our actions?

The best suggestion I have heard so far was from the late Beardsley Ruml, who was never afraid of a new idea. (It was the old ones that worried him!) Ruml suggested that we copy the Employment Act of 1946 and merely substitute the word *education* wherever the word *economic* appears. The preamble would then acknowledge that the Federal Government has a duty and a responsibility toward the well-being of our educational enterprise, comparable to the duty and responsibility it now acknowledges toward the health of our economy. The Federal Government has exercised this latter responsibility throughout the postwar years without taking over all the shoe stores and grocery stores. It is simply providing a frame of reference for evaluation and planning.

An education act modeled on the Employment Act would provide a council of education advisers, an annual President's report on the state of education and a joint committee of Congress to examine the report and give it a good public airing. There would thus be one sound and comprehensive overview on which public discussion would be focused. The Federal Government, under such an arrangement, would have no more control over American education than it has now, but it would be exerting far more effective leadership.

Perhaps Federal responsibility is not the best way to meet the problem. Perhaps we should invent a private or quasi-public instrumentality to perform this needed function of competent diagnosis, to monitor the annual progress of American education. But somehow the job must be done. The result of our present lack of knowledge is well illustrated by the conspicuous contrast between the administration's tax proposals to Congress and its education proposals. The tax proposals, whatever their merit, are at least set in a logical, analytical framework which reveals their relevance to the well-being of the whole economy. The education proposals, by contrast, though the individual items are undoubtedly desirable, can be described charitably as a shopping list in search of a rationale.*

The United States will not write the history of this century or the next all by itself. It can have, at most, only a marginal influence on the course of world events. Yet this marginal influence can be decisive, for better for for worse. How wisely we shall use it will depend very heavily upon our educational system, on how responsive it is to the new and vast needs for knowledge, insights and skills— needs that have been engendered by the revolutionary changes which have lately swept the world.

Just as the world is in a state of crisis, so is American education. If both crises are to be met, we must immediately apply more of our best brainpower to the rational development of our educational enterprise, on which we rely so heavily for rational solutions and progress in all other realms.

COMMENT BY . . . *David Riesman*
                        Henry Ford II Professor of Social Science,
                        Harvard University

[Mr. Riesman's comment is difficult at times to follow, partly because it is directed not at Mr. Coombs's major statements

---

*By 1965 there has been some improvement. The 1965 educational proposals of the Johnson Administration are better integrated with national goals than in the past.—Ed.

but at certain of his underlying assumptions, partly because its own premises and conclusions are often implied rather than stated explicitly. For both these reasons, brief editorial guidelines seem to be warranted.

[In the first section Mr. Riesman is apparently reacting to Mr. Coombs's proposal that American education be geared more closely to the nation's economic and other manpower needs. He is apparently suggesting that it might better be geared to a wider frame of reference—a fuller understanding of the American temperament. This leads him, a few paragraphs later, to recall Mr. Coombs's observation that the most serious obstacle to educational progress is the fact that "our knowledge of human beings and human society . . . is still in a primitive state."]

Mr. Coombs has given us an extraordinary proposal. I am in sympathy with what he said, and I want to take up right away his brilliant and clarifying analogy between educational planning and the economic legislation and institutionalization of the postwar years.

Let me suggest a course of action which, I think, would be a good way of beginning to carry out the larger challenge of understanding American life, which underlies that analogy. I would like a census to be taken of American attitudes, affects and developments in psychic structure, done with the seriousness of the Census Bureau. We have now various adumbrations of this in the polling by Louis Harris, the Survey Research Center of the University of California and other such groups; but these studies are totally unplanned, often partisan and always unconnected. There has been no census to determine the really underlying attitudes in our society. In fact, as our society becomes more complicated, we know less and less about these attitudes. One result is that the chances for educational reform are often blocked because of the decision-makers' uncertainty as to what would be accepted "out there."

It would also be an enormous boost to the development of the social sciences to have this kind of census, which would not have to question every American but could proceed for now by sampling. I am not convinced, any more than Mr. Coombs is, that more money is what the social sciences need in order to understand change and resistance to change. I think that the task of trying to frame questions and surveys which would encompass the whole country in a better understanding of itself—and of finding, at the same time, the mechanisms to isolate this census from both the instramural politics of social science and the extramural politics of the country as a whole—would be a great stimulus to the profession as well as to educational planning. And I think that we know barely enough to take the chance now, just as we knew barely enough about statistics in the eighteenth century to develop the modern census.

I agree that there is now very little progress in understanding human affairs, in comparison with the problems we confront. One reason, I think, is that there has been a general movement by the various social-science disciplines toward being at the service of the discipline, rather than of the society. The contempt with which the word "applied" is used and the sanctimonious vows toward so-called pure research are indicative of this great division. But what is called pure research is simply research done at the call of the discipline or subdiscipline, as against research done at the call of the outside client. Each is a client. The question of what research is relevant to the needs of society is not answered by who is the sponsor; and I think the guilds of academia, in their burgeoning sponsorship of the work in the social sciences, have tended to develop narrow trajectories which can only be broken into by the kinds of demands this census would provide.

[In the next section Mr. Riesman challenges directly Mr. Coombs's assumption that education should be geared more closely to the nation's manpower needs. He suggests that, in a profound way, it is already too closely geared to them.]

One of the problems of education today, certainly in its more advanced reaches, is that the young in our country are only too willing to see themselves as manpower and to decide their futures on the basis of a slight margin on an inadequate Strong Vocational Interest Test, rather than accept the much more difficult challenge of asking themselves what they *want* to do. The students—I am thinking largely of the better ones now, not of the more underprivileged and deprived —are being alienated from their own sense of what they really like, precisely because they are thinking of themselves as manpower being trained by a curriculum.

[Mr. Riesman then examines one of Mr. Coombs's major premises—that it is in the national interest for Americans to be educated to an understanding of world affairs. He identifies two contrasting points of view among people so educated, the nationalistic (which looks out from America at the rest of the world) and the global (which sees America as part of the world).]

Let me make one observation about the attitudes towards the rest of the world which are created by our present educational system, seen in its largest compass.

Education is today the greatest source, I would think, of both social and geographical mobility in our society. It pulls people out of their parishes. In the small town in America, the doctor, the lawyer, the school superintendent, the county agent—none of them came from that small town. They are from someplace else, and they are going someplace else. They are itinerants. And the young people from that small town who have gone to college have gone largely to get away from that small town (though maybe they are in some other small town). Even the parish about which there is the firmest patriotism, the South, is losing its patriotism, all political wigwaggings to the contrary.

As people find themselves outside their home locales, torn from their backgrounds and absorbed into new types of social structure to which they belong as units of manpower, I think they establish two identities to cling to. Both are forms of chauvinism: they identify intensely with America as a whole and with their own disciplines or professions. And while their nationalistic identity is a short-term advantage for the development of global awareness in American education, it is a long-run danger.

I offer as an illustration one still incomplete study done in a California state college for prospective teachers. The students were tested and scaled twice for authoritarianism, prejudice and so on, first on entrance and then after two years of college work. On entrance, they were bigots; they disliked Negroes, Jews, Mexicans, people from the next country, foreigners and so on. Two years later, this had been transformed: they had absorbed all the pieties about racial, interethnic and interreligious amity and comity. At the same time, they had become more nationalistic; they were more eager to win the cold war. In effect, they had shifted their allegiance to a new but still exclusive parish, the largest parish of all—more magnanimous in some ways, but also more heavily armed.

This development stands in sharp contrast to the much more sanguine development, for which the Peace Corps is the best exemplar, of young people who have shed their ethnocentrism, who are curious

about the world without being missionaries to it and who hope to
learn from foreign cultures as well as to instruct them. The Peace
Corpsmen will, I believe, come back to this country with a deeper
understanding of America, a deeper loyalty to its best hopes and, at
the same time, a sense of the problems of other global areas seen from
the perspective of those areas.

The result of these divergent developments—toward a nationalistic chauvinism and toward a perhaps too generous cosmopolitan outlook—is an enormous and frightening polarization. On one side are
those who view America in the perspective of a world society that
does not yet exist; on the other side are those who shrink into
America and try to pull the boundaries in because the global challenge
is terribly unnerving and threatening to them.

Mr. Coombs, in his brilliant talk, indicated how complex our
world is—how much people must be able to grasp, to grapple with
and to control in the modern world if they are not merely to feel
at home in it but to make a home of it. But there are many people
who cannot stand this necessity, who feel that the only hope for
them is to simplify the world somehow so that they can cope with
it more easily—if necessary, in a destructive fashion. I think this
polarization is growing very rapidly in our society.

[In the final section Mr. Riesman addresses himself to perhaps the deepest underlying assumption of Mr. Coombs's
speech—that the educational system should be used deliberately to indoctrinate students with certain predetermined
(and presumably beneficial) attitudes and commitments.]

One thought about education and what it has meant in this country
from the beginning, and then I have done. If one reads Horace
Mann and some of the other early nineteenth-century educators, one
can see in them a fear of the Wild West, which was then Ohio, the
Northwest Territory, Kentucky and so on—a fear which expressed
itself both in their fear of General Andrew Jackson and in their
fear that the western part of the country would break loose. Some
of these New England men felt that it was urgent to "educate" the
cowboys (as we call them now), and they managed to propagate
eastern values under the cover of an overt idealism, a quite genuine
sense of mission in spreading the enlightenment of education, reinforced by their fear that Old World culture would be lost in the
struggle for subsistence in this country.

That use of education as social control is one element, it seems to me, in the tension between the generations in America. There is, I believe, some connection between the advances of American education in its best reaches and the resistance of the young—the most highly gifted and qualified young—to the demands which they feel that the system increasingly puts upon them. This fear that they will be hemmed in, that they will not be allowed to act as free enterprisers of their own lives, is partly an illusion and partly a resistance to the plethora of choices which the greater opportunities require. But I think it is also due partly to their sense of being imposed upon, of not wanting the responsibility of the world put so heavily upon them, when they have so little chance to help define what the world needs and what they themselves need.

SUMMARY OF THE DISCUSSION

At one point early in the general discussion, after seeking to clarify a controversial issue, Mr. Coombs remarked: "I'm not trying to resolve all possible conflicts. I hope we can see more precisely what our conflicts are, but there is no need for artificial differences of opinion." His hope came true: several issues were defined with remarkable lucidity, but there was little or no consensus on solutions.

Four major areas of controversy came under scrutiny:

Planning education to meet manpower needs: "In theory," said Mr. Harris, "every young person ought to pick his own profession or vocation. In practice, the nation needs men and women who have been trained in specific fields. If the young person is not guided by rather narrow incentives, such as scholarships in the right fields, he may be inclined to pick the wrong field in terms of national needs. This is a tough problem; it is very difficult to reconcile these two objectives."

Manpower needs are certainly not the only determinant of educational purposes, Mr. Coombs declared. "The role of education in our society is not simply to make the Gross National Product rise. It just happens, fortunately, to do that. Maybe this is only a by-product." Still, the interaction of education and the national economy is a fact which cannot be ignored.

The importance of manpower needs is perhaps most obvious in the underdeveloped countries which are trying to build their economies rapidly. David D. Henry, director of the Harvard International Office, commented on this point: "In the developing countries, skilled individuals are needed to develop industries, to lay out roads, to tend to the medical needs of the people and so on—or these things will not be done. It is hard to see how these needs can be met without some kind of human engineering, some kind of educational system which tailors the students to the countries' needs." In the developed nations, such as the United States, these needs are less stark and less exigent but no less real.

Yet America's educational system, Mr. Riesman declared, to the extent that it pressures students to meet manpower needs, is "making it impossible or very difficult for them to choose the sort of lives they really want to live." The pressures are frequently blunt, as when the Federal Government helps to build schools for training in some fields and not others. But the pressures are often quite subtle, as when students are pressed to choose their careers before they can really know what they are choosing. "They need a chance to see what the world is like in the occupational realm. Education must open this realm for them to examine, not just tell them what they are expected to do. They should not act blindly out of an irrational, windmill feeling." All these pressures, blunt and subtle, are increasing today.

In pointing to the wider implications, Mr. Riesman noted "the inevitable narcissism of creative people," meaning presumably that they are concerned to develop those talents which they recognize as valuable within themselves, regardless whether these talents serve immediate national needs. Yet "if people are fundamentally unalienated, they want to do something that is of use, of relevance to their age." This double drive can be fulfilled under the right conditions: "The Germans developed great chemists at a time when the country did not need them, but they became so good that they made possible the growth of a tremendous chemical industry and thus created a demand for their services." Americans today, however, are alienated both from their individual selves and from the world around them. Considerations of status, rather than inner drives, point people toward one future or another; and "in order to offer them opportunities, one has to use very contaminated devices to compete against the other contaminated devices that are already there."

In brief, two sharp views were expressed—that education's concern with meeting manpower needs is (1) essential to the well-being of all Americans collectively and (2) destructive of the well-being of Americans individually. "These views appear to be diametrically opposed." Mr. Coombs observed, "and they may actually be opposed in part, but I think the conflict is not very serious.

"Our formal educational system is not an entity but a collection of institutional arrangements. Each student should have a wide range of choice as to what institution he will attend, if he fits it. Within that institution he should have a wide range of choice of disciplines, and he should certainly have a wide range of choice of careers. However, if the institutions within which these students exist and develop are not themselves enlightened as to what the future may hold, every student's range of choice and basis for choice are constrained more than they need to be.

"When I talk about planning for our educational system, I am not talking about planning for any individual student. I am talking about planning for the total structure, so that it will have some reasonable bounds within it and some reasonable relationship to the direction in which things seem to be going. For example, if we are ever going to raise the level of health and of health services in this country, somebody will have to figure out roughly how many more doctors and paramedical people we need in relation to the population. If this were done, it would actually open up for young people career opportunities that they now do not have. So I see no imcompatibility between planning for our institutions and full freedom of choice for the individual."

Nationalism vs. global awareness: The conflict between national chauvinism and a wider, more cosmopolitan world view, as Mr. Riesman had defined them, was discussed briefly from three angles. *First,* the charge was leveled by one discussant that the perspective of current educational development and planning is profoundly chauvinistic —that national, rather than individual or global, justifications are offered for all proposed advances in education. Two illustrations were offered: (1) the signal advances under the National Defense Education Act were conceived as furthering not education but national defense, and (2) international affairs are taught in social-studies courses in essentially chauvinistic terms. The latter illustration, perhaps because it was so vague, went undebated.

As for the NDEA, Mr. Coombs explained that the sponsors of the Act agreed, "invariably and behind closed doors," that is provisions are wholly desirable regardless of their impact on national defense. The "defense" label was added because the sponsors felt that without it the bill would not command enough votes to pass. "But I have asked a good many congressmen about this, and I have never found one who said that he would not have supported the bill without that label."

This disguising of generous motives, he continued, marks many of our public discussions. "I think it is only a slight oversimplification to say that most of the generous actions, most of the right things the United States had done since World War II in the field of international affairs, have been done ostensibly for the wrong reasons. I have been ashamed at times to watch people whom I know and respect give appalling reasons for doing fine things. Almost everybody involved has a sense of what is right and wants to do it, but each one assumes that the others will only respond to the wrong labels. So I think we are not quite as bad, not quite as competitive and cold-war-minded, as we seem from our words."

Second, the charge was leveled that American education presents world affairs in terms of competition rather than of cooperation and that this bias is very deeply engrained within our educational system. Mr. Coombs responded by questioning the assumption that competition is bad. "In the nature of society and of people, at least as we know them, can a society really be dynamic if it is not under some kind of pressure—competitive pressures, or natural disasters, or something else? Historians, pointing to the decline of the Roman Empire as an example, have said that as soon as a society is free of pressure and becomes affluent (which makes this a cue for us), it goes to pieces. I do not know whether this is inevitable or not, but surely much of our postwar performance, for better or worse, has been in response to what we conceive to be the competition of different systems, and maybe it has brought out the best as well as the worst in both systems."

Third, Frank Bowles, then president of the College Entrance Examination Board and now educational program director of the Ford Foundation, charged that our institutions of higher learning, quite apart from their academic instruction, are an obstacle to the student who is "becoming an international man." He cited as a prime example the experience of many college seniors who decide upon graduation to join the Peace Corps, rather than enter graduate schools or professional schools or take up Rhodes or Fulbright scholarships.

"A student may make this decision at a very great sacrifice and against the desire of most of his family and professors—especially his professors. If he joins the Peace Corps, which really will further his internationality or demonstrate his lack of ethnocentricity, he is immediately written off. He is regarded as an odd character who does not know which side his bread is buttered on and who does not have the really important qualifications for whatever career, academic or otherwise, he may have been considering. This is a very serious problem. If we really want to create international men, we must take some action at the university level. We must have a change of mind among the people whom the student respects."

Federal role in educational planning: In the course of the discussion, Mr. Coombs was asked to amplify his suggestion for planning at the national level. He replied: "There are a lot of meanings of planning, and I think we ought to be very clear what kind we are talking about. The Soviet style is more than planning; it is allocation —control over the flow of resources, including people, into different enterprises.

"At the other end of the spectrum is the kind of planning which the Council of Economic Advisers does. It is not planning in the sense of pushing the economy in specific directions. It is merely enlightening the marketplace with facts, giving perspectives and insights that otherwise would not be there, influencing people's free choices and decisions by giving them more information than they had before. In education, it means giving states and localities and institutions a national framework of information within which to orient their own planning. It is planning, but it is not control. This is really all I am talking about."

Several advantages, he continued, would follow from such planning. Properly coordinated, the national data would provide a basis for fairly confident projections about future demands on education and future resources available to it. Properly presented, the data could show "the flow of people through the educational system"—a set of information which could yield important insights and which is not now available in any form. Properly analyzed, the data could identify the frontier of educational knowledge and help to indicate the priorities for educational research. Above all, such planning would counteract the increasing and preposterous specialization being fostered by the schools of education. "We are turning out specialists on pieces of our educational system. We are not turning out people capable of looking at a total educational system and its relationship to our society. I am talking about taking a grand look at the total system."

A major weakness of this argument, Mr. Harris suggested, is its assumption that the mechanism created by the Employment Act of 1946 is really working as it was intended. Actually, political factors have made it fall far short. The Council of Economic Advisers does assemble data and draw precise interpretations, but these interpretations are not often made public. There has been general discussion of economic issues, and "the council has had considerable influence by making many facts widely available and by educating the public about these issues." But it "has been very careful not to say anything" in detail about possible courses of future action. Projections of the impact of alternative actions on the tax rate and the budget deficit have simply been too highly charged politically for general dissemination.*

Political inhibitions, then, are one major limitation to Federal planning. This is already apparent in education, Mr. Harris noted. "Congress has decided that it does not want the Office of Education to have great influence because the congressmen are terribly scared of Federal control. For that reason, the Office of Education is scared of forecasting or any similar activity." Mr. Coombs suggested that the Office might concentrate on gathering data and turn the task of interpreting it over to an independent or quasi-independent organization. But Mr. Harris noted that political considerations still operate. A recent report prepared by the Brookings Institution for the Council of Economic Advisers has been left unpublished because the administration is scared that its projections may prove inaccurate, "I think," said Mr. Coombs, "that we have to stop being quite so scared."

A second limitation to Federal planning was stated by Mrs. Joan Burstyn of the Graduate School of Education. "The goal for underdeveloped countries is a model which they can actually see, within certain limits. Their goal is a highly developed technological society along the lines of Western society. And although the politicians within these societies may disagree as to the methods of reaching this goal, I think that, on the whole, they would not challenge the goal itself.

"For us, the problem is different. Can we *see* any goals toward which our society is reaching? Have we models on which we can base our ideas? If not, the problems of development are political problems. Deciding the lines along which we shall develop is a political judgment. And that makes it very difficult, it seems to me, to plan educational development in any sense without immediately becoming involved in political questions."

Mrs. Burstyn's implication was that any serious educational planning at the national level would inevitably become a debate over the nature and vision of the American society. At such a level of generality, could any serious planning of specifics be accomplished

---

*This is less true in 1965 than in 1962-63.—Ed.

within a formal planning structure? The discussion was deflected at this point, and this question was not pursued.

Assuming that some form of national planning for education is desirable, what are the chances of its being accepted by Congress in the near future? "I think the prospects are not hopeless by any means," Mr. Coombs declared. "They depend a good deal on who advocates it and how the case is presented. But there would be much sentiment for it on the Hill. Many congressmen are very interested in education, and though their interest is divided by several issues— church and state, racial integration, the level of Federal spending— they would come together on an innocuous and inexpensive measure of this sort." Mr. Harris was not so optimistic, but under pressure he allowed that "I think you may get it—ultimately."

Education's resistance to change: Brief but intense mention was made of a fourth area of controversy. "I have been struck," said Mr. Riesman, "by how many of my academic colleagues are political progressives and pedagogic reactionaries. The explanation, I think, is that vested interest in ideas is the most important vested interest one has." But one result is a stubborn resistance by people in education to forces urging change, including the force of the changing world itself.

This situation was contrasted by one discussant to the situation in science, where "people seem to be more sure of themselves, more willing to criticize and to explore new and offbeat ideas. How can we begin to develop in education the kind of strength and viability which make that kind of dialogue possible?"

"Well," Mr. Coombs observed, "one reason why scientists can talk about their subject in a more objective way than social scientists, including educators, is that scientists are dealing with a much simpler subject. They are not dealing with people, and they are not dealing with the value structure of our society to nearly the same degree—except when they make a bomb. You can never expect the discussion to be as simple when you are dealing in the realm of human affairs."

Part II:
Qualitative Issues

6. Research in Education

Francis A. J. Ianni
Chief of the Cooperative Research Program, U. S. Office of Education

The Federal Government's concern for research in education might be characterized as both recent and long-standing, both diverse and narrowly focused. These seeming paradoxes result in part from the perdurability of education in American culture.

Education is a social process so vital to the preservation of our society that we are sure it will continue despite all obstacles. A lack of adequate research can hamper but not destroy it; what educators do not know, they will guess. One unhappy result of this durability is that research in education has never had the same urgency for the mind politic as research related to the needs of medicine, agriculture, the national defense or even the Fish and Wild Life Service. The Government spends, in fact, considerably more on research in the Fish and Wild Life Service than on research in education.

As a consequence, research has been ignored in most schemes of educational improvement. Efforts directed toward progress in education have generally centered around providing more of what already exists—more classrooms, more books, more courses, more visual aids —and improving the preparation of teachers, who are not fully using even the little that is already known. Though the Constitution says nothing about a Federal responsibility for education, this lack of important research and this indifference to it seem to demand from the Government, in its broad charge for the national welfare, a degree of concern. Certain professional educators may dispute this, but most educationally oriented interest groups today recognize the need for Federal support of educational research, usually as part of our concern for science.

Actually, the interest of the Government in both scientific research and education has a respectable antiquity. The creation of the Smithsonian Institution in 1846, the Morrill Act establishing the land-grant colleges in 1862, the founding of the National Academy of Sciences in 1863 and the United States Office of Education in

1867—all give evidence of this concern. In more recent years, the emergence of the Office of Naval Research in 1946 and the National Institutes of Health in 1948, the creation of the National Science Foundation in 1950 and the Cooperative Research Program of the Office of Education in 1956, the passage of the National Defense Education Act of 1958—all these are new evidences of continued interest.

As we look back over this record, however, one salient fact emerges. In each case, the motivating factor—or at least the manifest motivation—has been to enhance the national interest or purpose as conceived in broadly utilitarian terms. Thus research in agriculture, stimulated under the Morrill Act and developed under the Hatch Act of 1887, which brought about the agricultural experiment stations, was made palatable to the nation not as scientific research but as a means of improving agricultural productivity. In the same way, while it is becoming increasingly possible to obtain congressional approval for research and development funds for remedial programs for the deaf, the blind, the mentally retarded, the delinquent and even the gifted, appropriations for research and development for the general purpose of improving the quality of education have been extremely difficult to obtain. Even today, foreign language and area-training programs must be sold to the Congress as a means to bolster the national defense and to get on in a world grown perilously small.

Certainly one cause of this failure to view scientific inquiry into educational problems as vital to the national and individual interest is the lack of drama in educational research: no congressman's daughter has ever died of a split infinitive. But in large measure, educational research has failed to catch the political and public imagination because it has been unimaginative and, until recent years, almost wholly restricted to doctoral dissertations and small, uninteresting research projects. Think back over the years to the significant innovations in educational practice, and you will find, I believe, that all too often they grew out of the experience and insight of an individual or the pressure of society, rather than the findings of educational research.

The pattern of the Federal subsidy for research and development also reveals the lowly status of educational research in the United States. In comparison to amounts available for research in other areas, educational research funds are meager.

In the decade 1951-1961, an impressive total of $80 billion was expended by all sectors of the economy on research and development. The proportion of these costs assumed by the Government increased steadily, from about one-half of the total in 1951 to over two-thirds in 1961. By the fiscal year 1963 there was a Federal budgetary obligation of $12.4 billion for research and development activities.* Our present projections indicate that by fiscal 1970 the Government will bear three-fourths of all research and development costs. Estimates beyond that year are largely a reflection of the political orientation of the forecaster, but it seems safe to assume that the Federal Government will continue as the dominant source of support for research and development.

Research as a whole plays a relatively important role as a source of Federal support in institutions of higher learning. Of the approximately $1 billion expended in such institutions by the Government in 1960, about $450 million went for research, as against $488 million for scholarships, loans and fellowships, $17 million for various programs of instruction and $44 million for facilities. (Of the $450 million which went for research, however, 94 per cent went to only 100 institutions out of the 2,000 institutions of higher learning in the United States.) †

Almost all of these research funds were contributed by the seven principal sponsors of research in educational institutions—the Department of Defense (about 40 per cent), the Public Health Service (about 30 per cent), the National Science Foundation (about 11 per cent), the Atomic Energy Commission (about 8 per cent), the Department of Agriculture (about 6 per cent), the National Aeronautics and Space Agency (about 3 per cent) and the Office of Education (about 2 per cent).

If it is assumed that any research which improves the competence of the American educators is essentially educational research, then most of the money expended by these agencies must be assigned to educational research; but this is scarcely realistic. Actually, a very small portion of these moneys is given for purely educational research. The Office of Education is the principal agency which supplies support for studies of the *process* of education. We may safely say, therefore, that just 2 per cent of the research funds given to institutions of higher learning is for educational research.

---

*By 1964-65, the total was $15 billion.—Ed.

† *The Digest of Educational Statistics*, 1964, gives a figure of $829 million of income for research from the Federal Government in the year 1959-60.—Ed.

To narrow the focus somewhat more, if the categorical research-support programs (such as the Newer Educational Media Program of the National Defense Education Act) are excluded, the Office of Education's share falls to less than 1 per cent. In fiscal 1961, the Cooperative Research Program, the principal granting agency within the Office for noncategorical educational research, had a budget of $3.6 million. Over $3 million of this was needed to pay the continuation costs of research projects initiated in previous years. Less than $500,000 was available for new research.

It seems unnecessary to point out that this is a pitifully small amount for so important an enterprise. But, in all candor, education may be getting just about what it deserves in terms of its own vision of the need for innovation. Educators are prone to talk about the need for "big money" in educational research while clinging to small plans for innovation. It has become fashionable, for example, to deplore the fact that while many industries spend up to one-third of their budget on research, educational research and development expenditures amount to less than .2 per cent of total annual expenditures on education in the United States. But progress in education requires more than just additional money. Before we can even consider seeking the sums now expended on research in health or agriculture, for example, we must broaden the frontier of experimentation in education and create a pervasive professional mood which not only accepts innovation, but seeks and welcomes it. Here, I believe, is the challenge for leadership which we hope the Cooperative Research Program can meet.

Let me tell you just a little about the program and give you some idea of what does take place. The Cooperative Research Program was established during the post-World War II period. The reason for its establishment, very frankly, had nothing to do with the promise of educational research. It was founded because certain members of Congress had taken a strong interest in the problem of mental retardation and decided that some research had to be done in this area. So the Office of Education was authorized to do research, primarily in the area of mental retardation. The law, which is Public Law 531, was enacted by the 83rd Congress and signed by the President in 1954; it authorizes the Commissioner of Education "to enter into contracts and jointly financed Cooperative arrangements with universities and colleges and State educational agencies for the conduct of research, surveys, and demonstrations in the field of education."

Actually, though the law was passed in 1954, no funds were made available until 1957. In the fiscal year 1957, the Office was given $1.1 million for research. The following year this amount was increased to $2.3 million. By fiscal 1961, the research budget had reached $7 million; and anticipated for 1965-66, $25 million.

In its early years, the Cooperative Research Program was focused on ten areas of research interest which the Office of Education considered particularly important. In addition to mental retardation, these included such concerns as juvenile delinquency and school vandalism. But we were allowed to make contracts for other types of research, and the research areas serviced by the Program have been expanded rapidly in recent years. Today research is being supported in many fields of basic knowledge which hold promise of important contributions to educational knowledge.

We have also had, in recent years, growing numbers of social scientists coming to the Program. We have sociologists, psychologists, anthropologists, political scientists, philosophers, economists and—this year for the first time—a psychiatrist working on problems of educational research. Equally important is the fact that the Cooperative Research Program has continued as the one source of funds for the training of educational researchers.

Proposals for research are received from colleges, universities and state educational agencies throughout the year and are reviewed by panels of research specialists from outside the Office of Education. This process of review is very painstaking, and many proposals are not approved. To date, we have received 2,100 proposals and approved about 500. Many researchers, particularly those whose proposals are rejected, wonder at this rather high rejection rate. Some maintain that our researchers favor only experimental studies. We have checked ourselves on this, in a rather elaborate analysis, and I can assure you that the charge is unfounded.

What does seem to be wrong with the rejected proposals—and I think this will give you some idea of what is wrong with current educational research as a whole—is that usually they are marred by one of the following faults:

First, the problem to be attacked by the proposed research has no general significance to education. This fault may appear in several ways. In a surprising number of cases, the problem is simply a trivial one. Since a definition of a trivial problem is extremely difficult, let me give you an example of one that we received within the last year. (Incidentally, in quoting these proposals, I shall try to mask them as much as possible.) This study, which I consider trivial, was designed to prove that Zen Buddhism could be taught in physical education courses. Now, this seems trivial to us—though presumably not to the people who suggested it—primarily because the outcome of such a study would be virtually meaningless in terms of the total educational program.

In a surprising number of cases, the problem is not only trivial but is also limited to one institution. Many proposals seek to prove the excellence of a particular institution. Obviously, we cannot support this type of study.

Many other studies are lacking in significance primarily because the area which they intend to research is so vast that they simply cannot narrow their focus. One of my colleagues from anthropology, for example, recently applied for funds to study all the significant inventions from the Stone Age to the present—a really commendable undertaking, until one realizes that he intended to do this in nine months with the help of one graduate assistant.

Second, the objectives of the research are often too broadly stated. The objectives, hypotheses or questions of a research proposal represent the investigator's attempt to focus his attention on specific aspects of a problem. The sharper the focus, the more likely the investigator is to succeed in his task. Consider, then, the following objective quoted from a recent proposal: "The broad hypothesis is that a procedure can be followed which will lead to the initial formulation, revision, and final development of a broadly conceived theory of education based upon psychological and other relevant research findings."

When one reads this, one gets the impression that the researcher is going to come out with a magnificent theory. The way in which he proposed to do this was rather interesting also. He was going to sit and talk to his colleagues for a period of one year and, at the end of that year, gather together everything they had said into one broadly conceived theory of education.

Third, and finally, many proposals are poorly designed, usually because the investigator fails to recognize the complexity of the task involved. One proposal, for example, sought funds to provide a program of mathematics and English instruction to an experimental group of high-school graduates during the summer before they entered college. A control group would not have received the instruction. During the freshman year the mean achievement of the two groups would have been compared. This study says, in effect, that a group who have had instruction in English and math will be better prepared to cope with college English and math than a comparable group who have received no instruction. The intergroup analysis not only compares something (the instruction) with nothing (the lack of instruction), but it completely obscures the complexity of the problem. In reality, one would expect that some students—those who were highly motivated but who lacked certain math and English skills— would show significant improvements, while others, including those who lacked motivation for academic work, would show little or no improvement.

We have been greatly impressed by a study which was conducted in England several years ago by the National Foundation for Educational Research in England and Wales. The director of the institution, Professor Wall, introduced into several schools in England a new method of teaching reading based upon three processes: (1) reading nonsense syllables, (2) learning to read with one eye closed, and (3) learning to read while standing rather than sitting. At the end of two years, the children who received this type of instruction scored significantly higher on reading achievement tests than children who learned by the traditional method. The method, of course, had nothing to do with it. The teacher and the students, feeling that they were involved in an experimental situation, made much greater efforts.

As for those proposals which we accept: once they have been approved by the Commissioner of Education, a fixed-price contract is negotiated with the investigator. The dimensions of these contracts vary considerably—in cost, from a low of $800 to a high of $1,450,000 (though we have had only one $1 million project), and in length, from three months to eight years. The average project tends to run for about two and a half years at a total cost of $50,000. In all, the Cooperative Research Program has expended $26 million on 500 research projects during the last six years.

Despite my earlier pessimism over what educational research has done to improve education, some progress is now being made. The research conducted under the Program in the six-year period has been instrumental in providing new knowledge for education. As a result of these activities, I believe that we are now in a position to provide leads to the solution of some persistent educational problems. Let me say honestly—and this is something which is embarrassing before the Congress—that I do not believe we are ready to solve problems. I think we are ready to provide the information to take the next

step, which is to apply this knowledge in the school system. We have
not done that in the past.

Let me share with you just a few of the recent findings in the
area of educational practice, to indicate the range of data which
we believe we now have available for the schools. I am restricting
my examples to five sectors of educational practice, leaving aside the
many studies which we have funded in basic learning theory, sociological theory and other areas—studies which we feel will have a long-
range effect on the Program but which do not yet enter into practice.

First, education of the blind. As the result of one Cooperative
Research project, it is now possible to increase at least fourfold the
rate of listening comprehension of blind children, from approximately
60 to 240 words per minute. Until now, the blind have been limited
to receiving information at frustratingly slow rates of speed through
the Braille system or through ordinary voice recordings. Now, thanks
to the remarkable new application of "compressed speech," it is possible for them to learn not merely at 240 words per minute but,
experimentally at the present time, at 350 words per minute. The
average rate of reading for sighted children is 300 words per minute.

Second, studies of mental retardation. In the important area of
research dealing with mental retardation, the Program has new evidence which points to the possibility that at least some of the children
who have traditionally been handled as mentally retarded individuals
may, in reality, be the products of "retarded homes." Probably the
most remarkable finding in this area is that many children classified
as mental retardates can be taught to read at a very early age. These
preliminary findings are being tested experimentally with a large
number of children. Research to date indicates that, in many cases,
apparent retardation may actually result from a family environment
in which there has been no stimulation for young minds—a home
which lacks books, magazines and newspapers, and where there are
few interests other than in the most immediate material problems.

Third, mathematics education. Another recently completed
Cooperative Research project has shown that learning in mathematics
can be doubled in young children if they are taught basic mathematical ideas in the first grade. The researchers in this study have experi-
mented with the ability of first-grade children to learn mathematics
in terms of algebraic structures rather than sets of rules. This initial
experiment was successful, and they are proceeding to develop curricular materials for the first three grades, in which children will be

taught to view mathematics as a logical system of relationships rather than as a scattering of unrelated concepts.

Fourth, studies of the teaching-learning process. Many Cooperative Research studies have dealt with what is certainly a core problem in education: the teacher-student relationship. One recently completed study, for example, has developed new techniques for helping the inexperienced teacher in her first critical periods of teaching—and I do mean the *first* critical periods, the first ten periods in which she teaches.

An earlier study by the same researchers indicated that many experienced teachers may be characterized as "fearful teachers," lacking in confidence and often ineffective as a result. These experimenters are now developing a specific curriculum which can be used by fearful teachers.

Still another study with some fascinating implications for teacher education dealt with the ways in which teachers need to control their classroom and the importance that verbal behavior plays in this need. Thus, while research confirms that excessive controlling behavior on the part of the teacher is much more likely to impede than to facilitate learning in the classroom, the researchers indentified some teachers who devoted up to 44 per cent of their verbal behavior to simply controlling the children. Such teachers are as ineffective as the fearful ones, and indications are that such behavior represents a well-established and early-ingrained trend in personality. The researchers are developing instruments to test prospective teachers for these characteristics.

Finally, the identification and development of human talent. The first major phase of Project Talent, the large Pittsburgh study of the education of 440,000 American students, has been completed, and some preliminary results have been announced. These give some idea of the range of findings the researchers eventually hope to get from this particular study.

For example, in the area of English, the project found that twelfth-grade students are generally able to spell correctly 92 per cent of the 5,000 most frequently used words in the English language; also, that they are able to apply rules of capitalization correctly in 90 per cent of a set of examples based on all the rules of capitalization. Authorities in the field of English tell me that it is extremely important to ascertain these rates and percentages.

In reading, the students' ability was tested on representative paragraphs selected from current periodicals and from classic novels. Test

questions were developed to estimate the completeness of their understanding of these paragraphs. The average twelfth-grader was able
to answer correctly 78 per cent of the questions concerning matter
taken from typical articles in motion-picture magazines such as *Film
Fun*, but his comprehension declined swiftly to 28 per cent on material selected from the more literary periodicals, such as *The Atlantic
Monthly* and *The Saturday Review*. On reading materials selected
from writings of well-known novelists, it was found that the average
twelfth-grader is able to comprehend only about half of the broader
ideas of the authors of typical novels.

Most interesting to me—and this shows my social-science bias—is
the finding that of all possible correlates with achievement scores
in English, the highest positive correlation was with the socio-economic status of the child's parent. No matter how much additional
English instruction was given, the parental background still tended
to have the highest rate of correlation.

One important side result of Project Talent has been the development of a system of classification of types of schools which will allow
for meaningful comparisons between schools. In the past we have
usually tended to compare schools with a "national average," which
is meaningless. Project Talent has come up with a classification for
schools which will allow for comparison in terms of excellence in
particular areas. One of the most interesting results of this portion
of the study, by the way, is that the highest correlate with all possible
measures of achievement is the beginning salary of teachers in the
school system.

The summaries which I have just given you are taken from only
a few areas. Results of equal significance are emerging in many additional areas, such as identification and development of gifted students,
language achievements of the mentally retarded, teaching of spatial
concepts to blind children, motivations of youths for leaving school,
relationship of school experiences to juvenile delinquency, effects of
various teaching methods on the achievement of elementary-school
children, cross-cultural studies of education, development of language
and reading skills in young children, economics of higher education,
social climates in the schools, financing of education in urban areas,
and improving the effectiveness of college teaching. In each case, a
research project at a college, university or state education agency
has provided these important findings.

But, despite the obvious promise of these important findings,
it would be less than honest to suggest that they have had any wide-

spread effect on American educational practice. Braille still continues as the principal method of teaching the blind; the traditional patterns of the teaching-learning process have remained relatively unchanged, except for occasional minor refinements, usually in the direction of reinforcement of existing methods; and the chronological lock step from kindergarten through college seems to remain almost inviolate. Some progress has been made in revising the curriculum; but despite the combined efforts of the Office of Education and the National Science Foundation, the new mathematics programs, for example, still meet considerable resistance, at least some of which is led and organized by national associations of educators. (I want to make it very clear that I did not say specifically the National Education Association).

One of the problems, therefore, with which we have been troubled for a long time is that of getting schools to make effective use of our research results. One obstacle, as experience has shown in the past, is that research results can be interpreted in almost any way to suit a particular organization. Let me give you one short example from my own field, anthropology.

When the doctrine of evolution first became generally accepted in America, back in the early 1900's, one segment of the country took this doctrine to hold that each of the modern races was descended from a different grade of ape. The Negro was supposed to be descended from the gorilla, the Mongoloids from the chimpanzee. That left the white race with no visible ancestor, but this lapse was soon corrected. Its ancestor was located, believe it or not, in the white-faced baboon.

Well, this theory was held until about 1920, when Professor Robert M. Yerkes did a series of studies on the comparative intelligence of the great apes. He discovered that the chimpanzee is probably the most intelligent of the great apes, with the gorilla a close second. As a matter of fact, there is only one idiot in the whole family, and that is the white-faced baboon.

Another reason for our past failures to bring about a practical reification of the promise of educational research is more to our purpose now. The simple fact is that research aimed at improving education has been so timid in conception that it has never been taken seriously by most educators. This is equally the result of the researcher's ineptness and lack of vision and the educator's notorious tendency to cling tenaciously to the security of old, familiar practices.

Until very recently, educational research has not been regarded as a respectable field of endeavor by the best scholars in such fields as history, English, economics, anthropology, sociology and psychology. As a result, the responsibility for educational research was left almost entirely to faculties of education, who have labored valiantly but under great handicaps and with distressingly small results.

Faced with the smug scorn of his more respectable colleagues in the humanities and the natural and social sciences, the educationist retreated to small, manageable research projects, most of which have been on such a tiny scale, so fragmented, and often concerned with such minor problems that the really critical problems of education have remained unanswered. He has also tended, more and more, to turn to the behavioral and social sciences for his answers. I deplore this just as much as staying strictly with the educational psychologist or the educational researcher, because what is needed today in education is not additional studies in basic learning, as important as these are, but rather some good studies in the control of learning, which we have not done in the past.

As the scholarly community and, in more recent years, the Congress and the general public have chided the educational researcher for his lack of practical results, he has too often responded by attempting to spread the mantle of science over his efforts and pronounce the well-defined and exquisitely designed, small research project as the only scientifically tenable one for research in education.

This project-by-project approach has served educational research well as a means of establishing a firm base for the development of certain ideas and techniques, but the time has come to examine its value as a unique means of gathering usable data for the educational process. A scrutiny of research in the physical sciences, medicine and the behavioral sciences—all of which are certainly further along in the improvement of research techniques than education—reveals that the project approach loses its utility when it is applied to the resolution of major problems.

The project approach has proven most valuable in basic research, where the investigator has a particular hypothesis or series of hypotheses which he desires to test. The project is essentially a technique for focusing attention on some discreet problem within a relatively narrow area of interest—for example, to identify a particular strain of virus or to determine the effects of various forms of discipline on student achievement. In both cases the investigator is examining the interaction of variables under relatively controlled conditions. But because of the very nature of the rigid controls necessary to basic research, the operation of these variables outside the laboratory or the experimental classroom remains undetermined unless basic research findings are field-tested in a variety of situations. And after field-testing, they must be demonstrated and eventually disseminated to the educational community.

These four steps—basic research, field-testing, demonstration and dissemination—along with continuous research planning and development constitute the total research process. It seems obvious that if new "projects" have to be mounted for each of the four steps in a single area of research interest, there must be a significant loss, both in time and in continuity of research. Our estimate is that, over the past century, the time lag between the emergence of relatively wide discussion of a researchable idea in education and its final dissemination as a usable tool throughout the schools has approached sixty years. The time lag between the *completion* of a research project and the use of its results in the schools is closer to forty-five years.

The recent trend in scientific research has been to move from the project approach to the program approach, in which planned, continuous attention, through all steps in the research process, is focused on persistent problem areas until solutions are found *and translated into practice*. Each group of researchers follows a research program from development through demonstration. It is our belief that educational research and the Cooperative Research Program are now ready to make this shift. The research project remains the most valid method of conducting basic research, but the time has come to implement the results of basic research as soon as they are available.

The first actions in this movement to a program base have already been taken in the Cooperative Research Program. In 1962 "progammed research" activities in English and talent development were introduced as a means of focusing attention to these problem areas. This programatic approach will be gradually extended to the social studies, the arts and teacher education. In each programmed area, funds are or will be available for research planning and development programs, basic and applied research, field-testing, demonstration and dissemination.

It is in these final steps of demonstration and dissemination that we have made the greatest departures from our traditional approaches to educational research. The Cooperative Research Program has traditionally been a source of funds for basic research. We have not and will not abandon this as our chief function. But we have instituted several new programs in an effort to speed the demonstration and dissemination of results.

Early in 1962 a number of demonstration projects were instituted for the purpose of both testing and demonstrating the use of research results in the schools. One demonstration is now under way, for example, to test the use of an enriched mathematics program with talented youngsters; this grew out of our earlier basic and applied research project. Another will demonstrate the feasibility of early admission to the first grade for mentally advanced children.

Another new program has been the establishment of curriculum study centers to develop and test promising practices and materials in English and the social studies and to produce new curricula in these subjects. In coming years, we will expand the centers approach to cover the entire range of the curriculum.

We are also letting contracts for a number of regional demonstration centers in English and in the identification and utilization of talent. Our hopes are that as the results of research projects and curriculum development programs become available, they can be demonstrated to teachers and administrators at these centers.

During the fiscal year 1964, we hope to establish a small grant program which will allow a researcher with a "hot" idea to take the necessary time to plan and develop his approach to the problem and perhaps try it out on a limited scale. We hope also to establish our first program-research centers at a number of educational institutions. These centers, financed on a long-range, full-support basis, will bring together university scholars, state education agency administrators, and teachers and administrators from the local schools to work cooperatively on total research-dissemination programs.

In 1965, if our dreams come true, we shall establish a pre- and postdoctoral fellowship program, not only to upgrade the training of educational researchers, but perhaps also to try some new, experimental types of training—for example, training research administrators to direct the applications of research in the schools, or providing social-work training for teachers going into slum schools. In that year, we also would like to establish an international exchange of educational researchers, a series of model-demonstration schools in each state, and perhaps even a number of educational laboratories at universities or within the Office of Education, in conjunction with a clinical-training program and an internship program. We dream also of creating in 1965 a Center for Advanced Study in Education—not just a "think tank" for educators, but a center where scholars and researchers from all disciplines may come together to lend their talents to the resolution of educational problems.

Perhaps our biggest dream is for 1966. (By the way, we dream for 1966, so that we may have it by 1980.) That year we hope to move to the third stage of research mobilization: a national institute program. The function of these national institutes would be to stimulate, to finance and to coordinate research, demonstration, experimentation and dissemination activities related to specific areas of knowledge. A National Institute of the Arts and Humanities, a National Institute of Learning and a National Institute of School Administration are examples of possible approaches. Each institute would maintain a staff of interdisciplinary research specialists who would work with colleges, universities, state education agencies, local school systems and other appropriate agencies to develop new knowledge and new applications of knowledge in specific areas of concern.

These are our more important plans for program growth and development for the immediate future. Obviously, our hopes are high. But we will continue to dream, for the time has come to take bold, new steps in the improvement of education, and we cannot take those steps without a positive approach to articulation between research and practice.

COMMENT BY . . . *Jerome S. Bruner*
Professor of Psychology, Harvard University

Let me say first that I found this speech by Dr. Ianni a delight. I have not been in the educational field proper very long—if, indeed, I am in it now—but even in these short three of four years, it has been a pleasure to watch the change in the climate and the level of forthrightness in discussions of education. This speech was another evidence of it. So, thank you.

I would like to comment briefly on three very general issues: (1) what constitutes educational research, (2) how its impact on the educational system can be amplified, and (3) what is the proper role for the Federal Government in educational research.

First, the question of defining the limits of educational research. It seems to me very significant that the research into applications of compressed speech for the blind, of which Dr. Ianni rightly boasted, had its origin in an area of inquiry which, ten years ago, nobody would have thought had any bearing on education. This was communications engineering—in particular, the study of the relationship between signal and noise and message. Compressed speech was first investigated as a means of speeding communication across the trans-Atlantic cables, then as a means of communicating through the DEW Line. Now it is finding its way into education.

This points up what I think is a very important lesson: educational research is involved in any research that concerns itself with the transmission of information or knowledge. It is, therefore, involved in practically every field of human inquiry. And an awareness of this lesson is reflected in the trend of current projects in educational research. A number of research efforts, very frequently the best of them, are starting outside the usual context of conventional educational research. They are drawing on the behavioral sciences and many other disciplines.

One immediate reason for this trend is a change in our attitude toward the relationship between education and human development. For many years we have lived with an image of man—an image which Freud was principally responsible for formulating—as a being trapped between his own wild impulses and the inexorable, censorious forces of society, with the ego trying to maintain some identity and balance between them. The emphasis of education has been on shoring up the ego by encouraging such qualities as spontaneity and originality. It worked primarily, if you will, from the inside out.

We are now beginning to remember that there is also some education that goes from the outside in. We are shifting toward an intense concern with intellectual development as a facet of human development. And we are discovering that just as technology precedes progress in human culture, so the mastery of technology by the individual makes possible his great bursts of intellectual growth.

The child, for example, reaches a stage where he is capable of shifting from the single-word utterance (the so-called holler phrase) to grammar. He may start by combining two holler phrases—say, "All gone," which covers a variety of meanings having to do with departure, and "Sticky," which covers everything from jam to soap in his eyes. First he may say, "All gone, sticky," in which "all gone" is a pivot word and "sticky" is an open-class word. Then, within forty-eight hours, he will make several dozen attempts at combining "all gone" with other holler phrases: "mommy," "baby," "sister," "milk" and so on. This new technology for combining aspects of experience which he could not combine before corresponds to a tremendous increase in his capacity for problem solving. If the child does not reach this stage when he is supposed to, there is reason to worry and to search for ways to enrich his education.

Another example is the teaching of mathematical structures. Once the child grasps the ideas of commutativity, associativeness and distributiveness, he can run; but he needs the technology. And the challenge of how best to teach him this technology is one that demands far more than just calling in the behavioral sciences.

The second topic that I want to touch on is the problem of amplifying the impact of educational research and development. One of the grave weaknesses in educational research up to, say, 1948 was that it concentrated on evaluating bits and pieces of a static curriculum. It almost never focused on the nature of the educational process itself. To correct this, we are moving toward more extensive research into the concept of curriculum and the ways in which research results can be translated into curriculum.

One of the keys to research development, it seems to me, is that Turin's theorem holds true for human beings as well as for computers. This theorem dates back to a revolutionary paper which Turin wrote a generation ago; its results in the field of logic became known as Turin's theorem. (I am going to oversimplify it a little.) The basic point which he demonstrated was that any problem that can be shown to have a solution can be restated in such a way that it can be solved by simpler techniques than the ones which have just been used; that is, canonically speaking, there is always a simpler way of doing it. All you have to do, usually, is to take more steps in doing it. As you increase your speed, it becomes possible to use operations as simple as make-a-mark, move-a-mark, save-a-mark, which is essentially what a computer does.

In the same way, it is possible to take complex problems and restate them in a repertory of operations that a small child is capable of doing. For example, in teaching quadratic functions to children, it is possible to begin with the idea of the mathematical square, the notion that you are dealing with a set of sets such that the number of sets is equal to the elements of each set. You can do that by very concrete means, starting with an ordinary geometrical square, which everybody knows, and moving through very simple demonstrations until the child has learned the whole subroutine set. Then he can use it as a whole.

As research moves ahead on the nature of the processes by which people encode and transform knowledge—and I think we are learning a fair amount about that in psychology, linguistics and various other fields—it becomes possible to use those research findings to help shape a curriculum in history, in economics, in vector spaces, in any subject area. The next step is to try it out on groups of children in a few schools to find out how it goes. If it goes well, you can count on a sort of Gresham's law in reverse: when you introduce a better curriculum in which students learn more and so are accepted into college more easily, there is a sudden, enormous clamor among other schools that want the curriculum too. You may even, very frequently, be embarrassed by the curriculum's success because you do not yet have teachers trained to teach it. But that is another story.

So I would urge that, if educational research is to have an impact on the educational system, it must be translated either into curriculum that can be taught or into programmed instruction. The latter is a vast field; I shall not take time to go into it now.

The last topic I want to comment on briefly is the role of the Federal Government in educational research. It is perfectly clear that we need the Government's financial support. It is not altogether clear, in my mind, that the best way of organizing the research is in national institutes. On the contrary, I suspect that we will have to go through a period of rather sloppy pluralism for some time, particularly since the researchers will have to work very closely with the most able people in substantive fields and it will be difficult to draw them away from their universities. While it has become much more respectable in the last few years for these professors to spend their weekends on projects in education, I see no real possibility of drawing them into large institutes.

On the whole, I feel quite optimistic. There is no question that efforts like those of the Office of Education, the National Science Foundation and the President's Science Advisory Committee have been tremendously encouraging to people working in educational research. There are likely to be, I think, some very startling breakthroughs in the next decade.

SUMMARY OF THE DISCUSSION

The discussion took shape, not as a general exchange of ideas, but as a series of questions addressed to Dr. Ianni and Professor Bruner. The questions and answers are here rather tightly condensed.

Questions answered by Dr. Ianni

Q. Professor Bruner has ,said that educational research has not led to an assimilable content; it has not led to improvements in the process itself. Is the Cooperative Research Program trying to break this impasse? Is it assuming the role of change agent?

A. Not directly. Our philosophy is that we are to provide the means for others, especially teacher-training institutions and school administrators, to bring about changes in education. The Federal Government is simply too cumbersome for such a role. We can provide the funds and the mechanisms, but the actual changes will have to come through local institutions.

Q. To what extent does your Program initiate research projects? Do you simply approve or disapprove applications? Or do you sometimes suggest projects and invite individuals to apply?

A. We do not generally suggest research topics to individuals in the field. We do, at times, let it be known that we would like to support more research in a general area, but any applications that come in as a result are evaluated as stringently as all the rest.

English, for example, is an area of special emphasis that is showing good results. When we began special stimulation in this area, in February, 1961, we received sixteen applications, none of which seemed to merit our support. We then held an invitational conference of researchers and English scholars to suggest and discuss possible projects. As a result of this conference, we received forty-two new applications, of which we accepted ten.

Q. To what extent are you subject to pressures from Congressmen?

A. We do, of couse, get such pressures. But if they seem unreasonable, we resist them and stand our ground. When we first established Project Talent in Pittsburgh, for example, we came under fire because of the types of questions the researchers were asking. We weathered the storm, and now Congress is in favor of the project. Again, we were criticized for a special study, which we set up, of social-control techniques being used in certain Russian schools as a means of bringing about general social change. The criticism was vigorous, but we managed to stand up fairly well.

A third example is perhaps the most interesting. In 1961 we financed a project, at a small southern Negro college, seeking to teach southern Negroes a better use of standard English. The methods employed were those developed to teach English to foreigners. Within a few weeks we received a call from the chairman of the Education Committee, who happened to be a Negro. He wanted to know why we were treating southern Negroes like foreigners.

But the vast preponderance of congressional pressure is not so specific. It comes, rather, in the types of funds which Congress makes available to us. Congress still tends to prefer research for blind and disabled children, rather than for normal children. When we requested money to set up quality education programs for gifted students, one Congressman objected, "Why do you want to spend more money and attention on children who are already so well endowed by God?"

Q. Do your funds tend to go to researchers at institutions that are already strong in resources?

A. We try to avoid this, but without total success. The four criteria that we use to determine the worth of a project are its significance to education generally, its research design, the facilities and personnel available to carry it through, and its economic efficiency. The requirement of facilities and personnel makes the difficulty.

In 1960 we set out to compensate for this. We began looking specifically for young researchers at small institutions, and we gave 120 of them small grants to pursue research interests. The result was probably inevitable. Our grants made these young researchers better known, and within two years 85 of them had been hired by large institutions.

Q. Why are teachers not given more opportunity to participate in developing the new curricula? Teachers already know a great deal, by experience and in practice, that researchers say they are trying to discover theoretically. Teachers could offer the researchers a great deal of information, but the contact between the two groups is lamentably small.

A. We insist that schoolteachers who are actually teaching be involved in all projects in our curriculum-development program. These projects are supported for five years, and classroom teachers take part from beginning to end. Moreover, the most crucial phase of each of these projects is the central phase, where the tentative curriculum is tested in a variety of schools before it is revised into its relatively final form.

Q. At least three other Government agencies—the National Science Foundation, the National Institutes of Health and, increasingly, the National Aeronautical and Space Administration—are funding projects that seem to overlap those of the Office of Education. How closely are these efforts coordinated?

A. We coordinate in two ways: we eliminate duplications in funding the same type of study, and we explore the possibilities of joint support in particular problem areas. But education is not an exclusive preserve of the Office of Education. These other agencies have a large and proper concern for education, and I think the pluralism of efforts is beneficial. Professor Bruner pointed out the important contribution to education of basic research in related fields. Think of the range of studies which the Office of Education would have to support if there were no NSF, no NIH, no Space Agency. As matters stand, we can borrow very heavily from them.

Incidentally, unlike Professor Bruner, I am not convinced that there is any such thing as basic research in education. All educational research seems to me to be essentially applied research, since there is always a specific application in mind.

Q. What effect does your Program have on expenditures by other supporters of educational research, such as the foundations and state governments?

A. The foundations' approach is considerably different from ours. They tend to emphasize projects for applying what is known, rather than for adding to the store of as yet unapplied knowledge. So there is no conflict. Our projects tend to be developmental. Theirs tend to be operational, though we do finance some projects jointly with them—and they are able, of course, to take on some developmental projects which we cannot handle.

As for the state governments: we are in constant contact with their educational research organizations, helping them to develop and refine their own research ideas. We also hope to establish a fellowship program to train individuals as experts in research administration, partly so that such an administrator can be available for every state educational agency.

Q. How do you cope with the resistance to curricular change on the part of various forces in the educational community, such as the National Education Association?

A. Some of this resistance resolves itself—for example, the contention over new projects in English that arose between English educators and the traditional English scholars on university faculties. Other resistance is more tenacious. The NEA, as one example, is unalterably opposed to any movement by the Federal Government in the area of curriculum development and curriculum revision, primarily because it feels that this would lead to an attempt to establish a national curriculum for all schools.

Our solution has been to provide the means to develop the new curricula and then to make the results available on a request basis. We would much prefer, of course, to put the materials into the schools wherever they will be most useful. But our solution at least falls short of the NEA position, which is, essentially, that the Federal Government should take all the money earmarked for education and put it on a tree stump at midnight on a very dark night and then run like hell. That just is not our philosophy.

Questions answered by Professor Bruner

Q. (by Professor Wade M. Robinson, Graduate School of Education, Harvard University). It seems to me that a number of recent innovations in curriculum and methods—the use of television, teaching machines, and so on—tend to take away some of what the teacher has euphemistically called her autonomy, her right to be teacher and to be wise, her right to do what she will with the classroom. And this seems to me to be based, in part, on some recognition that our teachers are not as good as they should be and that we probably will never have the resources to upgrade them all to the required level.

·Must we, then, have an infinite redress to more automation, more outside control, more control by authorities in subject matter? Must we rely on this externalization to guarantee a level of excellence in the student's learning, though not necessarily in the teacher's teaching in the classroom?

A. This is a vexing problem, of course, but I wonder if we have yet made a serious attempt to upgrade the average classroom teacher. On the contrary, considering how little help we provide our teachers once their careers are launched, it seems to me amazing that they perform as well as they do. A widespread adoption of in-service training programs, weekend seminars and similar means for keeping them abreast of new knowledge in their fields might make a significant difference.

It should be very beneficial, too, to strengthen administrative control of the teaching situation. Without limiting the teacher's freedom to do well, the administrator can at least give her new ideas and enforce standards that will prevent her from teaching poorly.

Q. The discussions about early learning, with their emphasis on determining the age at which various ideas within a subject area should be taught, presuppose that we have defined the total body of ideas to be taught during the years of formal education. This presupposition may be accurate in disciplines such as mathematics, but it surely is not accurate in the social sciences, English and the humanities. How are we to make that basic definition in these disciplines?

A. This is, in effect, the question of what constitutes the educated man. And that question is a matter for general debate, not just for debate among specialists. It is a community issue.

7.

Accreditation:
The Quality of Institutions

F. Taylor Jones
Executive Secretary, Commission on Institutions of Higher Education,
Middle States Association of Colleges and Secondary Schools

"Accreditation" is one of those chameleon words whose meanings take on different complexions according to their environment. So let me begin by placing in context the sort of accreditation I shall be talking about.

The two forms of accreditation which people generally have in mind when they use the word are *regional* and *professional*. The first is carried on by six autonomous associations of educational institutions—in New England, the middle-Atlantic seaboard, the South, the Midwest, the far West and the Northwest. These associations are voluntary and nongovernmental; they accredit high schools and preparatory schools as well as colleges and universities; and taken together, they cover the United States. They confer (or withhold) general accreditation; that is, they accredit each institution as a whole —all its departments, curriculums and schools. It is this general or regional accreditation, particularly in relation to colleges and universities, whose function I shall attempt to define.

Professionally oriented accreditation, in contrast, is conferred (or withheld) by national bodies representing various professions. Such accreditation applies either to an entire professional institution or, in the case of a more comprehensive institution, to its individual professional programs. Mr. Selden [in the following paper] will describe this activity in more detail. In addition, certain procedures by states and by quasi-official agencies verge on accreditation or bear some resemblance to it. Mr. Selden will take note of some of these procedures, but they are not our direct concern here.

The six regional associations have much in common, but each began as a local response to local needs and problems—needs and problems which were not and are not identical in all regions. Until recently it was sufficient for them to work side by side in friendly independence. They still do, but now with increasing communication and coupling of their energies. They have no relation to state education departments or to any other outside bodies. They have no interest in merging into one national body or even in resolving all the discrepancies among themselves. Their regional quality and responsibility, with its resultant flexibility and responsiveness, is one of their great strengths.

How did the regional associations become involved in accreditation? They did not invent it, and to this day they do not consider it their main function or reason for being. Fundamentally, the regional associations are interested in facilitating an exchange of ideas. They do not want to control anything. They are less and less willing to establish or subscribe to formulas, rules or requirements—to "standards" in the old sense. The essential purpose of the regional associations is to increase the free exchange of ideas and experience among higher institutions of all sorts, looking toward a clearer understanding of the nature of education, seeking to strengthen and improve the rich variety of America's educational resources, and constantly striving to enlarge the horizons and educational opportunity of the people.

They entered into accreditation strictly as a means to these ends. Variety is desirable, but chaos is not, for it can eventuate not only in confusion and waste but also in abuses. At the time of World War I, when the burgeoning diversification of higher education cried for sorting out, this problem was widely debated, and a consensus of the educational community was achieved. This was followed logically by recognition within the profession of those institutions which were able to give practical expression to the ideas seized upon in the exchange. That meant accreditation. It began by the taking of quantitative measurements—of the library, the faculty's degrees, the endowment and so on. Any evaluating agency must begin with quantitative criteria until painfully won experience enables it to move toward a qualitative approach. The regional associations, by and large, have accomplished that transition. They are now completely committed to the principle of subjective, qualitative evaluation.

One other characteristic of the early years of general accrediting is worth noting, for it still is a cardinal principle today. The regional associations wanted—and still want—their lists to be inclusive rather than exclusive. Their governing bodies and operating agencies are actively helping institutions to gain accreditation. They refuse to separate evaluation from consultation, and they have no interest whatever in creating an elite.

In the evolution since those early days, several major concepts have emerged in their thinking. One is that liberal or general education is an essential element in all higher education worthy of the name. Another is that the purview of evaluation in higher education must remain the entire institution, not isolated parts of it, for an institution is an organism whose whole is greater than the sum of its parts. General accreditation is general, however, only in this sense of inclusiveness. It is not casual or superficial. Every program in an institution is examined directly and in detail before the institution as a whole is approved.

In the last generation, the regionals have made a complete about-face in their attitude toward uniformity. The earliest terms for accreditation were "classification" and "standardization," and many people still think of accreditation as a seal of conformity or equality, such that all accredited institutions are roughly interchangeable. Some of the professionally oriented accrediting agencies feel that this approach, carefully defined, is still relevant for them. They believe that graduation from an accredited school should justify employment in the profession anywhere in the United States, and this implies that all schools must assure a comparable preparation. The regionals tend to question this position as confusing accreditation with licensure. They draw a sharp line between accreditation of institutions and licensure of individuals; they hold that the former is properly the function of groups of educational institutions, while the latter is the function of the state advised by the professions.

The regionals' position is that uniformity is as undesirable among colleges as it is among students. They want each institution to strive for excellence in service to its particular constituency, working in the most intelligent way its trustees and staff can devise at the bewilderingly complex task of higher education. The regionals are highly interested in and eagerly encourage individuality among institutions.

This idea of seeking an institution's own genius, rather than bringing a set of requirements to it, is often described as evaluation in terms of an institution's own objectives. The regionals adhere firmly to this concept, though they realize quite well that it is tricky. The evaluators do not automatically accept whatever statement of objectives the institution happens to put before them. They apply critical intelligence and discernment to the objectives, making sure

they are apposite, precise and realistic, before examining their implications and implementation. Furthermore, if the evaluators' point
of reference is the institution's own declared educational objectives,
their concern must center on the institution's educational program.
Buildings, organizational patterns, endowment, administrative services
and the like are of secondary importance, deriving their significance
solely from their effect upon the educational program. This places
accreditation upon a highly sophisticated and highly subjective basis.

The regionals, then, have largely cast off the convenient and
reassuring conceptions with which they began. As a result, they are
wide open to the charge of inconsistency in their judgments. They
must accept that. They could go far to eliminate it by having a
small, employed staff do all their evaluating, but they reject that
alternative because it would fasten upon higher education the very
thing they wish to avoid—the promulgation of a particular doctrine
with an implication of ex cathedra authority. The regionals would
rather risk inconsistency than rigidity.

To state it most simply, regional accrediting asks only two questions, finding in them all that one really needs to know about an
institution. The first question is: *Precisely what changes does the
institution hope to bring about in its students by means of its educational program?* This question is deceptively simple. Generalizations
are essential—they identify the underlying purposes which all higher
education shares—but any meaningful evaluation of an individual
institution must delve far beyond generalizations. The challenge is
to say clearly, explicitly and realistically what particular educational
objectives the institution has set for its students, over and above the
universal purposes, taking into consideration all the circumstances
and conditions in which that institution operates.

When this first question has been answered, the second follows
inevitably: *Do the students actually achieve these objectives?* In its
most significant respects, however, this question is largely unanswer-
able. We can measure retention of factual information with fair accu-
racy, and we can assess the acquisition of skills, but these are not the
heart of the matter. The fundamental, long-range aims of educational
institutions are concerned with the students' quality of thinking, their
intellectual attitudes, their perceptiveness, their power to form independent judgments and to weigh values, their sense of personal responsibility. These characteristics are simply not measurable. We have
no tests for the intricate processes of intellectual maturation. So we
had better have no illusions about the evaluation process on which

collegiate accreditation is based. When it deals with the central engagement of higher education—that for which the institutions exist—the process is highly subjective, even intuitive.

In practice, an operative question is injected between the two big ones: *Does the institution appear to have gained the resources and achieved the conditions which are required for the accomplishment of its purposes?* This question provides a handle for the evaluation, but it remains largely subjective. There are no pat formulas as to what such resources and conditions are. One cannot define a library, a faculty, a student body or a curriculum in quantitative terms. The best we can do is to depend on the thoughtful judgment of experienced observers, plus bits of evidence and hints as to actual outcomes of the educational process.

Under the circumstances, can accreditation have any real meaning? Can a high-level consultation on mutual problems coinciding with a subjective evaluation, actually yield an appraisal of an institution which is searching and reliable enough to support accreditation? Strangely enough, it does. The operating commissions of the regional associations today find themselves, rather to their surprise, more acutely aware of the quality of an institution's performance and of the precise conditions which enhance or retard it than when a more formal approach was used. This may not sound wholly reasonable, but it is true. A good deal depends upon the open-minded, objective, professional atmosphere which the consultative relationship fosters. Nobody is attacking or defending. The evaluation becomes a project in group research around a common table.

On the other hand, general accreditation has its disciplinary aspects too. The system came into being forty years ago because something was needed—and nothing better was at hand—to protect the public and to inform the educational world about individual institutions. It still has those functions, and they are a necessary complement to the regionals' most important function, which is to stimulate and press each institution to reach its highest potential of educational effectiveness. If accreditation is to justify the confidence the public accords it, the possibility of withdrawing an institution's accreditation must exist. It does, though fortunately the delicate and sensitive balances in our complex body of higher education usually make such action unnecessary. A gesture toward it is normally sufficient. These warning motions are fairly common, yet the educational community rarely hears of them, for the relationship between an institution and its regional accrediting association is privileged. The admonitions and warnings are never announced. Publicity would harm rather than help the institution, and the regionals are in business to be useful, not destructive. They do not try their cases in the newspapers.

It seems natural that relatively unknown colleges and institutions should be avid for accreditation and its attendant prestige, but why do established and even renowned colleges and universities also support it and subject themselves to periodic regional re-evaluation? There are solid reasons why the system is more widely accepted today than ever before. The public still needs protection against chicanery and incompetence, and the established institutions still need to safeguard the sources of their future students and faculty members; but two other considerations are paramount. *First,* the voluntary evaluation and accreditation system places educators—specifically, the best qualified among them—in a position to establish their own standards and levels of expectation. And *second,* this system has proved to be the most effective stimulus yet devised to help institutions apprehend and approach the standards. Obviously, our prestige institutions have little need themselves for accreditation per se. They have great interest in supporting a program which raises sights throughout higher education and which retains quality control in the hands of those who know most about it.

So regional accreditation is not as simple or as tangible as it may first appear. It does not yield scores, ratings or comparisons. It pretends to no unchallengeable insights. It is simply the serious attempt of experienced educators, building on slowly accumulated knowledge, to define the characteristics which accompany excellence in higher education and to identify institutions which exhibit them.

The task of the regional associations, as they see it, is to foster a commitment to wholeness in education; to protect the integrity, unity and individuality of each institution; and to insist upon uncompromising quality in the performance of each institution's chosen task. Accreditation is their recognition, after as careful a study as they can make, that this quality is characteristic of a given institution. The accreditation is not the important thing at all. It is a by-product of a consultation which no institution can go through unchanged.

The regional associations know better than anyone else that their work is imperfect, uneven and inconsistent. They do not pretend to know the answers to the important questions in higher education. But they are convinced that we are more likely to find useful answers together than separately, that the answers to the big questions probably apply to all of us, and that the accreditation process can be a useful instrument in the search.

William K. Selden
Executive Director, National Commission on Accrediting

Accreditation by national professional associations or disciplinary societies (there are distinctions between them, but I shall use the terms interchangeably) is becoming increasingly important in the American society—fortunately or unfortunately, depending upon one's point of view. Perhaps the clearest way to introduce the issue is to describe very briefly the comparable situation in France, which offers a striking contrast to our own.

France has a national Ministry of Education entrusted with centralized responsibility for education throughout the country. Although there are many customs which provide informal checks and balances, the ministry retains the legal responsibility for the universities, and only degrees awarded by the state universities are accorded official recognition. In the case of medicine, for example, the attainment of the state university degree in medicine permits the recipient to practice throughout France. The degree is dependent solely upon the passing of university examinations, not upon separate licensure examinations. No school of medicine (or any other division) is permitted to exist at a university unless the ministry grants both final approval and adequate support, so that the school will meet the national educational standards established by the ministry.

In the United States, on the other hand, responsibility for education is one of the powers not mentioned in the Constitution. It is thus reserved, under the Tenth Amendment, "to the State respectively, or to the people."

The states also have authority to grant licenses to individuals to practice scores of vocations, including medicine, dentistry, engineering, nursing, osteopathy, podiatry, accounting, pharmacy, optometry, psychology, public health, veterinary medicine, architecture, teacher education, mortuary science and barbering. In contrast to France, these licenses are not granted automatically upon the passing of university examinations. Instead, each state has its own boards of licensure for the various fields in which licensure has been adopted, and each individual board has its own regulations with respect to licensure.

Among the regulations, however, is generally the alternate requirement that the candidate be a graduate of an approved institution or program of study. In these cases, an approved institution customarily means one accredited by the appropriate national professional agency. Accreditation or approval of institutions is, like licensure, a state responsibility; but in practice it is normally delegated to extralegal organizations—the national professional accrediting agencies and the regional accrediting associations.

The first accreditation of a professional field of study was in medicine. The Council on Medical Education of the American Medical Association published its first list of classified schools in 1906-7, but it was the publicity resulting from the critical report by Abraham Flexner in 1910 which gave real impetus to improvement in medical education and the strengthening of medical accreditation. Since then, all other professions and would-be professions have sought to imitate medical accreditation, even to the extent of adopting similar policies and practices, though they are sometimes quite inappropriate for other fields of study.

Today accreditation is being conducted by some twenty national professional agencies, and other groups are continually striving to perform the same function—to assume responsibility for publicly identifying those institutions which are offering programs of study adequate to meet standards agreed upon within the profession. Among the many organizations which are giving thought to the possibility of initiating accrediting activities are those representing political science, home economics, food technology, inhalation therapy, design, educational theater, microbiology, city planning, agriculture, and speech and hearing. The National Commission on Accrediting is in frequent communication with these organizations, endeavoring to maintain a proper balance between control and freedom in higher education—between the forces unifying a given institution, which may lead to negligence toward individual programs, and the forces strengthening the individual programs, which can lead to fragmentation of the institution as a whole.

These forces leading to fragmentation of our university structure and curricula are epitomized in the seemingly innate desire of each professional group to establish distinct standards in its field of study. Their tendency is reinforced by the increasing professionalization of society.

Let me call your attention to some of the social developments which are encouraging professionalization. The most obvious are the great acceleration in the growth of population, the increasing social need for highly trained personnel, the swelling college and university enrollments and the rapid spread of knowledge, both in depth and breadth. These developments can be partially demonstrated by a few statistics. In 1919-20, America's colleges and universities awarded 48,-622 bachelor's and first professional degrees, 4,279 master's degrees and only 615 Ph.D. or equivalent degrees. Forty years later, in 1959-60, they awarded eight times as many bachelor's and first professional degrees (394,889), over eighteen times as many master's degrees (74,497) and fifteen times as many Ph.D. and equivalent degrees (9,829).

As these figures indicate, there are more graduate degrees today than there were undergraduates forty years ago. Postbaccalaureate studies are of a specialized nature; they are concentrated in fields with which the professors identify themselves and to which they are interested in recruiting new members. The opportunity for the encouragement of professional identity is manifest, and it is intensified as the universities increase in size and as proportionally larger sums are granted by foundations and by agencies of the Federal government for the support of specific fields of study. This support tends to encourage both professors and students to feel more closely attached to their profession and their research than to the particular institutions with which they happen to be associated.

More subtle developments are also at work. Democratic societies, with their ever higher and more complex standards of living, require a multitude of organizations to operate the numerous social functions, to provide citizens with the means of expressing their diverse interests and to make it possible for individuals to develop a feeling of group identity. It is to his professional association that the professsional man turns. Membership offers him also a degree of social status, which many people desire especially during periods of social stress and strain.

From his association he expects a number of services, including professional protection. He expects to be protected against the entrance into the profession of inadequately and even shoddily trained men and women. Society supports this expectation by assigning to the profession, sometimes formally and sometimes informally, the responsibility for identifying, among other things, the type and extent of education needed to prepare an individual to qualify for professional practice. Accreditation is one of the major means employed by professional associations to meet this responsibility. (Let me repeat, so that there may be no chance of misunderstanding, that it is the state through licensure—*not* the professional association through accreditation—which indicates that an individual is qualified to practice his profession on the public.)

And now we find ourselves in a dilemma of growing importance. As professionalization increases—and I see every likelihood that it will increase much further—more and more professional groups will seek the power to accredit professional programs in colleges and universities. If this tendency is not held within reasonable bounds, our educational institutions, including our leading universities, will be subjected to uncoordinated demands from many different groups with relatively specialized interests—a centrifugal pressure which can only lead to damaging fragmentation. Not merely education but our entire society would suffer.

The opposite side of this dilemma is that colleges and universities can be chartered with relative ease in most states and that institutions, including those which are regionally accredited, have considerable latitude in adding programs of study at both the undergraduate and graduate levels, regardless whether, in the view of the professions, these institutions are adequately supported in personnel, finances and facilities to undertake these programs. To maintain the quality of professional preparation under such conditions is a matter of national importance.

We do not desire the French system of educational control in this country. We wish to continue to derive the many benefits nourished by the flexibility and freedom of our educational establishment. But as our society becomes more professionalized, as increasing reliance is placed on classification of individuals by skills, as institutions continue to add specialized programs of study and as licensure becomes more widespread, the professions are naturally intensifying their concern for the quality of college and university programs preparing future members of the professions. These forces above all are encouraging the proliferation of professional accreditation.

COMMENT BY . . . *David Riesman*
                            Henry Ford II Professor of Social Sciences,
                            Harvard University

One of the questions that troubled me as I listened to Mr. Jones's speech is: How does one go about casing the joint? How does one discover what the qualitative processes of an institution really are?

How does one see through the Potemkin village which confronts the visitor to any campus?

Let me draw on my own experience for an analogue. I worked in an interesting role as part of Paul Lazarsfeld's study of academic freedom for the Fund of the Republic. The study was based on interviews with a sample of social scientists on the campuses of a cross-section of America's colleges and universities. The survey was made by professional interviewers, and I visited some of the campuses shortly afterwards, spending from a few hours to several days on each, in order to form an independent judgment as one test of the adequacy of the survey.

My job was to evaluate the state of academic freedom on each campus I visited, and in preparation I tried to figure out the best way to learn this about an institution in a short time. What should my criteria be? What should be on my checklist of things to look for? Above all, how could I learn what the place looks like from below, from the student's point of view? How could I get through the official front of the institution to find out what is really happening?

I decided that I would look at the bulletin board to see who was speaking and what was going on in the line of culture and arts. I would get hold of the student newspaper and literary journal, if I could. I would talk to the student editor and, if I could, to local newspapermen, who often know a lot. I would go to the student center and to the coffeehouse, if there was one around. I would check various atmospheric indicators of this sort, which I am sure the accreditation teams take as part of their mandate, perhaps without even organizing their perceptions in this respect.

I felt that it was possible, in a very short time, to learn perhaps 80 per cent of what the much more formal, careful sample survey learned; but I would not be *sure* that what I thought I had learned was so. On the other hand, I doubt that one could be any more sure of the results of the sample survey. These two different approaches simply offer different ways of being misled.

It might be very instructive, I think, to study the visits of accreditation teams as forms of social negotiation and bargaining. What rhetoric would be used by the participants in these off-the-record encounters? What kinds of slogans would they use to defend what they are doing against criticism, or to incorporate in part the criticism they receive, or to give themselves special justification, which we all need? What defensive or aggressive rhetorics would be exploited to say, "I cannot be judged by a national or a transnational standard. My work must be judged in terms of my very special constituency, for whom I provide something which you cannot measure"?

To take one example, colleges which are too small to provide a critical mass in any discipline defend themselves by asserting the advantage of their very smallness. While there are some colleges whose smallness is testimony to their courage, there are many others whose smallness is testimony to nothing of very great value. It merely permits them to have a whole panoply of officials which they could not have if they were parts of larger institutions.

Let me turn now to some of the problems raised by Mr. Selden. In the first place, I certainly agree with his observations about the search for security within a profession. Education, especially higher education, is taking people out of their narrow, local parishes—ethnic, geographical and parental—and nationalizing them. It is throwing them into the national parish. One version of the national parish is the national corporation; another is the national profession. And as people are cut away from their local ties, it seems to me that they sometimes cling more ferociously than ever to these nationalistic ties.

This makes for a curious conflict: people pay lip service to localism, but their own new allegiance is national. They insist on the value of freedom and local flexibility, but they are apprehensive that local actions can sabotage the national equilibrium. How can they prevent that sabotage without undermining the principle of localism? The regional accrediting associations, like all the other compromises which society has worked out between centralized control and local cowboy tactics (which we call individualism and freedom), seem to me one response to that quandary.

Three other brief questions were suggested by Mr. Selden's closing remarks. *First,* what about the amorphous groupings in our society which have not yet invented their guild? What about a city, say, or a neighborhood? How are the nonorganized segments of society to compete with the organized segments? More generally, how can we organize quality outside the areas in which it is already being so highly organized? And is the differential increasing? As the national professional associations get better, is the ancillary territory around them getting worse?

Second, does licensure not only raise the floor of a profession by eliminating substandard performance but also lower the ceiling by excluding exceptional performance? This question was raised several years ago by Everett Hughes, professor of sociology at Brandeis, when the American Sociological Society decided to become the American Sociological Association. He thought that sociology should remain a learned society and not become a profession. He felt that there should be no system of licensing at all in scholarly life because, in his experience, the people who are outside the associations in the fields with licensure include both some of the worse and some of the very best.

Third, what actually is a profession, or a discipline, or a field? How are its boundaries established? Disciplines are, historically, very fragile affairs. When I hear the word "interdisciplinary," I have somewhat the same feeling as I do about the word "international." It seems to take for granted that disciplines are part of the intellectual map, just as the other assumes that we shall go on having nations. If one wants to transcend the discipline or the nation, one must think in terms of different forms of organization which are free of the hereditary character, based on geography or on intellectual tradition, of the nation or the field.

One last comment. A great danger in professional accreditation, it seems to me, is the self-confirming nature of the efforts toward improvement of any going concern, especially in recruiting new members. It seems an almost inescapable problem that as a profession improves, it will select new members just like those who comprise it. Students will follow the models they see, and guidance officers will direct toward the profession those students who seem most like the active members of the profession. When they enter, those will be the models by which the novitiates will be judged. No profession, it seems to me, can afford to allow this to happen.

COMMENT BY . . . *Owen B. Kiernan*
                  Commissioner of Education, Commonwealth of
                  Massachusetts

I would like to introduce another and darker aspect of this broad problem—the aspect of state approval of institutions of higher education, as distinct from regional and professional accreditation of them. The professions and the educational community have an obligation to upgrade themselves, and part of this effort must be self-policing to protect the public against substandard and fraudulent operations. Unfortunately, the sanctions available, such as denial of accreditation, are not always sufficient to accomplish the task. Action by the state may then be necessary in the public interest.

Here in Massuchusetts, from the early days of the colony, the Great and General Court [Legislature] has had a direct responsibility for establishing institutions. The first of these, in 1636, was Harvard College. Over the years there were occasionally problems: along with institutions of high reputation, we had some that were substandard. In these cases, though Mr. Jones indicated that a warning gesture is normally sufficient, our own experience has been that it is frequently necessary to go beyond the warning stage—not only in Massachusetts but in every state of the Union.

In 1943, therefore, the General Court established the Board of Collegiate Authority, a representative board of fourteen members over which the commissioner of education presides as chairman. The board is not an accrediting agency. It is an approving agency. Its mandate is to approve or deny, after a long and meticulous scrutiny, two types of petitions: (1) the petition of an institution to use the term "junior college," "college" or "university"; and (2) the petition of an institution to grant certain degrees. The members of the board are eminent persons in the Massachusetts educational community, including the presidents of distinguished junior colleges, colleges and universities. They have no axes to grind; they are simply interested in establishing a reasonable level of performance for institutions of higher learning in the commonwealth.

Tufts, for example, changed several years ago from a college to a university. Before the board would officially approve this change of name, the officials of Tufts had to appear before the board with a formal petition, supported by comprehensive documentation. In this instance, the petition was approved. The law makes no exceptions, but this does not mean that the board can require reasonable standards in *all* higher education. Institutions certified before 1943 are not scrutinized by the board unless they petition, as Tufts did, to change their names or to confer new degrees. Many of our legislators are directly connected with certain of these institutions, so there are political as well as academic implications.

The board's prestige and influence are such that its statements are given serious attention, even in cases where it has no statutory authority over an institution. One law school, for example, which had contributed significantly in the field of law, broadened its base by developing a liberal-arts division which was clearly substandard.

We called the president and the two deans before the board and explained to them why this lowering of standards could not be tolerated. They understood and have taken action which we consider appropriate.

Much more troublesome are the fraudulent institutions which simply sell degrees. Massachusetts has a remarkably fine record in protecting the public from these institutions, but there have been a few. Several years ago, for example, we were successful before the Federal Trade Commission in having a cease-and-desist order issued against an institution in western Massachusetts which was issuing a really beautiful document, made of parchment and replete with seals. It was sold for cash and was called an equivalency degree. There is no such thing, of course, in the law. There is no such thing in the field of education. The document was very impressive, and it could be framed, but it had no more value than Confederate currency.

This particular institution is no longer in business, but comparable ones open up and advertise again from time to time. We bring them to the attention of the Massachusetts attorney general and of the Federal Trade Commission, and they do not last long. But they move from state to state, and this raises a nice legal question involving interstate commerce and certain constitutional rights. An organization which issues degrees from another state to Massachusetts residents is beyond the jurisdictional responsibility of the Board of Collegiate Authority and of the commonwealth itself.

Inevitably, the board's vigilance raises the difficult issue of control versus freedom. To what extent is a paternalistic concern warranted, on the part of the state or Federal government, even to stamp out an operation that is obviously fraudulent? It might help to keep in mind the scope of the problem as Robert H. Reid assessed it in 1958. In his book *American Degree Mills*, he indicated that some 750,000 students are being shortchanged each year at a gross annual cost of $75 million. As I forewarned you, this is the darker side of the picture.

SUMMARY OF THE DISCUSSION

The general discussion touched on three broad topics:

Sources of authority for accreditation: "How does an association or society gain the authority to be an accrediting agency?" the discussants were asked. They replied that there are three sources of authority: (1) state and Federal law, (2) informal endorsement by state governments and (3) the consent and support of the academic community.

Two forms of indirect legal authority were specified by Mr. Selden. One is the educational requirements established by state licensure laws and practices. In many states, for example, admission to the bar is dependent upon graduation from a law school accredited by the American Bar Association. The other form is Federal: the U. S. Commissioner of Education is required by law to designate those accrediting agencies whose approval of institutions he will recognize as valid for particular purposes. Thus accreditation by one of these recognized agencies may indicate that an institution is eligible for, say, certain Federal grants.

Informal endorsement by state governments is also a significant source of authority. The simplest level, perhaps, is the referral of inquiries. Parents who write to a state department of education to inquire why a particular institution is not accredited may be advised to write directly to the accrediting agency. The implication of state endorsement is then unmistakable. But the endorsement is very often more explicit, as when a state, in deciding whether to approve an institution, relies heavily on whether it has been accredited. "In effect," Mr. Selden observed, "certain assumed powers have been delgated to these extralegal bodies. This is a situation which people from other countries find most difficult to understand."

(Mr. Harris asked whether the converse is also true: "Do the state governments interfere with the accrediting agencis in any way? There must be many disgruntled college administrators whose institutions have been denied accreditation, and I would expect many of them to put the heat on the government to interfere." No one replied.)

The third source of authority for an accrediting agency is the educational community itself. As one example, Mr. Selden offered his own National Commission on Accrediting, which was created in 1949 by its seven constituent organizations, "largely as a protest against the excesses of accreditation, especially—but not solely—by the professional accrediting agencies. Today over 1250 universities and colleges are dues-paying members. Our leverage resides in the fact that if an accrediting agency is not recognized by the National Commisssion, our members are expected not to deal with that agency on an accrediting basis."

The functions of accreditation: In his speech, Mr. Jones had identified three functions of accreditation: (1) "to protect the public," (2) "to inform the educational world about individual institutions" and (3) "to stimulate and press each institution to reach its highest potential of educational effectiveness." The first and third of these were recalled during the discussion:

(1) "To what extent," Mr. Harris asked, "does the average consumer of higher education understand the issues involved in accreditation and, as a result, express a preference for an accredited institution?" The reply was that this seal of approval has only limited effectiveness. Most students are aware of its meaning, but many are not, and the fact that three different types of accrediting may be applicable to a single college is extremely confusing to many consumers.

(3) The regional associations make a vigorous effort to help institutions qualify for accreditation, Mr. Jones explained. "I work full-time as executive secretary of one of these associations, and close to half my time is spent with unaccredited institutions, not trying to judge them but making available to them, in every possible way, the resources of their colleagues in other institutions. And they move up."

But what happens to those institutions which do not earn accreditation? Mr. Selden stated emphatically: "Any institution which is strong and good should construct and operate its program in the way it thinks best. It should not violate its own judgment to comply with any accrediting agency. Those which are deeply concerned about compliance are not strong in quality, regardless of size. There are cases where regulations prevent the accreditation of a strong institution, and I have said many times to such institutions, 'You are good. You don't have to worry about accreditation at all.' "

Under questioning, however, he conceded that "what I have said is very definitely subject to restriction." The drawback to an institution in disregarding accreditation and insisting upon its own sense of mission is that it may thus disquailfy its graduates for employment in their profession. A discussant noted, by way of illustration, "the new two-pronged program of the American Association of School Administrators. First, they intend to accredit institutions through the facilities of the National Council for Accreditation of Teacher Education. At the same time, they are undertaking a drive to persuade school boards throughout the country—that is, the employers of school superintendents—to hire only graduates of NCATE-AASA-approved institutions."

Mr. Selden commented on this illustration: "This involves the stress and strain between the necessity of insisting upon some standards and the need to do so in an enlightened and constructive way. If the demands affecting school administrators should become too severe, there will undoubtedly be reactions, and the National Commission on Accrediting will be one of the parties concerned. One of our jobs is to keep a weather eye open for such developments."

Mr. Harris suggested the possibility that the professions might tend to use their powers of accreditation in the service of restrictionist policies—in effect, to keep the number of schools and programs at a minimum in order to keep the professions small and exclusive. Mr. Selden agreed that this occasionally happens—and with the regional associations as well, despite the general policy Mr. Jones has indicated in his speech. The regionals were started by institutions committed to liberal education; teachers colleges were excluded for a long time and junior colleges even longer. Regional differences also exist: "One institution I know is excluded from the New England association simply because of the type of institution it is, whereas it might well be accredited if it were located in another region. This is a restrictive policy.

"So you are correct in your question. There are implications of exclusion which should be of concern to society. This is one reason why the regional associations, collectively, and the National Commission on Accrediting—both of which have essentially the same membership—feel that it is extremely important for the institutions, rather than the practitioners, to be the dominant influence in the professional accrediting agencies. Both influences must be represented, so that any conflicts can be resolved within each agency, but the agencies should not be controlled by those who are practicing in the professions."

Accreditation procedures: The discussants agreed almost unanimously that the greatest difficulty in evaluating an institution is defining the characteristics to be measured. "Accreditation is a fallible method," Mr. Selden said, "using gross measurements to evaluate the quality of education. One reason is that we have not yet refined our techniques well enough, though we are continually striving to do so. The other major reason is that we do not yet have—perhaps fortunately—a completely accepted definition of what constitutes quality in education. Certainly that quality is measured by some change in the student, but here we are dealing with individuals, and we do not know what makes one individual outstanding compared to another. Exploring this question is one of the great and intriguing features of education."

Mr. Riesman alone dissented. Education has been successfully defined, he reported, by Nevitt Sanford, professor of psychology and director of the Insitute for the Study of Human Problems at Stanford University. "Stanford's masterly studies give some sense of what it is to be educated, what the optimal changes are from freshman to senior—for instance, the growth of uncertainty and the shift from doctrinaire to exploratory positions. I think these can be tested, though not easily."

The other discussants remained uncertain. Mr. Selden pointed out that the institution's product is not the seniors but the graduates: "At what time do you measure the graduates, and on what qualities?" And Mr. Harris commented, with half-wistful irony: "Well, if we could only find out what the product is and define it, and if we could only know what the input is, then the problem would be relatively easy."

In professional accreditation, said Mr. Selden, a more precise difficulty arises. "Unlike the regional associations, the professional agencies are not interested in intangibles. They concentrate on identifying those features in a program which prepare students to practice well in a specific profession. As a result, there may be a social lag: they may be identifying those features which are important for preparing people for what was done yesterday. So we [in the National Commission on Accrediting] must continually encourage them to review what they are doing."

The complexity of this problem is exemplified by the field of engineering. "The accrediting society is still evaluating by sequences, at a time when the engineering schools are placing greater stress on basic science. What does the profession do? Should it become involved in accreditation of fields which emphasize basic science? If it does not, it is not in tune with some recent developments. But if it does, it extends its activities into areas for which we have not recognized it." And how far can such expansion be carried without infringing on other jurisdictions?

To a large extent, Mr. Jones suggested, this apparent division of interest between regional and professional accrediting is not actual. "In practice, many of the professional agencies are just as interested in the total quality of the institution as are the regional associations. The relevant societies are generally represented in the regional teams which visit institutions, and the societies welcome this an an opportunity to get a more general view. It is a good corrective factor for their own evaluations of the professional programs."

Apart from this aspect of accreditation procedure—the difficulty of deciding what to measure—the discussants offered explanations of three other key points. *First,* both Mr. Jones and Mr. Seldon stressed that accreditation is *not* rating. No attempt whatever is made to assess the comparative strength of accredited institutions or programs. The criteria would be virtually impossible to determine, since one would have to weigh the relative advantages each institution offers to each potential student. Besides, the institutions would never tolerate it.

Second, Mr. Jones and Mr. Selden agreed that the financial evaluation of an institution is not tied rigidly to such factors as the size of its endowment. The real question is: "What may reasonably be expected as continuity in income?" Tuitions, gifts and unit costs—as well as contributed services in the case of some church-related institutions—are among the factors taken into account in assessing the prospects for long-range financial stability.

And *finally,* in a response to a question, Mr. Jones explained that the regionals want institutions to prepare for the visits of evaluation teams, since this will lead them to face the basic questions of quality in education. There is no risk that an institution, knowing what the team will be looking for, could deceive it by a temporary display of quality. "The accreditation process lasts two or three years. It is not a one-shot visit of three days. In fact, the visit is likely to be the least important phase of the whole process."

8. College Admissions: The Qualifications of Students

Frank Bowles
Educational Program Director, Ford Foundation; Former President,
College Entrance Examination Board

As a springboard for this session, I have been asked to speak on the topic "Criteria for Admission to Colleges Abroad." This title really does not describe the situation abroad, so I had best begin by redefining slightly each of the operative words.

Critera, in this case, means the formal requirements for a given program. These requirements are uniform for all candidates, and meeting them automatically confers admission to the program. *Admission* thus means simply meeting these formal requirements. In contrast to the procedure in America, no personal selection is involved. *Colleges,* for our present purpose, means various types of educational institutions which would be considered higher education in America, though some of them are considered secondary education in Europe. *Abroad* could theoretically mean the entire world, but I shall take it here to mean only Europe. Since almost all countries in the world follow the European educational pattern, the systems in other countries and regions can be described in terms of their adherence to or deviation from the European pattern.

There is one important exception: Russian education, from an admissions standpoint, is more nearly like the American than the European system in terms of the opportunities it offers, though it retains many of the examinations and other selective features and devices of the European system. It was an adaptation of the nineteenth-century feudal German system, adapted for nineteenth-century feudal Russia and then thoroughly reorganized and overlaid with Marxism, as interpreted first by Lenin, then by Stalin and then by Khruschev. Throughout all these changes it was administered with that inimitable attitude of Russian administrators: "It doesn't matter what rules they change, as long as they don't change the operations."

167

In talking about countries abroad, it is important to note that all educational programs are controlled by the government. This means that the established criteria are enforced essentially by legal means and that the results of education, in the form of certificates and diplomas, are legal documents. This has unexpected significance. There is, for example, little likelihood of any private experimental operation rising up to challenge the existing order. There might be strong intellectual sanction for such an operation, but it could not function because it could not issue credentials with legal weight. The government, of course, has full powers to experiment, and it sometimes does so—but almost always administratively.

Control over education is fundamentally administrative. There are no bodies within the educational structure whose responsibility it is to evaluate and perhaps reconsider policy. Policy changes may come as a result of administrative action, such as the evolution of the French *lycée technique* in recent years, but this happens infrequently. In general, policy changes come from outside the educational structure and are politically developed, as in the British Conservative government's sudden discovery that England needed seven more universities, just when the Labor party intended to make higher education a political issue.

Let me, by the way, correct an error which I have seen creeping into many discussions comparing European and American education. Admiral Hyman G. Rickover, among others, has made the rather ill-tempered statement that American secondary education is administered by people who have had no teaching experience, people who have degrees and diplomas but do not know first-hand what they are administering. That, as it happens, is not so. There is admittedly a very high proportion of ex-football coaches among school superintendents, but they have had teaching experience, and they usually are fairly experienced administrators by the time they come to the job. In the European system, on the other hand, the actual adminstration is concealed: it is found in the ministries and is done by functionaries who, as a general rule, have had literally no educational training and no teaching experience.

In talking about criteria, it will be easiest to divide higher education abroad into three rough groups: university and engineering education, technical and semi-professional education, and training for primary-school teachers.

University and engineering education

European universities train students for medicine, law, government service, science and university teaching (including teaching in secondary schools which prepare students for university education). In some countries, they also train for the field of economics, either pure or applied. As a general rule, the universities offer no other programs, although there are a few specialized research institutes attached to the major universities. Training in engineering is offered in higher technical schools of university grade.

Entrance to universities and higher technical schools is based upon satisfactory completion of the university-line preparatory school. About twenty per cent of the youngsters in the appropriate age group enter this type of school, usually after passing entrance examinations. Fewer than half of these youngsters graduate.

The program in these schools is heavily weighted with languages, often including the classical languages, but considerable attention is also given to mathematics and the descriptive sciences. (There is surprisingly little laboratory work in the sciences.) The teaching is done by university graduates, who maintain university standards and apply European university methods. The teacher is often a lecturer; the textbook is used as a reference; recitation is based on an outline of the preceding lecture; and the entire program proceeds according to a formal study plan. The study includes substantial amounts of memorization, particularly in the literary classics. Emphasis is on factual accumulation, with relatively little attention to problem-solving, or to application of factual information, or to the production of new ideas. A final program, ordinarily of two years duration, permits a heavy concentration by the student in two or, at the most, three related academic fields. In these fields, the concentration carries the student up to approximately the level of the junior year in most American colleges.

Failure in the examinations given within the secondary schools is common and taken for granted; it is without stigma. Approximately 60 per cent of students taking the intermediate examination—for admission to the final, two-year phase—fail and repeat one or more times. A substantial number of students drop out at this point to enter other types of school which do not lead to the universities. Those who finally succeed at the intermediate examination encounter, two years later, the second and final examination covering their specialized studies. The failure rate here is lower, usually around 25 per cent. As a consequence of these two examinations, only about 8 per cent of the total age group graduate from secondary school, and only about half of these enter higher education. Not all of that 4 per cent, of course, complete their higher education.

Thus the line of schooling which prepares for higher education abroad is integral to higher education. It is so closely linked that its final examination constitutes the basic entrance requirement for higher education. Until recently there has been no other requirement, but a further examination (called the propaedeutic) is now administered within the science-oriented faculties of the universities—and increasingly in the humanities and law faculties. Success in this examination is an additional entrance credential which will doubtless be increasingly required.

This procedure for admission to universities and higher technical schools establishes essentially the following criteria: (1) Ability to pass detailed written examinations. Ordinarily, a minimum of three sets are required—the entrance examination to secondary school and the intermediate and final examinations within secondary school. A fourth examination, the propaedeutic, may also be required. (2) Ability to commit facts and even sections of books to memory, particularly in literary fields. (3) Ability to work according to a formal study plan and to handle the details of a scheme of outlining. And (4) High ability at verbal skills which in this type of operation are obviously more important than numbers skills.

Procedures for access to Russian universities and engineering schools are substantially the same as those for Western Europe, except for the important fact that no entrance examination is required for admission to Russian secondary schools. There is also no formal intermediate examination, yet a substantial number of students are drawn out of secondary schools at this level; they go either to technicums, for continued technical training, or to any of several kinds of vocational schools, which at the lowest level seem to offer a form of apprentice employment.

I asked repeatedly, when I visited the Russian schools, what causes these students to disappear at approximately the end fo the tenth grade and elect to go into these other schools. I never got a really satisfactory answer until I encountered one official who, instead of answering my question, talked about his daughter. She was a teacher in a Russian secondary school, and it finally dawned upon me that he was telling me that this was how the selection was made.

At the end of the tenth grade, his daughter, who was a homeroom teacher, nominated those of her students who were going to withdraw and enter other types of schooling. This is *de facto* an intermediate examination.

At the end of secondary school in Russia, there is a uniform examination, but it does not qualify students for admission to higher education. The entrance examinations are handled by the individual institutions, each of which runs its own preparatory school. In addition, one of the most important requirements for admission is two years of work experience, which is a firmly established part of the entire secondary-school curriculum, amounting to one-third of the time devoted to practical work. This requirement is waived only for those students who keep in the upper fifth of their secondary-school class. For any part-time student, work is an absolute requirement for admission.

After application, the Russian system again departs from the European and resembles the American in an odd way: entrance to universities, engineering schools and other forms of higher institutes is open in the day program to those who pass the examination at one level, in the evening program to those who pass at a lower but still sufficient level, and in correspondence programs to those who pass with even a barely good enough performance to establish a possibility that they might be able to succeed in a correspondence course. There is a fifty per cent dropout in the correspondence courses, which indicates that these are the Russian "opportunity programs," very much like our evening programs.

It may be noted, in passing, that in countries where secondary education has expanded much more rapidly than higher education, there has been a tendency to develop another important entrance criterion: persistence. In India, Japan, Chile and Brazil, where the student may have to repeat the entrance examination for six or seven years before he achieves a passing grade and can be admitted to the university, the evidence is clear that persistence is the most important single characteristic required for admission. This is confirmed by studies in Chile and Brazil, which show that students who have taken the entrance examination for six or more years have almost inevitably been admitted to higher education.

Students in India and Japan, by the way, are treated very badly. Costs against them are levied in various ingenious ways, including very high charges for entrance examinations and for training in private coaching schools. Since the income from these charges is an important source of support for higher education, it is reasonable to surmise that the entrance examinations in those countries are rigged so that the average student is unable to pass them, thereby creating a situation in which the repetition is enforced.

In addition to these standard forms of higher education, there is a distinctive system of superior-grade higher education, which, as far as I know, is found only in France. These programs are offered in certain of the *Grandes Écoles*, among them the *écoles normales supérieures*, the *École des Ponts et Chaussées*, the *École Polytechnique* and certain other higher specialized institutions, dealing for the most part with technical subjects.

Admission to these schools is based on a *concours*, or competitive examination, for which preparation is given in certain of the major *lycées* in the larger cities. This preparation usually involves two years of intensive study beyond the otherwise final secondary-school examination. Students then take the *concours*, with the understanding that the institutions will have room to admit only one-tenth of those competing. The graduates of these superior-grade institutions of higher learning comprise a very small cadre of elite personnel who are absorbed into the higher levels of the public service and education.

In Latin America, admission to the universities is established by the curious operation of the system of secondary education. Primary education in that continent, though by no means universal, is ordinarily free. In most countries, however, the state makes little or no provision for free secondary education. It is therefore offered primarily by church-related, tuition-charging schools. It may get subvention from the government, but it is under church control, and the churches charge tuition. The effective requirement for admission to higher education, therefore, is the ability to pay the tuition in secondary education. An anterior requirement is that the student must live in a city, for there is not enough primary education available in the rural areas, in any case, to prepare him for secondary education.

Latin American secondary schools operate on fairly low standards, and there is no reason why any student of normal intelligence should not be able to complete his *bachillerato,* once he gets in. Entrance to the universities is therefore relatively easy from an intellectual standpoint. Many Latin American universities are now using a propaedeutic examination to cluster up to three-fourths of this very large first-year enrollment. For example, the School of Medicine in the

University of Buenos Aires has about 5,000 students, but it graduates only about fifty a year. Most of the others are clustered in the first year, either waiting for the first-year examination, or having failed it and expecting to repeat it, or planning how they are going to avoid it this year. Avoidance is serious business at these universities. Students are allowed to fail the examination only three times before they are dropped from the university—this is considered quite a restriction—but there is no requirement that they must take it when the time comes. They may register, reregister and again reregister and never take the examination. Of course, if they take it the first time and fail, they may still take it twice again. Many students have thus become professional students—and, concomitantly, professional political agitators.

Technical and semi-professional education

The next level below the universities and higher technical schools consists of training for such vocations as librarian, accountant, documentalist, draftsman, engineering technician and social worker. In the United States these fields are generally considered semiprofessional, but training for them is offered at the college and university level. In Europe the reverse is true: such training is called professional, but it has a lower status, somewhere between secondary school and university. These programs are given in separate schools, very often private schools which specialize in preparing students for particular state examinations.

Two different groups of students enter this type of training. One group are those from the university-line preparatory schools who have failed either the intermediate or the final examination. Once that failure has established a permanent barrier in the student's path to the university, he is permitted to apply to this type of school, and he is usually admitted. Sometimes he is required to pass an entrance examination, but more often not, since it is always easier than the examination he has just failed. In some countries, on leaving the preparatory school, he is issued a credential—such as the French *brevet élémentaire* or the British GCE—which indicates an achievement about one year less than an Americah high-school diploma.

In the new school, the student undertakes a three- or four-year program which is largely technical in nature and which includes a substantial amount of on-the-job training. He graduates as an accredited professional, with a *brevet* or *diplôme* of some kind, ready for a functionary job within the Civil Service or within business. For this group of students, it has been fair to say that one criterion for admission is failure in the academic line. This is now changing, as requirements for the professional schools are raised, but it accounts for the relatively low esteem in which the semiprofessional fields have been held abroad.

The second group of students entering the professional schools are quite different. They have gone from primary school directly into technical training at the secondary-school level. A student entering this line may have failed the entrance examination to the university-line secondary school, or he may not even have attempted it. The technical schools are ordinarily open without entrance examination. If he does well in this lower technical study, which begins almost immediately at the age of eleven or twelve, he may move into the higher technical study, which eventually gives him a professional qualification.

It is within this professional line that much of the European social mobility is now beginning to occur. Children of men in this professional category are turning up in increasing numbers in the university-line preparatory schools—something they never did before World War II. This is the present extent of the democratization of European secondary and higher education. I must emphasize that this professional status is not easy to attain. It accounts for approximately ten per cent of the age group, at the most.

In other countries, even this level of democratization has not yet appeared. In Asia, Africa and South America, semiprofessional education scarcely exists at all. Indeed, very few of this type of professional worker are found anywhere outside of Europe and the United States. So if this kind of European education seems oddly below our own standards, remember that in most other countries these professions do not exist or, if they exist, are entered only by apprenticeship training of one kind or another.

Training for primary-school teachers

In Europe the higher technical training is considered, if not comparable to university education, at least significantly above secondary education. Most teacher training is not. In contrast to the United States, students who will become teachers in primary schools and in technical and special schools at the secondary level—in Europe these are called higher primary schools—are themselves trained in programs given at the higher primary level. (Only the university-line preparatory schools are called secondary schools in Europe. Teachers for these schools are trained, as I have indicated, at the universities.)

In the European system, then—and it applies as well in Asia, Africa and South America—entrance to teacher training is directly from the lower primary school; it may or may not be based on an entrance examination. The teacher-training programs last either six or seven years and include a very limited amount of practice teaching. After the candidate graduates, he is sent immediately into service. The teachers in these teacher-training institutions are graduates of the institutions who have had some years of teaching experience. No graduate work is attached to this program, and except in a few countries, graduation from it does not qualify the student for entrance to any form of higher education. This situation is changing, but there is a long way to go before the change will become significant.

The prevalence and persistence of this form of teacher education has a very strong, though possibly indirect, relationship to the procedure for admission to higher education and to the real criteria which control entrance. When the primary school is taught by teachers who have had no experience of university standards or university-level intellectual stimulus, there must be a very profound effect upon the pupils. The school has no one on its teaching staff who will stimulate students to *want* to move from primary education into the university line and eventually into higher education.

It follows that, as a general rule, the only primary-school students who have ambitions for higher education are those who have a stimulus in their homes. Other pupils—and the primary-school teachers themselves—are, in a sense, locked into their primary-school environment. Intellectually they have all too little opportunity to escape it, even though technically and legally the opportunity is fully present. In a very real sense, therefore, any cataloging of the criteria for admission to higher education abroad must include the existence of a stimulating—or at least a motivating—environment outside of the school.

This locked-in environment of the European primary school has another serious consequence. The schoolteachers themselves, the *petits intellectuels*, do not generally encourage even their own children to seek a higher education. There are two important exceptions to this generalization: it does not hold true in the Netherlands, where the children of schoolteachers are one of the largest groups enrolled in universities and by all odds the most successful, nor does it hold true in Austria. However, it is significant that in both these countries, teacher training at this level does permit some access, although perhaps limited, to higher education.

One other set of facts relating to criteria for entrance to higher education should be noted. It is clear from what has been said that the vast majority of students in school systems abroad never get into any line of study that may conceivably lead them to higher education. In fact, most training of the labor force in countries abroad is by an apprentice method, which may or may not be coupled with formal schooling. Schooling in most countries still terminates at age 12, although the age limit is rising to 14, 15 and even 16.

There do exist, although they are not widely used, various means of working up through the apprentice and labor-force training into higher education. For example, a student going from the lower to the higher primary school can get into a technical program there; by doing well, he can move into a middle-caliber technical program; by continuing to do well, he can move into an advanced technical program and finally into a higher technical school at the university level. This does not happen often, but it does happen.

It is of interest that the new technical university at Eindhoven, the Netherlands, includes—for the first time in any Europen country that I know of—a higher technical school, which is actually giving work that is recognized as of university grade. The French have opened at least one faculty of engineering which admits applicants without examination and without consideration of previous schooling, allowing them to earn their degrees as regular students solely by the quality of their work in the institution. In England tens of thousands of individuals are enrolled in what is called further education, which provides a route whereby a student may earn a credential, the higher national certificate, which is of higher-education status. Again, this does not happen often, but it does happen. Also, in England as in Russia, it is possible to take degrees by correspondence programs.

A Russian correspondence course, incidentally, includes two months of actual laboratory work and sitting for examination before the faculty. It thus includes a substantial contact with the faculty, which is not found in the correspondence programs of other countries. The Russians have also begun what I think is a very interesting process in establishing, in some of the outlying cities, a series of helping centers where students taking correspondence courses can go for assistance with particular sets of problems.

By way of summary, the following points seem to me worth noting:

First, educational systems abroad offer a wide choice of programs at the primary-and secondary-school level. This narrows down suddenly, so that the range of choice at the level of higher education equivalent to the American college and university is very limited indeed. Our own pattern is quite the reverse: we are tending increasingly to a unitary pattern in secondary school, with a very limited range of choice, leading to a wide spread of choices at the level of higher education.

Second, the limitation of choice in educational systems abroad is accomplished mainly by examinations. It is therefore an impersonal elimination, involving no individual assessments whatsoever, which produces a highly examination-oriented and highly learning-conscious group at the end of the process.

Third, money is not an important criterion for entrance to higher education. But persistence is, often the kind of persistence that is associated with the possession of money and/or social status.

Fourth, there are no professionals engaged in controlling admission to higher education or in any related activities, such as guidance. Most guidance and counseling for schoolchildren are essentially clinical, conducted as part of the public-welfare or public-health programs. However, the development of loan and scholarship programs is beginning to produce a few professionals, and there is some recognition that guidance is an academic specialty involving professional skills.

Finally, the lines of demarcation among various segments of educational systems abroad are clearly marked, and the operation of the system is such that these lines are self-perpetuating. They can, of course, be broken down; but if they are, the present system of admission to higher education abroad is also broken down. The admissions system, in turn, is essential in maintaining the present lines of demarcation.

An example of what happens when a traditional system breaks down is that of England, where the reform of secondary education, effectuated in 1944, has produced an entire generation of secondary-school students who have no roots in the old, selective, quasi-feudal system and who are therefore not awed by the limitations they find on their further progress. By their refusal to be awed, they are creating a continuing educational crisis, and in time they will create a political crisis. They almost did so several years ago, but the Conservative party got the word in time and announced the opening of seven new universities, as I mentioned earlier. Still, the existence of this crisis in England shows the extent to which the criteria for admission to higher education in colleges abroad have, in the past, been enforced through the instrumentality of the secondary shcool.

SUMMARY OF THE DISCUSSION

The general discussion developed in a somewhat fragmentary and inconclusive manner, touching upon four areas of concern:

European vs. College Board examinations: "What are the similarities and the differences between the final examinations in the European secondary schools and our own College Board examinations?" To this question Mr. Bowles responded that he sees very few similarities and four marked differences:

First, the European examinations carry with them diplomas and titles which are conferred on those students who pass. The College Boards do not.

Second, the European and Middle Eastern examinations have at times been rigged to reduce the number of graduates and consequently the number of university entrants, though "this has never been admitted officially." In Europe such tampering has never been successful. "Every time they tried the experiment, there has been such a political uproar that the examination was invalidated and a second one administered."

Third, the European examinations are based on a long-established curriculum. The College Boards, except for the so-called Writing Sample, attempt not to influence or control the curriculum. "The attempt is perhaps not always as successful as we try to kid ourselves it is, but the attempt is there and is recongized."

Fourth, the Scholastic Aptitude Test has no equivalent overseas. "It is an abhorrent concept to Europeans. They simply will not have any part of it." In practice, however, there is comparable screening at the end of primary school, as under the English 11-plus examinations, and the regular examinations are narrowly directed to "pick out students with quite high verbal skills, who would score very well on the Scholastic Aptitude Test." A discussant asked Mr. Bowles to explain "what the Europeans have against aptitude tests." He did not reply.

In Russia, the objection to aptitude tests is ideological. Marxist dogma "does not permit any difference among people on the basis of inherent ability. The Marxist concept is a very firm belief that environment changes ability. As a matter of fact, this belief seems to be supported by more evidence than would have been expected a few years ago."

General vs. specialized education: One salient contrast between American education and that in other countries was sharply drawn. "The European principle," Mr. Bowles explained, "is that the secondary-school final examination is the ending point of general education. Students who pass beyond this point are going to specialize. The universities are therefore not at all concerned with general education. The students enter immediately into training for their professional fields."

The American principle was defined by Paul M. Chalmers, associate director of admissions and advisor to foreign students at the Massachusetts Institute of Technology: "We are moving ahead very strongly toward a system of higher education which offers not one choice but a series of choices. The university is not content merely to provide a certain amount of organized knowledge. Another of its major roles—perhaps even more important—is to help the young person find his way. It is perfectly acceptable for him to change his objective rather radically, at least in his early undergraduate years. Indeed, most academic programs allow for it."

This contrast becomes a personal dilemma for many foreign students who attend American universities. "A nineteen-year-old Frenchman, say, when he comes to MIT, knows exactly what he intends to do in his higher education and in his professional career. We then have a hard job helping him adjust to our approach, conveying to him what we are trying to do. After he realizes that the choices are still open, we may have another hard job counseling him when he tries to explain this to his government or to whatever other sponsor sent him here. How can he tell them that he was quite sure, when he arrived, that he was going to be a sanitary engineer, but he has discovered that it is much more fun to work with computers and that, as a matter of fact, he is extremely good at it?"

A challenge to the American principle of general education was posed by Mrs. Joan Burstyn, of the Graduate School of Education. "Is it always an advantage to have the maximum choice at university level? Is it necessarily a good idea for the universities to concern themselves with general education? Why not let the secondary schools do this and the universities be more specialized? After all, with people marrying younger, the pressure toward some sort of specialization is probably going to increase. Other industrial societies at the same level of development as ours have found a specialized system of higher education functional. Shouldn't we at least consider this possibility? Can we always assume that whatever America happens to be doing is best?"

The challenge was taken up by Ronald B. Greeley, director of admissions at MIT. "There may be a great difference on this score between the typical American of seventeen and the typical European of eighteen or nineteen. Certainly the American college freshman is not sophisticated enough, not sufficiently crystallized in his interests and habits, to know precisely what line of work he wants to enter and which of his strengths are most valuable to develop. I speak partly from our own experience at MIT. We are in a position to take students who are relatively crystallized; we certainly place a far greater stress on achievement tests and correspondingly less on aptitude tests than most colleges do. Yet nearly half our students make significant changes in their specific line of professional orientation after they enroll. It seems to me that a system which does not incorporate this sort of flexibility would be an unfortunate system, as far as the American student is concerned."

Another danger of specialized higher education was pointed out by Mr. Bowles. "In some less developed countries, the lack of diversity in university offerings may be a serious problem. India and Egypt, for example, have enough universities, but the drastic limitation of the science programs forces thousands of students—in India hundreds of thousands—into the nonscience programs, in which it is much easier to get a degree but from which it is very hard to find a job. In Egypt there are many more lawyers—and many more students of law—than the economy can possibly accommodate at the present time."

(Much of the general discussion was devoted to the questions of manpower planning and the relation of education to a country's economy. Because these parts of the discussion were irrelevant to the issue of student qualifications and because both questions are dealt with more comprehensively in other chapters, they are not summarized here.)

Democratization of education abroad: In response to questions, Mr. Bowles amplified the observations in his speech concerning the increasing pressure for democratization of the total educational structure in Europe. There has not yet been any serious modification of that structure, he reported, but there is very heavy pressure for changes, largely because a higher proportion of children are enrolling in schools and because those who enroll are staying in school longer.

"This traces back to a political action which was taken by the governments formed in Europe just after the end of World War II. Virtually all were left-wing governments, and one of their very first actions was to create universal primary education, not merely in principle but in fact. This was a brave undertaking, but to their surprise, it was not enough. The primary-school graduates demanded more education; they snowed under the old form of higher primary school, which terminated at age eleven or twelve, and forced the governments to extend this to a higher age.

"Next the graduates of these schools asked for higher education, and at this point the university cadre reacted with grave misgivings and something like anger. They said, in effect: 'Look, we have just given you primary education and now secondary education. Please go away and don't bother us. We don't want you in higher education. We have no room for you, and we will make no provision for you.' And they have not made room. While university enrollment in Europe has increased by twenty-five per cent in ten years, only eight new universities have been founded in all of Europe, and two of these—in England—ars still on paper. But the pressure is on in Great Britain with many more on the way.

"There are very large differences, of course, between developments in higher education in England and in the rest of Europe. The English, having made a major move toward democratizing secondary education twenty years ago, are facing these problems much before any of the other European countries."

In Africa, he continued, the problem is different. "The university-line preparatory schools are very expensive and very beautifully run, although the teaching staffs are sometimes a bit undermanned. We could not afford this kind of secondary education for our mass enrollments. However, these are the only schools at the secondary level." There is virtually no training available for potential teachers in primary schools. As a result, the educational base is weak, and the system cannot direct enough students toward higher education. "Even in Nigeria, which is an exception in important ways, the same trouble exists. There is a tremendous demand for access to higher education, but the students who are clamoring are not qualified by Nigerian standards. The country has not expanded its primary and secondary structure enough to support its higher education."

Corrections and clarifications: Under questioning, Mr. Bowles acknowledged a few inaccuracies and overgeneralizations in his speech. With regard to teacher training, he agreed that teachers in England

and Germany are now receiving a university education before entering the classroom. He added that this "is becoming a strong movement in all the European countries." No participant invited him to revise, in this light, his observations on motivating schoolchildren to seek a higher education.

England is an exception to the European pattern in two other significant ways, he acknowledged. Educational credentials are not government controlled, although the government has negotiated the value to be given to Examining Board credentials by other countries. And teaching in the college-preparatory schools is not characterized by lectures, recitations and fixed courses of study. "Indeed," one discussant noted, "such teaching appears to be appallingly frequent in American high schools, but I never saw it in any school I visited in England."

At two other points in his speech, Mr. Bowles had erroneously implied a contrast—or so the discussants felt—between the conditions he was describing and the prevalent conditions in the United States. The first point was his description of *de facto* screening of secondary-school students by homeroom teachers in Russia. A discussant asked how this is different from the American procedure, which relies heavily on the recommendations of the guidance counseler. Mr. Bowles replied that there is no difference: the Russian homeroom teachers are acting as guidance counselors.

The second point was his emphasis on political pressures as a source of educational change in Europe. When asked about the United States, he stressed that "our changes have been very heavily politically developed." Asked when a change is "just educational," he replied: "That is a very fine line." But he offered no examples, and the questioner did not press for them.

Coda: A brief comment interjected into the discussion by David Riesman, Henry Ford II Professor of Social Sciences at Harvard University, offered one possible unifying perspective on this session. Mr. Riesman said: "I have thought for some time that the great advantage of American education is that Americans consider it inferior to European education. They do not believe themselves cultured unless they have been abroad, and so they keep on educating themselves insatiably to make up for this supposedly very bad education they have had. When the truth that Mr. Bowles told us sinks home—that in global perspective, however bad our system is, it is not the worst in the world—I wonder whether we shall lose that great advantage."

Part III:
Economic Issues: The Cost of Education

9. Productivity in Schools and Colleges

Joseph A. Kershaw
Professor of Economics and Provost, Williams College

The growing interest of economists in the fields of elementary, secondary and higher education is gratifying. Education is second only to national defense as a voracious consumer of resources; perhaps even more important, the old saw that today's schools are training tomorrow's leaders just happens to be true. So the economic problems of education are quite properly a matter of national concern. They are also very difficult, and since educators have demonstrated their inability thus far to solve them, perhaps it is our turn now to try.

The problem of productivity in schools and colleges ought to be a natural for us, yet it is one on which we have made surprisingly little progress. Most studies of the economics of education devote a few pages to productivity, but I have found in them no really pungent analysis, only a lament that productivity should be higher and that output is hard to define. This paper, unfortunately, will be no exception. For the simple fact is that there is no consensus on what the output of education is or should be; and until we define output, we can never know whether we are combining our resource inputs in an optimum way.

Certainly, at the insistence of educators, we have become increasingly lavish with our input of both capital and labor per student. If we contrast the facilities pictured in that wonderful book *Mark Hopkins and the Log*[1] with the equipment in any modern institution of higher learning, we see that the difference is immense. In the public school systems the contrast is, if anything, greater. And this capital investment has not been used to displace labor; rather, it has been accompanied by a large increase in manpower per student, so that both major inputs have increased faster than the student population. Thus, if the student-teacher ratio could be used as a measure of labor productivity (which I think it cannot), we would have the curious spectacle of an industry trying its best to worsen its productivity—and bragging about its success.

Still, the student-teacher ratio is a measure of our use of labor resources, if not of productivity, and we should pause to look at it briefly. In elementary and secondary schools, a maximum ratio of thirty-to-one has become virtually enshrined. Any larger ratio is regarded as indecent; it is considered axiomatic that the quality of education falls off rapidly as this ratio is exceeded. The fact is, however, that the "best" ratio undoubtedly varies greatly according to the subject, the teacher, the method of instruction and other variables.

Naturally, it is harder to teach more students than it is to teach less, but the prevalent ideas about this subject are scarcely based on rational analysis. Some time ago a colleague and I studied the matter briefly and interviewed a good many teachers and other educators. We concluded that, according to our informants, the optimum size of any class is three less than are in it, and we came away with the impression that each teacher can name the three she wants out. But in spite of this mystique, the student-teacher ratio will almost surely have to rise in the future under the impact of the rapid growth in enrollments. The challenge that confronts us is to enable this to take place without diminishing our educational output, either quantitatively or qualitatively.

Colleges are also clinging desperately to their current ratios in the face of severe shortages of supply. A fortunate few may be able to keep within the ten-to-one ratio that is widely regarded as sacrosanct, but it seems clear that ratios here too will rise. How this will affect the quality of education is probably even less clear than for the schools. Marginal changes can surely be made without impairing educational achievements, but it will be far more difficult to make substantial changes, which are the only ones that can really help.

What is necessary, then, at both the school and college level, is not merely to increase the put-through of students per faculty member—this would be easy—but to increase the number of students while maintaining the quality of their education. Before we can have any confidence that a specific measure will contribute toward this goal, we must understand what educational output is. This is the heart of the productivity problem.

To consider the schools first: what is it that they are trying to do? The old-fashioned notion was that they should produce students who have some familiarity with and appreciation of the culture in which they are living. But many additional or different objectives are now being urged. The child should emerge from high school adjusted to life, or a creative being, or a conformist, or a nonconformist, or trained to enter a trade.

In practice, the schools are setting different goals for different groups of students. The top group is following the college preparatory route; its curriculum emphasizes the liberal-arts subjects. Another group, which is deemed unsuited for college, is strongly counselled into vocational subjects. This latter policy seems to me particularly questionable, and I note with some dismay that Dr. Conant has afforded substantial encouragement to it. I should think that the terminal student would have the greatest, rather than the least, need for exposure to books and other things intellectual. For him this is really the last chance.

Finally, there are the youngsters who are virtually ineducable and whom the school accepts merely to keep them off the streets. I agree that this job must be done, but it is not clear to me why the *schools* should be expected to do it, nor why teachers who are adept at communicating enthusiasm about English literature or algebra should be presumed to be competent in dealing with this group of students. Nevertheless, almost all schools these days rate themselves in part in terms of how low they can keep the dropout rate.

I have categorized too sharply, of course, but I hope that even this simplified scheme indicates the complications involved in deciding what the output of the schools is or should be. Any rigid solution is bound to seem drastic. Admiral Hyman G. Rickover, for example, strongly urges that standardized Federal examinations be administered to all public-school children, so that the taxpayer in each community may judge how good a job his schools are doing.[2] The idea has great appeal, but note that its adoption would force all schools to accept one set of objectives—a set, incidentally, which is by no means universally preferred at present. This, of course, is one of Admiral Rickover's main purposes: to force all schools to de-emphasize the nonacademic aspects of their curricula.

Yet it may be that a rigid criterion of some sort is the only way out. A few years ago I took part in a study for the Ford Foundation,[3] one of whose goals was to see whether a public school system could be analyzed systematically so that one could evaluate the productivity value of different ways of combining inputs. For this, some generally applicable measure of output was necessary. After looking at the problem with some care, we concluded that it would be possible to rely on achievement tests, such as the Iowa tests, which are widely given in the schools. We recognized that the criterion is imperfect, but it is single-vectored, quantifiable and, we think, correlated with most other desirable features of education. But it is admittedly far from ideal, and the vocationalists would reject it as completely inappropriate.

Another problem in defining educational output is to neutralize the significant effects of influences which have their source outside the school. The most important of these are family education and family income, which may be much more important than the school experience. Indeed, anyone who examines the educational process over a period of time must experience moments of despair when he wonders whether the educational process really has any effect at all! But putting this heretical notion behind us, we recognize that we are seeking to define the educational *value added,* not the gross value. This raises our difficulty by another order of magnitude.

With respect to colleges and universities we can be briefer. Most of the definitional difficulties found in the schools are found at these higher levels as well. The major addition is the problem of how to measure research as a factor in educational output. To the extent that research makes a scholar a better teacher, the effect belongs in almost any measure of output. But there is also a more direct product of college and university research which ought somehow to be included. This is the scientific discoveries and advances of many kinds which benefit mankind directly without passing through the teaching process. These are as much a product of the university as is the education of a person destined for leadership in the society.

Educational output, then, is a slippery notion indeed. It is possible, I think, to do some constructive productivity analyses below the college level, though the procedure would be expensive and the results partial. At the college level, more preliminary research needs to be done—for example, by following the performance of graduates of various kinds of institutions. Some work of this sort has been undertaken, particularly in terms of income-earning experience and performance in graduate schools, but we still lack both data and appropriate conceptualization for understanding output at the higher level. It is important that such work go forward, so that we can someday evaluate proposed changes and know which will really increase output per unit of input and which will simply reduce both input and output. The former, of course, will increase productivity; the latter may not at all.

Meanwhile, even without a clear definition of output, there are many areas where changes can be made which will enable us to do our job more efficiently. Education at all levels has a particular obligation to seek out these areas now, for it is going to need major new resources in the coming years if it is to accommodate the growing population, which, all agree, has a right to be educated. At the college level we are told that operating expenses will multiply two and a half times between 1960 and 1970, even without inflation. And with enrollment doubling or more, new construction will add more billions to the budgets. These resources are well within our capabilities, as many observers have pointed out; but alumni, businesses and legislatures are bound to demand assurances that funds are being used wisely. School systems, too, can expect difficulty. Indeed, it is already on them. In 1961 one-third of the school bond issues submitted to the voters were defeated—an ominous statistic.

Fortunately, a number of suboptimizations can be achieved immediately, regardless of over-all educational goals. Some of these are fairly obvious: better office procedures, better accounting, better plant utilization, and possibly the development of institutional research staffs. Both schools and colleges could re-examine seriously the number and value of their small classes. If a home economics teacher can teach cooking to twenty girls at once as effectively as to ten, she ought to have twenty in her class, whether or not a knowledge of cooking adds to the output of the school. The schools could also look at their curricula with care, particularly at some of the vocational offerings. (It is ironic that math is inexpensive to teach, whereas machine-building is not.) Attention to matters of this sort is desirable no matter how educational output is defined.

A few other, more fundamental changes ought to be considered if education is to use its resources efficiently. One is a correction of a strange admissions policy. Some colleges admit large numbers of freshman and allow many to fall by the wayside at each examination period, until only a small fraction survive. This is not only wasteful of resources but cruel in the bargain. Why it continues I don't know.

A second and more significant misuse of resources arises from the nearly universal use in the public schools of the single salary schedule, under which all teachers in a school system are paid the same if they have the same length of service and have taken the same number of courses. The market plays no role whatsoever; the kindergarten teacher and the high-school physics teacher are treated identically.

Roland McKean of RAND and I studied this phenomenon in our book *Teacher Shortages and Salary Schedules*. The result, we were not surprised to find, is that severe shortages of some kinds of teachers coexist with surpluses of others. Different skills are scarce in different areas; but we found shortages generally in math, science and English, while social-studies teachers are in fairly good supply and male physical education teachers are in surplus. So long as the schools are unable or unwilling to take market forces into account, this situation will continue. We expect it, in fact, to get worse as the market demand for some kinds of skills strengthens in the coming decade.

If the public-school system has to pay every teacher at the rate necessary to attract the scarcest skill it wants, the misallocation of resources will run literally into tens of billions of dollars. Schools will not do this, of course; rather, they will fail to get the teachers with scarce skills, and instruction in those subjects will fall even further into mediocrity. Our hope is that the public and the school boards will come to understand the issue and that the single salary schedule will yield to the community's desire for good education at reasonable cost.

Colleges and universities are paying a premium for scarce skills, but even they worry about the "inequities" brought by the market, and they show a great reluctance to depart far from uniformity. Frequently they resort to subterfuges; for example, new Ph.D.'s in math are appointed assistant professors, whereas in languages they become instructors. For some reason, this sleight of hand is supposed to be better for morale than would an actual pay differential, facing up frankly to the fact that math and language instructors are in different markets.

I would like to conclude with a caution about educational changes and productivity. Education at all levels is going to be subjected to more and more pressures to increase its productivity, to introduce economies, to conserve resources, to operate more efficiently—all of which mean the same thing. I think it proper that education should be under these pressures. But there is danger that we will be asked to do things which *seem* to work in the direction of efficiency but which really do not, or which are really ambiguous because our concept of output is still somewhat vague. A couple of examples may be helpful.

The suggestion is often made that we reduce from fifteen to twelve the number of hours the college student spends in the classroom and that more independent work be required. This would diminish the faculty load by twenty per cent and thereby, it is held, increase productivity. This shift toward more independent work may be a sound notion, but it can be considered an increase in productivity only if educational output does not fall—at least, not more than twenty per cent. This, of course, brings us back to our output-measurement problem. If changes of this sort are made in the name of efficiency, I believe they should be regarded as experiments and accompanied by careful study of the impact on the students.

To take a second example, we have a tradition at Williams College that most members of most departments teach at least one section of the department's introductory course. Since our salary scale is a good one, this means that our costs per introductory student are among the highest in the country. We *think* this is efficient; we think that using our senior staff adds more to the educational process than it costs. But in this respect we are clearly out of step with many of our contemporaries, and the present state of our knowledge does not permit us to determine in any definitive sense whether our practice or the growing use of graduate assistants is more efficient.

I think it follows from these examples that we need to be careful about instituting changes for reasons of efficiency, unless it can be ascertained that they will really increase productivity. There are instances where this can be demonstrated; there are others where the character of the output will be altered in such ways that even the direction, to say nothing of the magnitude, of change is not clear. Unless we recognize the slipperiness of our output variable, we are likely to propose and accept changes which diminish, rather than increase, the productivity of our educational system. We ought not accept such changes—and surely not in the name of economy.

REFERENCES

1. Frederick Rudolph: *Mark Hopkins and the Log; Williams College, 1836-1872*. New Haven: Yale University Press, 1956.
2. See *The New York Times,* September 3, 1962, p. 17.
3. J. A. Kershaw and R. N. McKean: *Teacher Shortages and Salary Schedules,* McGraw Hill Book Co., 1962.

COMMENT BY . . . *Seymour E. Harris*
                                  Littauer Professor, Political Economy, Harvard
                                  University

I want to speak briefly, only to make a few points that supplement what Professor Kershaw has been saying.

We hear a great deal of talk these days about how little money is being spent on education. It seems to me that a good corrective for this impression is to look at some figures. These were compiled as of 1956; they would be higher today.

Since 1900 our total expenditures on public-school education jumped from $215 million to $11 billion* an increase of about 55 times, which far exceeds the increase in the Gross National Product. The total expenditures for day schools per pupil in average daily attendance increased almost 20 times, from $20 per year to $388 per year.

These rises are only partly explained by the expansion of faculty and enrollment. The number of teachers has not quite tripled, from 423,000 to 1,150,000. Enrollment has barely doubled, from 15.5 million to 31 million though the rate of increase in average daily attendance is greater—a jump from about 10 million to 27 million.

Two other factors also help to explain the rises. The number of days in the school year grew from 132 (somewhat earlier than 1900) to 178. And the average pay of teachers climbed from $325 at the turn of the century to $4,200. This is one very important explanation of the rise in total expenditures.

But if the number of students being educated has only doubled or tripled, while the total cost of educating them has increased 55 times, what does this indicate about productivity? Does it suggest, perhaps, a decline in productivity?

Professor Kershaw has pointed out, in this connection, the significance of our changing objectives of education. We turn out an entirely different product now. We give the youngsters health care, lunches, recreation and other nonacademic benefits. This reflects not only a change in educational philosophy but also a change in the standard of living of the average American. We see this also in the great increase in the price of teachers, which is due partly to inflation, partly to a change in the standard of living.

When you examine the dynamics of productivity in the economy as a whole, you see another reason why the costs of education have

---

*By 1963-64, educational expenditures of all kinds had risen to $33.7 billion and were increasing at a rate of almost $3 billion yearly.

gone up so steeply. The general economy shows very large rises of productivity, right up to the automation stage. As a result, industries can afford to pay steadily higher rewards. This economy does not prevail in the schools and colleges; they do not have equal advantages of rising productivity. Yet in spite of this tremendous disadvantage, they have to meet the competition. They have to meet the market test on prices, or their product deteriorates.

Another important factor in educational productivity is class size. There have been hundreds of controlled experiments, in both schools and colleges, that try to compare what can be accomplished with a class of 10 as against a class of 50 or a class of 100, and so forth. I myself believe strongly in the small seminar of 10 to 15; I think it offers very important educational products. But I am not at all convinced that there is a great advantage in having 25 as against having 75. And most of the experiments show that, all other things being equal, you do not get a larger educational product with a class of 25 than you do with a class of 75. Note that I say "educational product." In the schools there may be a greater case for small classes because of the disciplinary problem and considerations of that sort.

I think there is a good theoretical argument for this as well. At Oxford they used to say that half of the student's education comes in the classwork and the other half comes outside. When you tabulate all the factors that determine what a student learns during his school years, class size must be relatively unimportant compared to his motivation, his training at home, what he learns from his schoolmates, and so on. The higher the level of education, the more important these other factors become. I am convinced that we can save a tremendous amount of money with no loss in quality by having small seminars and very large classes.

One other factor in this lack of productivity that I want to mention now is that we build our schools and colleges in the wrong places. This is the result of all kinds of extraneous influences from individuals and from chambers of commerce, among others. The economic issues are submerged. Administrators usually fail to look at this problem as, for example, a business man does when he plans to establish a new plant. Not that the economic issues should be decisive here, but there is no doubt that they should be taken into account.

Not long ago I wrote to some 150 or 200 colleges that had established new schools or, in some cases, had established a new college, a new law school or a new graduate school of arts and sciences. I tried to find out what decisions had led to the establishment of these schools. It soon became obvious that most of the respondents had no idea about the economics of determining an optimum location. Most of them had never even asked themselves whether they should place the school near the students, or near the teachers, or near the labor market; whether they should place it so as to minimize transportation costs; and so on. They had never thought about issues of this kind. Inevitably there had been an awful lot of waste.

SUMMARY OF THE DISCUSSION

The general discussion focused on six topics:

Faculty salaries: A number of questions were elicited by Mr. Kershaw's suggestion that the salaries paid to teachers be determined in part by the market value of their skills. In response to these questions, he clarified several aspects of his proposal. The most essential was his explanation that the differentials paid for scarce skills are likely to be self-cancelling in the long run. A school must pay a premium now to attract a teacher of, say, mathematics; but as this higher salary attracts more teachers of mathematics, the differential will no longer be needed. The salaries paid to teachers of other subjects will increase faster than his, until eventually his salary and theirs are on a par. At that point, the shortage will be solved.

Some questioners wondered whether these differentials involve a moral issue. Mr. Kershaw pointed out that they are not personal (in contrast, especially, to a merit-pay system). "These people bring different skills to the market, and the buyer has to pay different prices for different commodities. We do it all the time." True, the prospective teacher is taking a risk. He may choose to major in mathematics and expect to teach at a preferential salary, only to discover, when he graduates, that many other college students have had the same idea and that his skill, being no longer scarce, no longer commands a premium. But he takes this risk no matter what career he plans to enter. "Ours is a mobile society, and it should be. This is the way the economy seeks its equilibrium."

Mr. Kershaw emphasized that price is only one of several factors that attract scarcer skills, and he acknowledged that some skills may remain scarce because they require an unusual intellectual ability. He noted also that the National Education Association and the American Federation of Teachers are resisting salary differentials based on market value. "The hope, I think, is that communities will insist on good education at moderate cost, and they cannot get it if we let the scarcest skill determine the entire pay scale."

There was general agreement that the present pay scale, though relatively high, is not high enough to attract competent teachers in sufficient quantities to meet the sharply increasing enrollments. A major problem is the narrow spread, with the highest salaries only about double the lowest—a situation which tends to drive out individuals who want to progress continually in their careers, in responsibility as well as in remuneration. Merit pay and differentiation in teaching roles were mentioned as possible solutions.

A less soluble problem which aroused some discussion is "the economically disruptive effect on salary schedules" caused by the predominance of women among schoolteachers. In Mr. Kershaw's words: "The public school system is a peculiar animal when you examine it in terms of its economics. And the main thing that makes it peculiar is the women. Frequently they work only because they want to supplement their husbands' income. They move when their husbands do. Very few are looking forward to long careers, and they are much less sensitive to pay differentials than men are. This keeps the differentials down—and keeps the men out of the schools." There was some dispute as to whether the increased costs of training and supervision —one result of the high turnover of women teachers—is or is not balanced by the high proportion of new teachers at low steps on the pay scale. But Mr. Kershaw concluded: "The question was, 'Would the wage system tend to be more rational if men dominated?' And I said, 'Yes.'"

Dropouts in school and college: Mr. Kershaw acknowledged the complexity of the problem of secondary-school dropouts, primarily because there is no alternative for them now except the school and the street. He argued that a different and more productive alternative must be found. Meanwhile, they must be kept in school; but he suggested that this expediency may be harming the entire system. "It depends on two evaluations—the extent to which these youngsters can be improved by even a grudging exposure to the educational process, and the extent to which they detract from what the rest of the student body is getting."

Some debate was occasioned by his challenge to the practice of admitting many more college freshmen than are expected to graduate. Is this a failure to use resources where they will do the most good, or is it an instance of freedom of opportunity, which is fundamental in a democracy? "I am pretty well convinced," said one discussant, "that one of the keystones of American higher education—and of our democratic system—is that there is no barrier based upon

social status or family connection or economic ability to keep a
youngster from trying his luck in higher education." The suggestion
was made that one standard might be appropriate to a small private
college, another to a state university; but the issue was not resolved.

Assuming that excess admissions are a waste of resources, what
can be done to minimize them? Discussion centered on possible adjustments in tuition: offering a partial rebate to those who graduate,
decreasing tuition for those who earn higher grades, or reducing the
tuition for junior and senior years. These incentives might be balanced by a significantly higher tuition for the freshman year, so that
the basic decision to enter college will be less casual than at present.

Two collateral issues were raised: is it a weakness in productivity
to have so many students changing their areas of concentration, and
is it uneconomic to provide higher education for women who marry
on graduation and never put their skills to work? To the first question, the consensus answered: Yes, and better guidance would help.
To the second question, Mr. Kershaw replied: "I like to think of
college-trained women as being better people than they would otherwise be and enjoying life more. I do not begrudge them that at
all. As for graduate schools, I think you get on terribly delicate ground
when you say that a woman cannot train to be a doctor because
she is married or is going to be married. Who knows? She may lose
her husband on the day she graduates and may put her training
to work for the rest of her life. I guess we all play God a little
bit, but that seems to me to be playing God a little too much."

Quality of students: Variation in the academic ability of students
—and the colleges' response to that variation—was suggested as a
factor in productivity in higher education. Mr. Harris reported the
result of a poll of two hundred economists, most of whom felt that
colleges should invest proportionally more resources in able students
than in others. Able students would meet in seminars with the best
of the faculty; other students would be taught by lecturers in large
groups. Two major objections were advanced by Mr. Kershaw: our
knowledge of how to divide these groups is very inexact, and relega-
tion to mass lecture courses would not be fair to the slower students,
whom the college did, after all, find worthy of admission.

The difficulty of assessing variations in quality was generally acknowledged. The "increasingly strong emphasis on academic excellence, in a very narrow sense," for college admissions was decried.
Tribute was paid to experiments in admitting freshmen whose academic records are not brilliant but who are extremely promising in

one field or who show potential in other important ways. Mr. Kershaw also questioned the schools' policy of separating college-bound from terminal students in the ninth grade: "If the school makes a mistake and puts a potentially good student into a terminal curriculum, he will never be challenged. The school will merely confirm its own mistake, and the student will be lost."

Some discussion centered on the question of acceleration and delay as factors in productivity. What might be gained by encouraging very bright students to complete their college studies in three years? What might be gained by encouraging some students to delay entering college, on the assumption that greater maturity will make them more serious students? These issues were not resolved.

Course offerings: The excessive number of courses offered in some colleges was identified as a serious drain on productivity, partly because proliferation leads to many courses with only a handful of students, partly because it seems inefficient to concentrate on absurdly narrow specialties within specialties. There appeared to be agreement that the fault lies with the faculty, especially those members who are either coasting on their last books or obsessed with their next ones. Praise was given to two solutions which some colleges have found successful: (1) pooling their faculty resources with those of neighboring institutions, so that duplication in offerings of small-enrollment courses can be minimized, and (2) encouraging each department to eliminate and alternate courses, thus reducing the size of the department, by allowing it to use the savings for salary increases within the department.

The suggestion was raised that colleges could increase productivity by having senior professors teach (or help teach) the introductory courses, thus assuring the students a more solid basis for their advanced studies. In rebuttal, the observation was quoted that younger faculty members are, in fact, better teachers and more willing to take time with the students. This observation closed off the argument.

Optimum size: A crucial factor in productivity of colleges, the discussants agreed, is the determination of the optimum size of the institution. Examples were offered of institutions which had set their size by totally uneconomic considerations, especially some nebulous concept of "the character of the college." The president of one of the leading universities, however, was quoted as offering a sound and pragmatic insight. Asked how he had decided the correct size for each campus, he replied: "There is one test. If your students cannot get from one class to another in eight or nine minutes, you are through. Then you have to start a new unit."

Mr. Kershaw set the issue of optimum size in perspective with a recollection: "When I first went to California, I met a man who taught at the University of Santa Barbara, which was then converting to what he characterized as a really first-class, small liberal-arts college. 'This is to be the Amherst of the West Coast,' he said. 'We are not going to have more than 12,000 students.' It was my introduction to gigantism in California."

Defining productivity: Scattered comments were made on the problem, which Mr. Kershaw had shown to be crucial, of defining educational objectivity. There was a feeling that academic measurements (such as the proportion of freshmen who later earn Ph.D.'s) are insufficient and that they might well be supplemented by such factors as the ratio between the best annual income of the graduate and his father. The point was also made that definitions will vary among institutions and will change with time. There was no consensus on whether these changes were superficial or fundamental.

10. Economics of School Management

E. Gil Boyer
Assistant Commissioner of Education for the State of Rhode Island

In order to understand the financial dilemmas of the school manager, we must refresh our knowledge of the cultural context from which his mandates and the resulting problems stem. America's very survival seems to be based upon the competitive ability of our economic system; at least, many people would have us think so. Thus education must not only foster the meaningful and effective consumption of our expanding productivity; it must also supply the technical competence necessary for the continued growth of our economy.

We produce and consume more than any other nation on earth, but our resources, both geographic and human, are rather small. Our population is rapidly shrinking as a percentage of the world's total population, and this fact necessitates an increase in the value that we place on our human resources. Our very survival demands that we educate all our citizens; the uneducated in our population are a luxury we can no longer afford. We must educate the masses, all of them. It is this pressure within our culture which is forcing the rapid and costly expansion of our school system in three dimensions: nursery schools, continuing education and higher education.

The amelioration of destructive cultural privation is being successfully attacked through formalized early-childhood education. Private nursery schools are on the rise; and public schools, pushed to solve the problems of failures in the city slums, are moving in this direction too. Nursery school experiments, such as the Grade City School Improvement Program in the Detroit area, are gaining wide attention.

As a nation, we were committed early to universal public elementary education, and we have succeeded in meeting this commitment. The latest refinement is a growing emphasis on school-community contact, deliberately designed to attack early the blight of intelligence-stunting cultural privation. This emphasis is typified by such projects as New York City's Higher Horizons Program in its schools in Harlem and elsewhere. We shall see many more developments along these lines.

The commitment to universal secondary education has also been generally accepted, but our success is far from complete: we are still graduating only six out of ten of our population. Moreover, a widespread demand is being pressed for universal higher education. The exigencies of cultural survival are pushing us rapidly in this direction. The last generation witnessed a shift in the level of what was considered an adequate education—from an elementary education to a high-school education. In our generation the shift is still upwards, to a thirteenth and fourteenth year. A high-school diploma is no longer considered adequate.

The demand and need for adult-education opportunities, both public and private, are also increasing. Our culture requires continuous education. It is no longer possible to acquire in one's early years an education that will suffice for one's whole life. Today change is so rapid that students who have been formally educated in the context of one world (particularly in a technical sense) are graduated into a world that is significantly different.

The school manager, in short, is faced with an expensive three-way stretch in his school population. The students are starting earlier, staying longer and coming back more as adults. At the same time, the population is expanding. Thus our national commitment to educate everyone is compelling us to provide more years of education for more and more people.

How are these masses to be taught? This is the subject of tons of professional literature, much of it polemic and controversial. All the usual discipline divisions of curriculum are undergoing scrutiny, and recommendations for change abound. Our persistent inability to understand what the scientist, especially, has been telling us about how to transmit mastery in his field is forcing him directly into textbook writing and teacher education. New programs are proliferating and are being labeled like Rooseveltian programs: SMSG, GCMP, PSSC and so on.

Although much new knowledge is being pumped into these new curricula, the more advanced theorists and the university-oriented practitioners of these various disciplines agree that their new content is not so important as their new approach to learning. *What* is being displaced in importance by *how*.

The scarcer literature of learning theory, when stripped to its essence, reveals the interesting conclusion that an effective process of education directly improves learning at its core. In other words, this acquired and therefore mutable characteristic that we call intelligence can itself be taught. Curriculum, then, takes on a new meaning. It is the vehicle for the teaching of intelligence.

For over a century, since the advent of compulsory attendance in schools and the graded-school system, we have confused the mandate of educating the masses with the method of mass education. They are not the same. Education of the masses is a goal, an aim. Mass education is a method, a technique, and this technique cannot be used successfully to educate the masses. It works for some, but too many fall by the wayside. No way has yet been found to eliminate the need to consider the variation among individuals. On the contrary, it is our wish to preserve this individualism that limits the effectiveness of mass-education methods.

The challenge, then, is to find the way to supply millions of people with an individualized education within a viable economic structure. One way to achieve this is to gear our teaching to individual students, who, for convenience, happen to be gathered in groups. This is no new concept. The one-room schoolmaster, who preceded our graded school, knew this. He had to. How could he teach children of all ages as a group? They had to be taught as individuals, each with a curriculum geared to his own age and his own talents. The wise schoolmaster treated his class in much the same way that a wise parent rears a large family. The ten-year-old is not expected to act like the five-year-old, even though they live and learn together. How educators, while building our graded-school system, could lose sight of so obvious a truth is difficult to understand. Apparently the economic pressures of numbers was blinding.

If we direct our teaching to groups, we cannot know with any certainty what each individual in the group has learned. If we direct our teaching to individuals, even in a group situation, we can assess individual progress with adequate certainty. Unfortunately, the certainty level falls off sharply as the size of the group and/or the complexity of subject matter increases. This is the phenomenon (which is, incidentally, common to many applications in information theory) that dictates the small class or small group size so dear to our schools. It is an expensive phenomenon, from the school administrator's point of view, but it is the only solution consistently employed by all levels of education whenever schools get really serious about learning.

A growing sophistication in the combination of learning and information theory is fostering a new approach which we are coming to know as machine teaching or programmed instruction. The designers of this technique claim that it effectively lessens the need for a teacher in supplying individualized learning. This is a promising development; but, unfortunately, it is being generally used to improve the quantity and the quality of mass-education methods, rather than to supply a greater measure of individual attention. In any event, schools have yet to be tooled up with these machines to a level even remotely near their requirements for a really increased productivity. I think we are on the fringe of a dramatic change, but the fringe only.

Where does all this leave the administrator who is responsible for the economics of school management? He knows that human power is expensive and that he should, as in any great industry, have it augmented or replaced by horsepower whenever possible. But his choices are limited. He buys power where he can, and the only power that is consistently sure to work in the education of people is the power of other educated people.

There are many tasks in all levels of our school system which are not strictly educational, and the application of technology to these tasks has been growing apace. We are utilizing the technology of both the first and second industrial revolutions—the replacement of man's muscles by machines in the first, and the replacement of man's nervous system by machines in the second. Where these noninstructional tasks have been split off from teaching duties per se, we have made progress.

For instance, with the advent of the graded-school system, the chores of tending the fire, cleaning the building, shoveling the snow and mowing the lawn have been assigned to the second group of teachers' aids that we have developed, the janitors. In this area, the thermostat attached to the automatic oil furnace, the vacuum cleaner, the power buffer, the snowplow and the power mower—all are in use, following the increased efficiency patterns so dear to American industry.

In the case of the first teachers' aid to be invented, the school principal or the college dean, similar progress has been made. The front office proudly displays its electric typewriters, mimeograph machines, telephone and public-address system and, more recently, electronic bookkeeping and test-scoring devices. Most of this equipment, incidentally, is operated by labor cheaper than that which is available for the classroom.

In the area of transportation, we have buses equipped with power brakes, power steering and even, in some school systems, two-way radios. To feed the children we use thermostatically controlled ovens, electric garbage-disposal units and automatic dishwashers. The school's progress in these areas has been quite impressive.

In the classroom, a similar rate of progress has been thwarted by our persistent habit of dumping masses of students into an unsuccessful assembly-line curriculum taught via mass-instruction methods. In spite of this, however, some progress has been achieved. Witness the growing use of movies, slides, overhead projectors, tape recorders and, more recently, television. Unfortunately, all this hardware has been used to improve mass-education methods and has added very little to the individualizing of instruction or to the creation of an environment conducive to the growth of intelligence, which is the school's prime task. What is more, even for this narrow purpose, few teachers have at their command the type of facilities available to most school secretaries or cafeteria workers. Machinery to lengthen the teacher's arm is apparently just not made available in the schools; or if it is, we forget to teach him how to use it.

Meanwhile, the administrator, who is pushed to produce with limited funds, falls back on the one item he knows—manpower. A brief examination of the typical school budget might help to make this more clear. The common format includes seven categories: general control, instruction, maintenance of plant, operation of plant, fixed charges, auxiliary agencies and minor capital outlay. When money is tight, the first to go is capital outlay, including audio-visual materials and mechanical devices. Maintenance and repair of plant follow, and the nonpersonnel supplies for instruction go next.

The first obligation of the school administrator, in short, is to assemble a faculty, either a few good teachers who are well paid or many mediocre teachers who are poorly paid, depending on whether the administrator's faith is primarily in quality or in brute numbers. Only after he has fulfilled this obligation can he begin to invest in hardware to extend their efficacy.

In the financially poor school, as much as ninety per cent of the operating budget may be allocated to the salaries of teaching personnel alone. In the very affluent districts, this item may account for only sixty per cent of the budget. The difference lies in the affluent district's purchase of more nonteaching personnel and far more supplies and equipment for the teacher.

In practice the rule seems to be that only after a fairly adequate minimum is invested in personnel—enough to bring the staff-pupil ratio up to over six per hundred—does the administrator invest in what industry would consider necessary specialized personnel or in other than manpower types of resources. The newest programs and devices can usually be found first in the affluent school districts—the ones that already exhibit some measure of success, the ones that need technological help the least, the ones that can affort to experiment. Less affluent schools cannot afford to take the chance.

School spending patterns are governed largely by the extent to which the school's performance is endorsed by the community, the extent to which the taxpayers believe in it enough to back it with money. But to win this endorsement, the school should be able to measure its achievement, and this is far more difficult than might be supposed.

A school's job is to educate, to add value to the incoming student. But it is not rated for this. Instead, it is rated by the gross value of its output—that is, the total value of the graduates, not by the value added by the school. No accounting is made either for the value of each student when he enters or for the value added by the neighborhood. Thus a very good school with a low student-input value is rated far lower than an ordinary school with a high student-input value, since the latter has a guaranteed high student output.

If you want recognition as an administrator in this business, therefore, pick your students with care, and your chances for success are already half guaranteed. If you would have fame, spend your money on selection, and ignore the pressure for educating all Americans. If, on the other hand, you want to go brilliantly into oblivion, spend your money on the mentally retarded. Be successful, and no one will know it.

Higher education avoids this dilemma because it is not committed to educate everyone. Its success is predicated on its freedom to drop unwilling or unable students from the rolls and to keep only those students who will succeed. If colleges and universities are ever forced, not just to accept every applicant, but to make certain that every applicant is educated and graduates, then higher education is in for trouble too.

School spending patterns are governed not only by the availability of funds but also by any restrictions that may be attached to the funds that are forthcoming. For public elementary and secondary schools, the typical financial pattern across the country is reliance on local property-tax resources, augmented by state assistance through flat grants, equalization formulas and precisely earmarked, control-centered aids. A fuller implementation of the commitments that we in education have to our country requires that more adequate resources be made available to administrators with less control.

The pattern of state and, possibly, Federal support through a reallocation of tax resources may be emerging along the line of Rhode Island's new, locally variable foundation program. At present, this approach is being explored further by schoolmen in Maryland and Delaware; New York has already moved in this direction.

In higher education, the public school is being extended into the thirteenth and fourteenth years, either by local support from the districts themselves or through an extension of the rapidly expanding higher education enterprise operated by the state. But the funds available for this higher education are restricted. They must be spent to provide more rather than better education. The pressure of numbers will not be resolved by the increased selectivity patterns so many of us hold dear. The public will not tolerate this. They will make room for their children. America's public higher-education institutions are being expanded to meet this problem in spite of anything we administrators may say.

The shortage of unrestricted funds is being felt also in the private sector. In the private elementary and secondary schools, their superior promise for individual success through individual attention has raised the demand for their services at the very time that our economy is lessening their support through philanthropic channels. They are being forced to seek financial recognition from the public sector in order to continue to compete.

In private higher education, a similar pattern is emerging. As the percentage of the population that is being educated by public institutions becomes greater, the private institutions are losing out, at least percentagewise. They are growing, however, in absolute terms, and the ordinary philanthropic channels are proving inadequate to meet their economic needs in competition with public, tax-supported institutions.

There seems, curiously, to be an almost schizophrenic split in public policy with regard to private elementary and secondary schools, on the one hand, and private higher education, on the other.

In the former, public funds are very hard to come by. In the latter, a degree of public support is available. Such techniques as unrestricted scholarship aid, which is available to the private as well as the public institution, have been employed as a means of publicly financing private higher education. The classic case, of course, was the G.I. Bill, which has been copied in some form by several states.

How long this public aid can be counted on, however, seems to me an unresolved question. With the profitable freshman and sophomore classes being increasingly drained off from the private institutions by the public thirteenth- and fourteenth-year institutions, the education of people is being displaced, it seems to me, as a primary objective of private universities. It will not be abandoned, but it is becoming substantially dominated by the more remunerative contractual research. This shift will grow more pronounced as public and private research funds become increasingly abundant.

This leaves me with one last comment, a sort of pie-in-the-sky hope that one important advance may be emerging from this different pattern. The janitor in our schools now lives in a world where he keeps the grass cut with a power mower, while the teacher lives in a world where there is no power, much less the necessary machinery. Is it too much to hope that the pressure of economic demands and the urgencies of our culture will encourage these research-oriented private universities to build curricular machinery for the public-school system?

Harold B. Gores
President, Educational Facilities Laboratories, Inc.

Under the general topic of the economics of school management, I shall stress the physical, primarily because that is the small piece of education with which I am most concerned these days. However, I shall also draw on my memories of my previous position. I was superintendent of a city school system until 1958, and the basic relationships in the economics of education seem not to have changed greatly since then.

To oversimplify the matter, a school, in our culture, is one or more groups of children brought together under one or more roofs. Each group under this roof consists of 25 children, if the community is rich; of 35, if it is poor; or of 50, if it doesn't care. And each group acts as a self-contained, one-room school. The schoolhouse itself is a shell filled with little, equal-sized boxes called classrooms. A 20-room elementary school has 20 boxes for 20 groups. A secondary school may have 50 or 100 boxes; when a signal is sounded (usually some sort of bell), the pupils and teachers swap boxes and reconstitute, in a slightly different pattern, the collection of 50 or 100 one-room schools.

Education has long been organized around groups of children, usually according to the annual crop of births. As far back as 300 A.D., Rabbi Raba decreed that when a class grows to more than 25 pupils, an assistant is to be added, and when the class size reaches 40, the class is to be split. This handy formula remains unchanged in the professional kit of every principal today, along with a knowledge of how to turn on the public-address system.

Having established the organization of education by uniform, standard groups, it is our cultural habit to assign a teacher to each group. In the elementary school, the teacher and her class are locked together all day, all year, in a so-called self-contained classroom. At the secondary-school level, the teacher sets up shop in one of the boxes and meets with groups of students who are scheduled to appear at intervals of forty-five to sixty minutes in a kind of game of musical chairs.

Fortunately, this mystique of equal boxes is breaking up, and for a very good reason: it violates the overriding principle of equal access and equal opportunity for children. In one first-grade classroom, for example, the students may have the best teacher in the country, a great teacher, an old pro who can teach children to read and to love to read. Four inches away—just beyond the cinder-block partition separating the classrooms—the teacher may be both incompetent and unable to maintain simple order. Yet in both classrooms the children are locked in from September to June.

The discrepancy in access to education and to opportunity for growth in the presence of first-rate teaching is obvious. It is a kind of academic Russian roulette for the child—and for the teacher, it makes teaching one of the few professions where great performance does not result in an enlarged sphere of operation. However good she is, her domain remains the box; if she is eager to extend her influence to more children and to education generally, she typically leaves the classroom for supervision or administration. The ultimate professional reward for great teaching, under this system, is nonteaching.

The curriculum is similarly bedeviled by ancient ways of organization. Instruction is mostly by jawbone and chalk, with the teacher transmitting the culture eyeball-to-eyeball, as though the complexity of our society and the speed of its change were indistinguishable from those of the South Sea Islands.

The building itself is simply a shell containing the boxes. Of the school's educational dollar, 27¢ is currently devoted to the containing of education. In terms of capital expenditure, the shell consumes about 75% of the cost, with 25% allotted to books and other tools of education. In business and industry the percentages are reversed: 25% for the shell and 75% for the tools. (At the Ampex Corporation in California, the proportion is 90% for tools and only 10% for the shell.) Industry realizes that money is not made from the building; money is made from what the people inside the building are doing. Education is housed as though we made money from the building itself.

The economics of education are dominated by the fact that our culture locks us into ancient ways of organization. Salaries, the biggest item in every budget, are locked in by salary schedules. Dean Francis Keppel described it best some years ago: "You can predict a teacher's salary by how many hash marks are on her sleeve and how long she has been on the premises." Salary has become a function of training and longevity; of master's degrees, doctorates and, more recently, certain intermediate certificates which are awarded for dogged persistence.

We are locked in a system. A superintendent who thinks he is truly managing the economics of the enterprise is deluded. In my days as superintendent in Newton, Mass., there was really only one act exculsively within my power, only one act that could not be reversed by some other body in charge of the conventional wisdom. That act was to call off school in event of inclement weather; once the announcement was made that there would be no school that day, no governmental or judicial power was capable of reversing the child's intention to accept the offer I had tendered him. In the last analysis, educational management has no more power than this—the consent ot of the persons affected by the order.

This 27¢ container, the schoolhouse, is locked in the system. Its physical characteristics are determined, by and large, by codes and statutes; and the codes which determine how the building is put together are based on the conventional public image of a schoolhouse. Both industry (unless it is new and trying to get established) and labor have a great affection for codes. Indeed, the plumbers of one of our major cities are so dedicated to the public welfare that if a school should purchase a pre-assembled plumbing facility, the plumbers will disassemble the fixture on the site and then re-assemble it—all to protect the health of the people of that state. The codes are the principal means of freezing our technology; and for practical purposes, particularly in our big cities, the schoolhouse is frozen against change. Many architects are happy collaborators with the status quo because their meagre six per cent commission allows no margin to cover the cost of thought.

So it is easy to understand why the debate about school buildings is conducted at its current low level: Should the classroom be square or rectangular? Should the ceiling be nine or ten feet high? Should the corridors be tiled? And how can we maximize the indestructibility and antisepsis of the institution?

The biggest obstacle in approaching the economics of school management is education's inability to equate input with output. Educators talk mostly about input: "What are you paying teachers these days? How are you fixed for books? What do you pay the superintendent?" Most educational statistics are about input; per-pupil cost of instruction, of operation, of maintenance, of debt service. About output, as Dr. Boyer has already said, we are fuzzy.

The situation with respect to educational research is equally disconcerting. Frequently, what passes for a new discovery in learning turns out to be a measure of Hawthorne effect. Educational Facilities Laboratories are currently supporting a study by the University of Michigan School of Architecture, which is abstracting the available research on the relation of environment to productivity in education. When I last visited their shop, they had abstracted eight hundred studies. The largest single file in the office was labeled *Nothing*. When I asked what was in this largest of all files, they replied, "This is where we file the research studies that say nothing."

In the old days, when I was interviewing prospective principals, one of my favorite questions was whether the principal was running an experimental school. The answer was always yes. I would then ask the candidate to tell me about some of his experiments that had failed. Believe it or not, I rarely if ever encountered a candidate who had engaged in experimentation that had failed. It is small comfort to realize that some educational research has found a way to take the risk out of risk.

Yet there are some ventures that have serious implications for the economics of educational management. Watch educational televi-

sion, for example. The superintendent of Dade County, Florida, testified before a committee of the Congress that his county had saved
$3 million during the first year after a television network was estab-
lished for the Miami schools. He asserted further that in the next
five years his district would save $12 million in construction of schools
by taking advantage of the large-group instruction that ETV makes
possible.

Watch the use of programed instruction in many of the
more alert communities. Instruction is swinging away from the uniform, standard group toward the individual learner; programed instruction is bringing education to each individual at his own pace of
learning. The avid learner, especially, will no longer be frustrated
by finding a classroom teacher interposed between himself and the
facts he wants to know. And the teacher will no longer be shackled
by the business of dispensing facts. The learner will pick up his
facts from programed materials, books, tapes, films, television and
other inanimate media; and the teacher will be free to do what only
a teacher can do—to deal with values, with applications, with concepts
and with the meaning of it all.

Watch also team teaching, which in one form or another is already in use in fifteen per cent of our elementary schools. In some
schools it is only a new label on the old bottle, but it clearly presages
the breakup of the tyranny of the standard group.

It is understandable, therefore, that the design of schools is changing toward malleable space that can be shaped and reshaped constantly according to how teachers and children choose to arrange
themselves. The traditional school design—the oversized egg crate or
ice-cube tray—is giving way to radically new designs. Schools are now
being built with interiors that respond, at will and at once, to the
various ways in which teachers and children prefer to work together
—in ratios of 1-to-1, 1-to-10, 1-to-30 or 1-to-100. In these new schools,
space is clustered into zones, frequently four classrooms around a
central library-like space. The classroom as the standard measure of
volume within a schoolhouse is disappearing, and educators are coming to describe volume in terms of zones of space, rather than numbers
of standard boxes.

The handwriting on the walls of academe can be illustrated by
Dean Keppel's description of the proposed new Harvard School of
Education building: "a great loft space put in a medieval shell."
The School of Education has sensed that the building will be there

to at least the year 2020, and who can tell how the enterprise will arrange itself over those years? It is cultural arrogance to design a building around only this present moment in time.

One of the great problems in school design, and therefore in school costs, is that school boards think of themselves as living at the end of time. They need a schoolhouse because they need more seats, so they buy a new school, tailored precisely to their present habits of instruction. But they are not at the end of time. They are in a stream of change, and buildings should be designed to consent to the future rearrangements that must occur if progress is to continue.

I see many school buildings being abandoned these days. The buildings are usually structurally sound; they are being abandoned because they are culturally repugnant and no longer useful. They depress the neighborhood and its real-estate values. They advertise that the town died two generations ago. (Incidentally, if you are seeking to persuade your town to abandon an archaic though structurally adequate school, you will find your task easier if the school is built of red brick. If it is of yellow brick, people will say, "What a fine old school! Just put some ivy on it!" But if it is red, they will say, "That old hulk demeans our town. Even the chamber of commerce says we have a future, so let's get a new school for the children.")

There are great stirrings in the design of schools and colleges. Let me cite as an example St. Patrick's College in Hartsdale, New York. St. Patrick's concept for a four-year, 350-student institution of liberal arts for the training of priests was simply this: Let us create a college that will be mostly one great arena—one great library-like place, one learnery. In the morning it is our habit to teach in groups, so on the periphery of this arena there should be classrooms, like the teeth on a gear, where groups can gather in acoustic and visual privacy. In the evening, when the student body is gathered together under the lamps of the library, these classrooms should be absorbed into the general arena. The peripheral classrooms can then serve as alcoves where small groups can meet and talk together; yet each person will retain a sense of being part of the organic whole, of being one among many studying together in a great arena where scholarship is obviously the fashion.

This building, I believe, is a straw in the wind. It has implications for economics because it will not become obsolete so fast. The building will be malleable and mutable; it will bend to the future. It is, in effect, a great envelope slipped over the process of education.

Another matter worth watching is the use of deployable space. Such is the mobility of people in America that to pick the location for a schoolhouse for the next half-century, with a predetermined and frozen volume, is hazardous at best. Systems are being developed whereby space can be sent out to the children wherever they appear, just as we dispatch teachers and books to their neighborhood.

Unfortunately, in the past, transportable space has been regarded as second-rate, a temporary expedient, a stop-gap substitution for a real schoolhouse. It is understandable, therefore, that many of these transportable schools look like chicken coops whipped out by a designer whose main criterion for design is cheapness. But this is not necessary. I am happy to report that a number of communities are creating deployable space which is aesthetically pleasing and educationally useful. Educational Facilities Laboratories has also employed an industrial designer to try to create transportable space with units that fit together as an organic whole, so that when the child enters his transportable classroom, he will feel that he is also entering an institution larger than his classroom—a school. The era of creating academic trailer camps, consisting of a dozen temporary classroom boxes, is behind us.

School design will also benefit from new developments in using computers to improve the arithmetic of education. MIT, under a grant from EFL, has scheduled a thousand freshmen students with twenty alternatives in eight minutes. It is now putting a proposed new college on the computer in order to determine its volume before it is built. Very soon we should be able to take the educational specifications for a new college (of which there will probably be a thousand in the next fifteen years) and not only compute the volume by machine before actual construction but also turn out the engineering drawings by an electronic process known as computer-plotting. The potential of the computer-plotter is suggested by two examples. The engineering drawings for a bridge, which may ordinarily take six months to prepare, can be turned out over a weekend. And while under ordinary conditions a civil engineer can turn out plans for eighty feet of highway a day, the computer-plotter ups this to eighty *miles* a day.

The effect of this machine will be to relieve architects and engineers from sepnding inordinate amounts of time as draftsmen on the tedious and routine business of planning in detail. The machine will enable them to rise to their real challenge—creating major concepts of building design—without having their energy drained by the drudgery of drawing lines. I have been told that computer-plotters assembled in one room could do one-half of the engineering drawing done in the United States each year.

No important assault on the economics of educational management will occur, however, until education breaks away from the rules of thumb, the formulas, the standards imposed upon it by our conventional image of education. We need more risk-taking in education. School boards and boards of trustees of colleges especially must be willing to look ahead, to pitch the design of their buildings and the organization of their people beyond that narrow moment when the new school first opens. Granted, we are captives of our past and keepers of the present culture. But if education is to be what Agnes Meyer said it must be, "the first business of a modern state," we must pitch our designs into the foreseeable future.

This is a hard thing to do. It is contrary to the way we now operate and to what is expected of us. Some people even ask whether it is morally right to guess about the future and to design for the unknown. Personally, I believe that it is immoral to accommodate merely present habits and to disregard—indeed, to trap—those who follow us.

SUMMARY OF THE DISCUSSION

The general discussion touched first on three topics suggested by Mr. Boyer's paper:

Earmarking of funds: In response to questions, Mr. Boyer emphasized that state support for local schools should not be earmarked for particular uses. The state should recognize that some communities are more able than others to support their schools through local taxation, and it should allocate state support in such a way as to give every community an equal opportunity to build a fine school system. But it should not require any community to use the state funds in any special way—or, indeed, to use them at all.

Earmarked funds have three major faults. (1) They tend to be inflexible and self-perpetuating. "After World War I, for instance, we became excited about vocational schools and agriculture, and Congress passed the George-Barton and Smith-Hughes Acts. Twenty years later, half the activities in every state were based on those acts, even in such unlikely places as Rhode Island, where people scarcely knew what a farm was." (2) "They proliferate like mad." And (3) "the really insidious flaw is that they usually result from some vested-interest group bringing indirect pressure to bear—persuading the Federal Government to earmark funds for the states, or the state to earmark funds for local communities." Control over what happens in the schools is being exerted at the wrong level.

The classic variety of equalization formula, in which the state guarantees each community a minimum dollar-volume per pupil, is also inefficient. Schools need money, but a good system cannot be built on money alone. The school managers must have a vision that they are trying to achieve; otherwise the funds may not even be used, let alone act as an incentive to greater local support. In Delaware —to take an extreme example—the state guarantees the total cost of every teacher hired in every community, in any number and at any step on the statewide salary schedule. A town could, if it wished, hire only teachers with doctorates and long experience in the class-room. Yet "the six school systems still hire them straight out of college or on an emergency level, and hire far too few of them."

Class size: There was general endorsement of the recommendation by Beardsley Ruml that students meet in large groups for formal presentations and in small seminars for discussion, with no groups of intermediate size. Only a few qualifications were offered. The standard-size class in schools may be justified, it was suggested, by the need to maintain order. "If the instruction is mediocre," Mr. Gores asserted, "it had better be intimate, or the teacher will have trouble with discipline." In colleges, the groups of twenty or thirty students may occasionally be necessary; but small seminars are generally preferable, and the price of seminars—if the college is to maintain a reasonable productivity—is a counterbalance of quite large classes. The use of closed-circuit television to make physics experiments visible to large groups was offered as one present possibility.

Classroom technology: Mr. Boyer was asked precisely what technological devices might be used at the interface between teacher and student—devices comparable to the janitor's power mower. He replied that we can move in either of two directions: (1) We can concentrate our teaching in small seminars, taking the challenge of education seriously and supplying the kind of interpersonal relationship that real education requires. When the student is not in a seminar, we would provide him with factual instruction—or at least divert him— with televised teaching, "which does the same thing movies do at fifteen to twenty times the price."

(2) We can blend our interpersonal teaching with a shrewd use of programed instruction. This type of gadgetry is quite different from television; it is coming from a wedding of psychology, influenced by learning theory, with the technological skills being derived from

information theory. A programed text, for instance, teaches many kinds of information and many skills as quickly as a teacher does —and, with a bright student, even more quickly. By using these tools, we can "free the teacher to do the things we have not found ways of automating yet."

The classroom today is being operated as a primitive society in a highly technological world, and it cannot remain so for long. We cannot rest content with graduating only sixty per cent of our secondary-school students. But to meet our commitment with the remaining forty per cent, if we relied on the technology now actually in use in our classrooms, we would have to double our dollar-investment in the schools. Improved technology, however, will make possible a continuous cycle of improvement. As it increases the school's productivity, it will permit the school to compete in salary range with business and industry; and as better teachers are attracted to the school, the technology will be used ever more skillfully, leading to ever higher levels of productivity.

The discussion then settled down for an extended examination of issues concerning school buildings:

Measures of cost: The traditional measure of the cost of new construction, cost per square foot, is often misleading, Mr. Gores pointed out. "It puts a premium on loose planning. If you design an efficient compact building—say, to minimize solar-heat gain for air conditioning—you are driving up your cost per square foot. If you want your figures to look good, throw in some corridors that are too big or an attic that isn't needed." A sounder measure would be cost per occupant, reckoning the efficiency of its usefulness to teachers and students over its expected lifetime.

Utilization of space: There was unanimous agreement that a important cause of the economic pinch in higher education is the appallingly low utilization of space. While a few institutions keep their space in use as much as 70 per cent of the time in a 40- or 48-hour week, the rate for all institutions, taken together, is only 25 per cent. It can and should be much higher. The problem is claiming the sharp attention of administrators, state and Federal legislators, state budget commissioners and Federal loan officers. Unfortunately, one other group seems unaware of this exigency. That group is the faculty, and there most of the trouble lies.

For the most part, college classrooms are used only during the morning, laboratories only during the afternoon. When courses meet at the pleasure of the instructor, many classrooms are not in use on Fridays or Saturdays at all. While the administration can theoretically require departments to schedule a reasonable percentage of their classes during afternoon hours, this is often impossible in practice. The faculty balks; so does the football coach. As a result, the institution finds itself pressed to build more expensive buildings, which will also stand idle 75 per cent of the time. And the faculty's obstinacy boomerangs, for the new construction drains away funds that might have gone to raise faculty salaries.

"From my observation," Mr. Gores reported, "there seems to be a correlation between the academic prestige and pretensions of institutions and their conspicuous consumption of space. The richer they are and the greater their academic halo, the more necessary it seems that they not utilize space highly. This allows some very prestigious institutions to have abominable environments, but since they are not used intensively, nobody gets mad. Your classroom may be dilapidated, but no other class will be meeting there in the hours before and after yours. As bad as the room is, it is all yours.

"When you increase the utilization—when people start piling up at the door, the drinking fountain, the toilets—you begin to get friction, and you have to make the environment more amenabbe to cool it down. One of the best methods of cooling is carpeting; it hushes the sound and imputes a dignity to the place. People will consent to more collision of bodies and more competition for the same space, as long as it is higher-quality space."

Operational costs: The harassing question of economy versus aesthetics in maintaining and operating buildings was posed, though not solved. Over a period of time, operating costs can far exceed the initial cost of construction of a building. These are, therefore, very large sums, and it seems reasonable that the materials used and the structural techniques employed in construction should be calculated to keep operational costs to a minimum. At present, colleges and universities are spending less than fifteen cents of each dollar on maintaining the physical plant, and nearly all administrators are seeking ways to reduce this figure. On the other hand, this fifteen per cent seems insufficient to keep most college buildings from looking rather grim. If the physical plant in an educational institution is supposed to be an aesthetic experience, we should probably be spending more.

Related to this issue is the question of so-called temporary construction. At present, temporary buildings are permanent blights on most campuses. Since they were supposed to be torn down after a few years, they were built cheaply—and they look cheap. For the same reason, maintenance is scamped, and the buildings are allowed to run down. But the construction materials were made to endure, and the buildings remain serviceable long beyond their intended lifespan. They are almost never torn down. (In the case of transportable structures, the same problem exists in an exaggerated form.)

Designing for the future: Two challenges were raised to Mr. Gores's appeal for schools that will adapt to future as well as present patterns of instruction. The first challenge concerned the economic value of the services which school buildings provide. Economists discount future values, so that, on the average, value returned after an investment of twenty-five or thirty years is worth less than half of the same value received immediately. Building for the present may therefore be economically sound. In rebuttal, Mr. Boyer indicated that the dispute may be semantic: "Most school buildings are designed not by present knowledge but by the suppositions of the past. They are forty years old before they hit the designer's drawing board. It would be an achievement to bring them at least somewhere near today."

The second challenge concerned the higher construction cost of flexible buildings. The current fad of movable walls, for example, forces the cost up as much as fifty per cent, from $30 to $45 per square foot. Rather than plan to adapt and readapt the school's interior continually for the next sixty years or more—at such a high immediate cost—it might be more sensible to build now the bulding that is needed now and, when the need changes, tear it down to make way for a new one.

Three counterarguments to this challenge were presented. (1) The buildings would not, in fact, be torn down. Instead, teaching patterns would be cramped and frozen to fit them. The present reluctance to tear down even "temporary" structures allows little dispute on this point. (2) Cost per square foot is a misleading measurement in comparing costs of flexible and nonflexible buildings. Comparisons based on cost per occupant might show no significant difference. They might even show a balance in favor of flexible construction, which permits a higher utilization of space. "It costs more," said Mr. Gores, "but it is worth more." (3) Federal loans for school construction must be repaid over a period of forty years. If the building is torn down before that and ceased to produce revenue, the loan repayments will have to be drawn either from permanent capital or from other operational income. Demolition is not, therefore, to be undertaken lightly.

Splitting schools: While Mr. Gores was superintendent at New-ton, Mass., the community decided to build a second high school to accommodate its burgeoning enrollment, rather than enlarge the existing school. Asked to explain the factors on which such a decision is based, he replied: "Not on any formula about how small a school must remain to avoid the law of diminishing returns. By adopting a house plan, in which students are clustered in groups of 400 or 500 which stay together throughout their high-school years, it is pos-sible to make each student part of a small unit in which he feels known and comfortable—in effect, a school within a school. And by adding new facilities proportionate to the enrollment, it is possible to maintain a constant level of quality of education.

"No, the decisive factor is logistics: how many children live where, at what distance from the school, and how can they be transported safely to school and home again? At Newton, our problem with enlarg-ing the existing school would have been: How shall we transport five thousand young bodies to an area of nineteen acres? Shall we take fifty-three homes, occupied by sixty-four families, by eminent domain to provide a parking area for the students' cars? Or shall we move them by bus, which means buying $50,000 worth of gasoline every year, with no educational benefit except that of riding in a smoke-filled bus? Logistics determined that we had better split the school.

"There were other factors, of course. The split was the less expen-sive alternative, largely because of the difference in transportation costs; and it was the more efficient way to maintain adequate space and facilities for quality education. On the other hand, there was a genuine apprehension that splitting the schools might drive a wedge through the city as a political entity. But in the long run, the decision was made this way: I got out on the PTA circuit and said that the ideal solution, which we should seriously consider, was to have not one or two but three high schools. Then we got two."

Intercollegiate cooperation: In many parts of the country, neigh-boring colleges are learning to share their resources to keep down costs, especially in new construction. They are planning common li-brary and laboratory facilities, and they are reducing duplication of courses (which means, among other things, duplication in the utiliza-tion of space). Through advances in closed-circuit television with two-way audio systems, they are coming to share the services of their finest teachers. They are even beginning to eliminate costly intercollegiate athletics and, though not yet very successfully, to collaborate in fund-raising drives.

The school as a symbol: There was general agreement that a school building is not merely bricks and mortar and investment. It is a symbol of the community's belief in the value of education. One can, to a large extent, judge the cultural tone of a city by its school buildings. And, Mr. Gores added, "a child has a right to attend a school building that says, 'The older people in this community, in which you find yourself something of a stranger, think you are pretty good, and they gave you a schoolhouse worthy of you.' If the building doesn't say this, the child can only feel that he isn't very important to our society."

11. Planning for Institutions of Higher Learning

Sidney G. Tickton
Program Associate, The Fund for the Advancement of Education, now
Secretary-Treasurer, Academy for Educational Development

In 1959, President Sharvy Umbeck and his associates at Knox College
in Galesburg, Illinois, helped me put together the first long-range
planning projection for an institution of higher education. A short
while later I polished the material, inserted some revised figures and
produced the "Ashford College" case study, *Financing Higher Education, 1960-1970* which the publisher, McGraw-Hill, described as "a
new tool for college and university management."

In the next three years, that case study was used as a basis for
projections by more than three hundred private colleges and universities. More than two hundred of these institutions have debated their
own assumptions, their own figures, and their own problems in laying
out a course of action for the future at one of the long-range planning
seminars sponsored by the Fund for the Advancement of Education.

Recently the question has been raised as to why a technique
such as the long-range budget, which has been used for many years
by business but never before by colleges and universities, has suddenly
caught on. The answer is that colleges and universities have recognized the need for a new tool of management because higher education has been feeling the first puffs of the breeze that is about to
develop into a hurricane of changes.

These changes will be dramatic, probably traumatic and possibly
fantastic in dimension. Jesse Hobson, former director of the Stanford
Research Institute, predicted in January 1963 that the changes in
our economy, our society and our culture during the next thirty-eight
years—that is, to the year 2000—would equal in significance all the
changes made during the past four hundred years. Even if his observation proves to be only half right, it is intriguing. It prompted me
to send my statistical colleagues searching for facts and figures at

221

the Census Bureau, the Office of Education, the Bureau of Labor Statistics and other agencies in Washington. Some of the materials they found were published, but much remains in unpublished, worksheet form.

The purpose of these investigations was to come up with the best possible answers to five questions: (1) What is the outlook for population changes for the country as a whole and by categories of the population? (2) What is the outlook for jobs, and what does this imply for the training of the labor force? (3) What is the outlook for college and university enrollments, particularly with respect to the distribution between private and public institutions? (4) What is the economic outlook; what can higher education be expected to cost; and if it costs more proportionally over the years, can the country afford it? (5) What does all this mean for the private liberal-arts college?

In order to pin down some answers to these questions, I asked my statistical associates to make projections for a generation ahead where possible—that is, from the actuals of 1960 or 1961 to, arbitrarily, 1985. These projections could not be considered precise, but they would provide magnitudes to be kept in mind as policy decisions for higher education are made within the next few years. The answers to my questions, the major considerations involved in arriving at these answers, and the most relevant statistics are summarized briefly in the following charts.

1. *What is the outlook for population changes for the country as a whole and by categories of the population?*

The first chart shows the anticipated growth of the population of the United States between 1960 and 1985 is more than 100 million in the coming generation (from the projection files of the U. S. Census Bureau). They assume that the birth rate will remain at the level of 1955-57; this is not the highest level of the postwar period, but it is reasonably high, nevertheless.

The chart also shows that as the population increases, there will be an increasing concentration in metropolitan areas—that is, in the two hundred largest cities and their suburbs. This nation-wide shift in concentration from rural and small-town to urban and suburban areas started during the Depression, accelerated during the war and early post-war period and has continued persistently since. The Census Bureau believes that it will continue for at least another generation.

U.S. POPULATION 1960-1985
GEOGRAPHIC AREAS

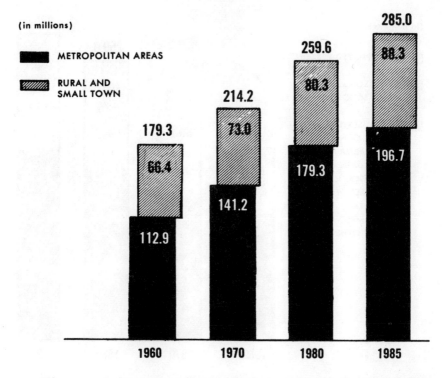

The second chart takes the population totals and distributes them among activity categories, which indicate what people are doing and can be expected to do.

As the total population grows, there will be changes in the rates of growth in the various activity categories. The best guess is that by 1985 the nation can expect a seventy per cent increase in the number of employed persons and a seventy-five per cent increase in the number of children and young adults going to school or college. There will also be increases in other categories (which have been consolidated for the purpose of this chart), but these increases will not be as great proportionately as in the first two categories.

These are "indicative" statistics, not as precise as I would like them but useful nevertheless. Different forecasts could, of course, be

U.S. POPULATION 1960-1985
ACTIVITY CATEGORIES

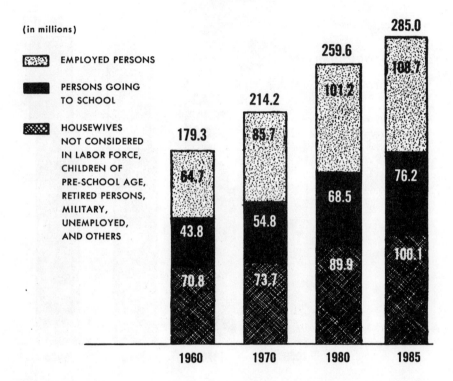

(in millions)

EMPLOYED PERSONS

PERSONS GOING
TO SCHOOL

HOUSEWIVES
NOT CONSIDERED
IN LABOR FORCE,
CHILDREN OF
PRE-SCHOOL AGE,
RETIRED PERSONS,
MILITARY,
UNEMPLOYED,
AND OTHERS

285.0

259.6

214.2

179.3

108.7

101.2

85.7

64.7

76.2

68.5

54.8

43.8

100.1

89.9

73.7

70.8

1960   1970   1980   1985

made for the various categories, but we consider ours the most reasonable in light of the nation-wide trends in births and deaths, the
tendency of women to return to the labor force when their children
no longer need all-day care at home, and the tendency of young people
to stay in school longer than heretofore.

We have, then, a background showing a large increase in population and a large increase in the labor force in the generation ahead.

2. *What is the outlook for jobs, and what does this imply for
the training of the labor force?*

The following chart divides the total number of employed people
into the major categories of activity—skilled, service, unskilled and
farm:

EMPLOYMENT IN THE U.S. 1950-1985
BY CATEGORIES

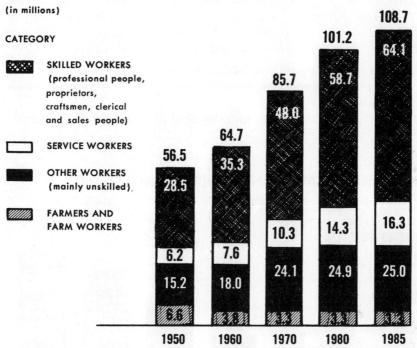

(in millions)

CATEGORY

SKILLED WORKERS
(professional people,
proprietors,
craftsmen, clerical
and sales people)

SERVICE WORKERS

OTHER WORKERS
(mainly unskilled)

FARMERS AND
FARM WORKERS

This chart indicates that (1) there will be a continued increase in employment in skilled occupations; (2) skilled workers will constitute a greater percentage of the labor force than heretofore; (3) unskilled workers will constitute a smaller percentage of the labor force by 1985; and (4) the number of farmers and farm workers will decline until 1970 and will then level off.

In arriving at these projections, my statistical associates predicted that the trend toward mechanization and automation throughout the country, both on the farm and in industrial activities, will continue and even accelerate in the future. Thus there will be fewer jobs proportionately for unskilled people—many fewer than there were when the country was primarily an agricultural economy. They also predicted that the number of women employed outside the home will increase but that older people will leave the labor force more rapidly than, say, a generation or two ago.

What do these job projections imply for the training of the labor force? By 1985, it is clear, we can expect to live in a nation that requires a high degree of training and skill for a large percentage of the labor force. Most of these people will have obtained much of their academic and technical training in schools, colleges and universities. The job for educational authorities, therefore, is to establish a system of education—from kindergarten through graduate school and professional school—which will provide the sort of training that is needed, when and where it is needed, at a reasonable cost.

3. *What is the outlook for college and university enrollments, particularly with respect to the distribution between private and public institutions?*

The fourth chart shows enrollment estimates from 1950 to 1985:

CHART 4

COLLEGE AND UNIVERSITY ENROLLMENTS
PUBLIC AND PRIVATE INSTITUTIONS

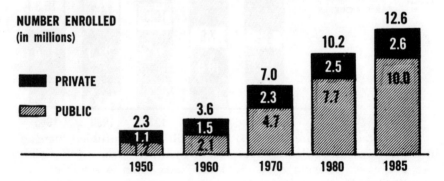

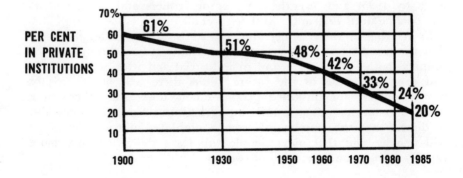

In the generation ahead, the number of persons attending colleges and universities, full-time and part-time, can be expected to double between 1960 and 1970 or thereabouts, triple by 1980 or thereabouts, and continue upward thereafter for years to come.

As to the distribution of these very large increases between public and private institutions, our best guess is that private education will expand fifty per cent between 1960 and 1970 and then grow rather slowly in the years beyond. A much greater expansion will occur in public colleges and universities, including public junior colleges and technical institutes, some of which will be established in areas not now served adequately by public institutions. As a result, the percentage in private institutions will continue to decline.

The enrollment totals for 1970 shown at the top of the chart are somewhat greater than the estimates that have been published until recently by Government agencies. My guess is that our figure of seven million is realistic; that it and our subsequent projections recognize two main factors whose combined effect has been underestimated everywhere in the past—the increasing number of college-age people, and the increasing percentage of young people attending colleges and universities, both full-time and part-time. The trends are illustrated in the following chart:

CHART 5

TWO FACTORS IN BOOMING ENROLLMENTS

1. MORE COLLEGE AGE PEOPLE (18-24 YRS.)

2. LARGER PER CENT IN COLLEGE

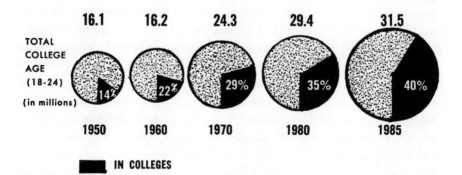

These estimates are conservative. The emerging evidence is that a college education is rapidly becoming as important to many individuals (and their parents)—and as necessary to the welfare of our country—as a high-school education became during the period between the two world wars.

Moreover, going to college is economically possible now for much of our population. This results from the increase in the national income since the war and its wide dispersion among the people. Proportionally fewer parents now must require their children to support themselves or to augment the family income after they finish high school. Many parents now consider a college education a kind of consumer good, which can be purchased instead of a new car, or a long vacation trip, or a new home.

Against this background, we believe that if business continues at prosperous levels and if personal incomes remain high, a large proportion of parents can be expected to send their children to college, despite the costs involved. If business falls to relatively low levels and if there is substantial unemployment among unskilled young people, many can still be expected to enroll in colleges and universities, possibly with scholarship aid from government agencies.

4. *What is the economic outlook; what can higher education be expected to cost; and if it costs more proportionately over the years, can the country afford it?*

The sixth chart compares the expected growth of personal income and of expenditures for higher education.

Since the war, economists of this country have been studying and projecting the economic, demographic, political and sociological factors that affect the activities of this country. Economists at the National Planning Association of Washington, D. C., a leading economic organization, estimate that by 1976 the gross income of all individuals in the United States can hardly be less than $803 billion, compared with $440 billion in 1961—an 83 per cent increase, with inflation excluded. We as a nation can achieve this great increase in income because, day after day, we are bringing to bear on the expansion of industrial productivity all the ingenuity, the inventiveness and the ability of our people. Moreover, we are concentrating more time, effort and money on research and development in relation to the problems of mankind than the world has ever known.

CHART 6

EDUCATIONAL EXPENDITURES
AT COLLEGES AND UNIVERSITIES
COMPARED WITH GROSS PERSONAL INCOME

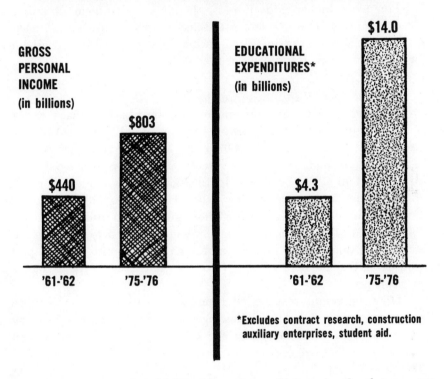

GROSS
PERSONAL
INCOME
(in billions)

$803

$440

'61-'62   '75-'76

EDUCATIONAL
EXPENDITURES*
(in billions)

$14.0

$4.3

'61-'62   '75-'76

*Excludes contract research, construction
auxiliary enterprises, student aid.

To estimate what higher education will cost in the future, my statistical associates looked at more than a hundred long-range projections in my files, as well as at government data. Their conclusion is that the cost of higher education is rising and can be expected to rise rapidly in the future. A good guess is that the total operating cost—including all educational and general expenditures, but excluding construction, auxiliary enterprises, scholarships and contract research—will more than triple by 1976. This is obviously a rough estimate, but it is close enough for analytical and planning purposes.

Can the country afford such expenditures? If personal income rises along the lines set out in the chart—and this appears reasonable and possible, in the absence of war or other national emergency—the answer is clear. Certainly we can, if the people of the country are willing to allocate the additional dollars that will be required. The amount involved will be only a small percentage of the increase in personal income and productivity; it will be an even smaller percentage of total income.

Financing higher education is, therefore, a problem of policy, not of resources. The problem is to select the basis on which to make a small portion of the increased income and productivity available for a service which the people need and desire.

5. What does all this mean for the private liberal-arts college?

In order to arrive at some answers, we went back to that creation of our imagination, Ashford College. Ashford is a 125-year-old institution located in a town of 30,000 in the Midwest. Sixty per cent of its students are men. The student-faculty ratio has grown moderately from 12-to-1 in 1952-3 to 15-to-1 in 1962-3, partly as a result of filling up the junior and senior classes. Ashford graduates 190 B.A. degree candidates a year, 55 per cent of whom go on to graduate or professional school. The students are better than they used to be; the average CEEB scores have jumped more than 100 points in the past five years. The faculty is better, too, and much better paid than a few years ago.

How the twenty-year period from 1953 to 1973 looks at Ashford is shown in chart 7 on the following page. The outlook is for a 60 per cent rise in enrollment over the 1953 base, a 25 per cent rise in faculty and a 200 per cent rise in faculty salaries.

I next asked my statistical associates to take these estimates and draw up budgets for Ashford College for 1953, 1963 and 1973. Chart 8 on page 232 shows the resulting trends.

The operating budget jumps about 400 per cent in the twenty-year period. This budget includes educational and general expenditures, scholarships and auxiliary enterprises. Expenditures for construction are excluded because of their irregular timing, but they are in addition to these totals and will average nearly $1 million a year during the second half of this period.

This rise in expenditures has moved Ashford from a little corner-store type of activity to a big-business operation. Five million

CHART 7

ASHFORD COLLEGE REVISITED — I

STUDENTS AND FACULTY

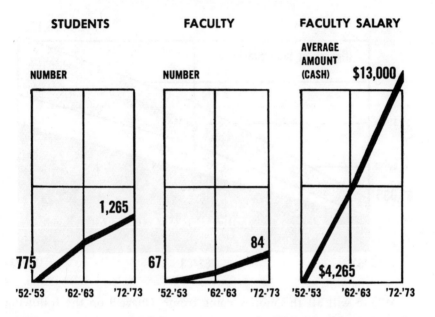

STUDENTS	FACULTY	FACULTY SALARY

dollars a year plus a million dollars of construction is a sizeable total. Management practices consistent with this expenditure level are certainly required. Ashford has already found that it needs much more experienced operating personnel. It has also found that it must be zealous in avoiding mistakes, for even a small error can be very costly. For example, the president observed recently that putting a faculty member on tenure is a $300,000 decision, not the sort of decision to be made casually one afternoon just before tea. He also observed that the main building is 105 years old and still in very active use; he drew the conclusion that if a building mistake is made, the college must live with it a very long time.

I believe that this rate of rise in expenditures shown in Chart 8 is typical of what will be experienced by private liberal-arts colleges. At universities, with their expanding research budgets and professional schools, the percentage of increase may be even higher.

ASHFORD COLLEGE REVISITED — II   CHART 8

OPERATING EXPENDITURES

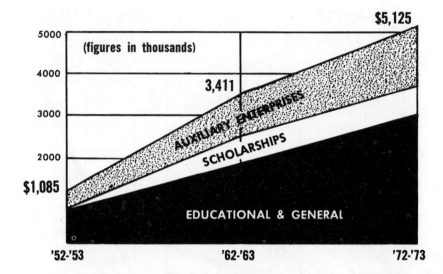

. Where will all the money come from? Chart 9 on the following page indicates the sources.

Most of Ashford's operating money comes from students. Ashford is one of those colleges that by 1962 had already balanced its educational and general budget without gifts and grants; it also balances its auxiliary budget every year, including a charge for supervision. The gifts and grants shown on the chart after 1962 are for scholarships only. The amount would certainly be bigger if the administrators at Ashford thought they could raise more scholarship money.

Can students afford to provide for such a large increase in the operating budget of a small college? I believe that they can and that the future financing of the operating costs of most private colleges lies mainly in appealing to willing students, rather than to reluctant donors. The students will be there; they can afford to go to college; and many will be willing to pay a good price for the high-quality education that many private colleges can provide. The future of private colleges depends, it seems to me, upon their ability to do the job required.

CHART 9

ASHFORD COLLEGE REVISITED — III

SOURCES OF OPERATING INCOME

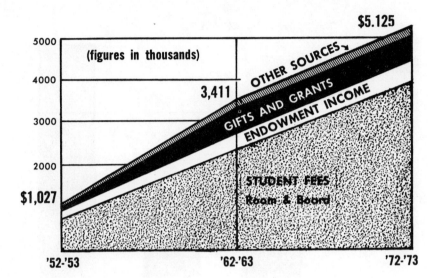

Before leaving Ashford College, I should like to present two final charts. The first is on assets (Chart 10, the following page).

Ashford expects its plant to expand from $3.3 million (at cost value) to $18 million during the twenty-year span. This will involve a great enlargement of the library; the construction of a new college union building, a new fine-arts building, a new service building and a number of new dormitories; the conversion of an older building to new purposes; and general refurbishing of the century-old campus. As to endowment, Ashford would like to see a faster growth than these figures indicate, but the administration knows from recent experience that endowment is hard to raise. Also, the college has many other urgent needs, particularly "people needs," that take first priority.

Chart 11 (p. 235) covers fund raising. To show the magnitude of the fund-raising problem at Ashford, the chart presents three five-year averages. This procedure smooths out irregular fluctuations due to fund-raising campaigns and the unregulated timing of receipts from bequests. Ashford was in the midst of a special fund-raising campaign

CHART 10

ASHFORD COLLEGE REVISITED — IV

PLANT AND ENDOWMENT

(BOOK VALUE)

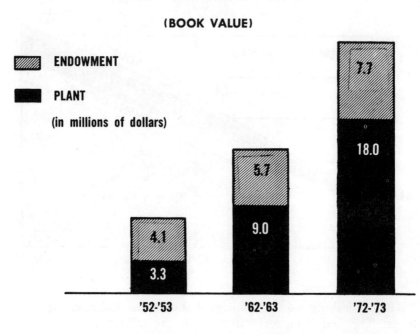

in 1962-63, so its figures are a little higher than they would otherwise have been. Its average annual fund-raising effort, however, can be expected to quadruple during this twenty-year period. And in the 1960's and 1970's fund raising has and will have only three purposes: scholarships, endowment and plant. None of it, as I have indicated, is for current operations.

These charts are, I believe, more eloquent than any words I might say about the need for long-range planning at private colleges and universities. I have made this presentation a number of times to groups of presidents and other officials, and it is usually greeted with an uneasy silence. Then come the questions, which usually boil down to one: "What can private colleges and universities do now to protect their future?" My answer, roughly, is that if higher education—private and public—is to meet its responsibilities in the decade

CHART 11

ASHFORD COLLEGE REVISITED — V

FUND RAISING — 5 YEAR AVERAGE

(From all sources and for all purposes)

(figures in thousands)

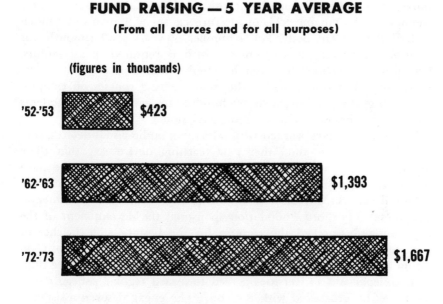

'52-'53 $423

'62-'63 $1,393

'72-'73 $1,667

or two ahead, everyone in authority or in a position of leadership should be at work now, planning for the future.

This means, as a start, eliminating the slack which characterizes higher education today. There must be a better utilization of time, space, personnel and financial resources. Colleges and universities the country over could provide millions of dollars a year for academic programs if they used their resources more fully. The opportunities are tremendous, yet the possibilities have hardly been touched by most institutions.

Take, for instance, the matter of better utilization of time and space. My guess is that by 1975 most colleges and universities in the mainstream of higher education, both public and private, will be offering regular classes from 8:00 a.m. to 10:00 p.m., five days a week, and half a day on Saturday, eleven or eleven-and-a-half months a year. (A few institutions in the big cities are demonstrating that this is already possible.) They will fill their student stations—the seats in the classrooms, the benches in the laboratories, the chairs in the library—sixty to seventy per cent of this time. In addition, students will be encouraged to carry on independent study in their dormitories, in their homes and in libraries and laboratories throughout the country.

As for personnel: my guess is that by 1975 most colleges and universities will have much higher student-faculty ratios than are now common and that, on occasion, lecture classes will involve as much as half the student body. For a number of years at Dartmouth, for example, the Great Issues course, which is required of all seniors, has provided lectures to seven hundred students at a time. At the University of Arizona, one of the most exciting courses on campus, freshman geology, is taught to five hundred to seven hundred students at a time by the use of closed-circuit television.

Those who have worked with television, audio-visual devices, programed instruction and other new teaching devices say that these methods offer a vast opportunity to extend the range of the most competent faculty members. As an example, they point to what was accomplished three years ago in the physics course on Continental Classroom. The Ford Foundation sponsored the development of the program and searched the country for the best possible teacher of introductory physics. It chose Harvey White of the University of California at Berkeley, whose televised course was so good that three hundred colleges and universities agreed to award regular college credit for it. As he proceeded with the course, he engaged seven assistants, all Nobel Prize winners. No college or university in the country could have afforded such a faculty. Similar courses could be developed in a wide variety of fields if it really became necessary, and my guess is that in the years ahead it probably will.

With regard to better utilization of financial resources: In recent years colleges and universities across the country have discovered what can be accomplished with imaginative use of money. Most institutions now have a good portfolio of common stocks. Many invest unused cash in short-term obligations. Some have invested part of the endowment in dormitories and reap two benefits: they receive a well-secured return and are able to handle additional students. Also, some colleges and universities are borrowing from private lenders for the construction of classroom buildings, on the theory that a long line of students waiting at the door to enter is as good collateral for classrooms as it is for dormitories and dining halls, whose revenue is already pledged on a self-liquidating basis. Moreover, some colleges are building dormitories financed by banks and consumer-credit organizations, where opportunities for imaginative design and quick action are better than with the U. S. Housing and Home Finance Agency.

Better utilization of resources can be achieved by any part of the college family, but to be most effective, long-range planning must be carried on at the highest level of authority. In private colleges, planning should originate with the president and should involve the dean, the business manager, key faculty members and the board of trustees from the very beginning.

For public institutions, planning must likewise originate at the very highest level—the board of regents, the governor and the legislature. All parties must be involved, or the efforts will not be very effective. In New York State, for example, the Committee on Higher Education was formed in 1960 by a joint effort of Governor Rockefeller and the Board of Regents, at a time when the governor's political associates had a majority in the legislature. There was a commitment to action and a mechanism for achieving such action. A great deal was accomplished in the first and second legislative sessions that followed the presentation of a long-range plan.

In Kansas, on the other hand, the planning was commissioned by the Board of Regents in its own capacity. The governor stood aside during the planning process and later expressed his own ideas, which differed from the report by a panel of out-of-state educators and from the attitude of the Board of Regents. The Legislature split wide open. The main political issue was whether Wichita—a municipal university offering a Ph.D. in a single, very specialized area, but with expansion ambitions for the future—should become the third state university, or a state college, or a university center under the jurisdiction of the two existing state universities. The situation was finally compromised, but the heat of the battle made action on other recommendations in the report unlikely for quite a while.

A third example of long-range planning where the tangible results were even smaller is the planning for the sixteen southern states carried on in 1961 by the Southern Regional Education Board, an interstate cooperative organization, which formed a committee composed of a number of educators, former governors and businessmen. There were so many problems, the structures of higher education were so diverse in the several states, and the mechanism for action was so nebulous that the report could merely emphasize general principles. As a result, the prospects for action in individual states are slim indeed.

Long-range planning for colleges and universities involves full collaboration on a great many details because all the factors are interrelated. Within a single college or university there is an intricate interrelationship among curriculum, plant, salaries, class size, the size of the institution, the student-faculty ratio, graduate work, independent study, the distance to the students' homes and so on. For public institutions, these factors are interrelated again at the state level, and a change in any one factor may have a substantial effect on the others. A decision on the establishment of junior colleges or technical institutes, or on the open-door policy, or on the number of state universities and their location, for example, will affect the volume of funds available for such uses as graduate work, research and scholarships.

A decision to build or expand a university in a rural town far from the center of population is frequently made on political, sociological or emotional grounds. Frequently no one recognizes that this may have far-reaching consequences with respect to improvements in curriculum and programs. For example, the University of Mississippi has a serious problem of location. Twenty years ago, Senator Theodore G. Bilbo tried to move the institution from a small rural town near the northern border of the state to an industrial town in the center. He failed because of local political opposition. Today the university must provide a dormitory bed for every student it brings to the campus, though the funds could be more usefully applied for academic improvements.

I see little hope, unfortunately, in joint planning by cooperative groups in higher education, such as the Claremont group, the Atlanta group of Negro colleges, the Connecticut Valley group, the Richmond Center, the Associated Colleges of the Midwest, the Great Lakes Association and the Big Ten Chicago Group. These are not planning organizations; they are joint-venture arrangements, in which the cooperating institutions try to gain something by working together which they could not achieve separately. Important though these operations are to the institutions concerned, they are of minor importance to the over-all educational planning picture. Even to the institutions concerned, their significance to date, as far as I can determine, has been greater on paper than in fact.

The Claremont group, for example, emphasize the advantages they gain from cooperative academic activities; but when I visited the campus, I found that the colleges were offering simultaneously two Chaucer courses, three Shakespeare courses and three courses in labor problems—and they had never questioned this until I questioned it. The group now has a women's college (Scripps) with two hundred students, yet they are about to build a new women's college (Pitzer) for another six hundred students on the same campus. No one there wants to face the fact that it is terribly expensive to finance two women's colleges, with a total of only eight hundred students, within a couple of hundred yards of each other. No one wants to plan because no one wants to put the size of the problem down on paper.

The Claremont group has, it is true, only one business office and one maintenance crew for the 2,500 students now enrolled in the five institutions but there is the overhead of five presidents, including their homes and Cadillacs, and five administrative staffs. The set-up costs as much as it saves, and it can hardly be recommended as an economy device for other institutions. In Toronto the chancellor told me that their similar arrangement was the most inefficient ever devised by man.

Some of the other cooperative groups are mainly joint-purchasing arrangements. At Richmond, for example, the various institutions are able to share a visiting-scholars program which is much more effective than any one institution could afford separately. This is also true at the College Center of the Finger Lakes. The colleges included in the Associated Colleges of the Midwest were able to obtain a $300,000 government research contract, participate in research activities of the Argonne National Laboratory, establish a wilderness research project and manage a Latin American project that would have been too large and too complex for a single liberal-arts college. However, the enabling force in this case has been the introduction of foundation money. Without it, the association's activities would be impossible to maintain at present levels, for despite the benefits involved, each college still puts up a maximum of $3,000 a year for ACM activities. And the structurally comparable Great Lakes Association, which has no foundation money, has never really gotten off the ground.

In conclusion, my thesis is that the problems in higher education are going to multiply, even faster than students. The students are likely to carry a higher percentage of the operating costs. The president at a private institution will be mainly a builder and a fund raiser; at a public institution he will be mainly a lobbyist with the legislature. Better utilization of resources will occur everywhere because it is necessary to survival.

Except in a few places, the colleges and universities of the far tomorrow will bear only a faint resemblance to the institutions we know today. Movers and shapers of education, as soon as they recognize this, will start planning the way.

COMMENT BY . . . *Owen B. Kiernan*
                              Commissioner of Education, Commonwealth
                              of Massachusetts

I would subscribe with great enthusiasm to some of the points Mr. Tickton has made. I would also raise a few questions.

The shift in heavy enrollments from private to public institutions, which Mr. Tickton indicated, is certainly being borne out here in Massachusetts. Up to 1960 we had fifteen public institutions of higher learning with tiny enrollments. Since then, thanks to Seymour Harris and some other far-sighted individuals, five additional institutions have come into being. These are the junior colleges. We call them, by statute, community colleges, but they are two-track institutions: some youngsters terminate with an associate degree after two years and enter business or industry, while others transfer to senior colleges and work toward a baccalaureate degree. We expect to open four more community colleges in the next two and a half years.

The enrollments are skyrocketing. We have about 25,000 youngsters in our public institutions full-time; many others are enrolled part-time in continuing-studies programs for advanced degrees at the various extension centers. And we will triple our enrollments by 1985, without any question. We are oversubscribed now many times, and it is rather discouraging to note the number of fully qualified youngsters who must be turned away.

Mr. Tickton mentioned that, in 1900, 61 per cent of the total enrollment was in private institutions and that this dropped to 42 per cent in 1960. He predicts only 20 per cent in 1985. This is happening; there is no question about it.

Yet we are concerned. The costs will be staggering and the General Court [Legislature] at the moment—and the people generally—do not seem willing to underwrite education. Here are some of the implications, related to this concern, that I drew from Mr. Tickton's presentation.

First, he said that more of us will be living in urban areas as we approach 1985. If this is the case, and if we truly have a metropolitan area from Boston to Washington, what are the implications for the location of public and private institutions? And what are the implications for dormitory construction? Do we forget dormitory construction? Do we concern ourselves only with self-liquidating dormitories? After twenty-five or perhaps fifty years, will we have only commuting colleges? What is the role of the so-called residential institution?

Second, I was very interested in the proposal that the students carry almost the full load of operating expenditures in these institutions. In our twenty colleges and the university, we now draw, for the most part, from a middle- to low-income group. Some of the community-college students feel the pressure of even the $200 tuition —which is, of course, the bargain of the century. The full cost of sending a youngster to the University of Massachusetts is approximately $1,500 a year, including tuition, room and board, textbooks, incidental costs, everything. In private institutions the cost runs from $2,500 to $3,000 a year, so a great many people are moving in the direction of the public institutions. But can this lower economic group support higher tuitions?

Third, there is certainly little justification for leaving any of these costly institutions, these multimillion-dollar compuses, vacant for good portions of the year. But most of the feet-dragging on this question of better utilization, including a longer college year, seems to be done by the faculties, though in some cases also by administrators. How do we convince the professional body to accept this need to use our plant during the full year?

Fourth, a question on salaries in relation to over-all budgets. I noted with some interest that between 1952 and 1972, Mr. Tickton moved salaries up on an average from $4,265 to $13,000. I agree that we can afford it, but will taxpayers accept an average salary of $13,000 for instructors? At the moment, they are not buying this in the public schools, and they are certainly reluctant to accept it in our institutions of higher learning.

And *lastly,* I was much impressed with his observation that cooperative efforts among colleges are not paying high dividends. We have such a program in the Pioneer Valley, involving the University of Massachusetts, Amherst, Mt. Holyoke and Smith, and the wheels are turning rather slowly. It is not long-range planning. Basically, it is a cooperative effort in which we will share library and laboratory facilities—and perhaps the services of distinguished professors who may be on campus and who could contribute to the four institutions, rather than to only one.

I said "lastly," but I should like also to comment that the tool of television, to which he referred, can certainly deliver quality teaching to a much larger group than does a seminar such as this, when, for one roomful of students, we are picking the brains of authorities like Sidney Tickton, Seymour Harris and James Coles.

COMMENT BY . . . *James S. Coles*
President, Bowdoin College

A friend of mine offered to lend me his car for the drive to Harvard this afternoon, and I must say I'm delighted that I didn't accept. He happens to drive a Cadillac, and after Mr. Tickton's crack about college presidents' Cadillacs, I might never have lived it down.

There is, it seems to me, no room for disagreement with the economic facts that Mr. Tickton presented or with most of his criticisms of planning for higher education. For that reason, I shall comment in a rather fragmentary fashion. This may tend to make my comments seem picayune, but I don't mean them that way.

With regard to long-range planning: I would point out the economic incentive has been a very important factor in persuading a large number of institutions to plan ten years ahead on the Ashford College model. They know that unless they are planning ten years ahead, large foundations—and one large foundation in particular— will not really consider them for a major grant. At present this sort of economic incentive is not unhealthy at all. Parents use it to encourage their children to get better marks in school, until the children pick up interest in their subject. Colleges use it to make the professors teach at night. And the foundations can use it to make colleges plan better and operate more efficiently.

A few colleges, however, were planning ten years ahead prior to 1959. For example, our own long-range planning was clarified in the middle 1950's by very able trustees who were in business and were used to business planning and brought the same techniques to us. We had been raising tuitions so that we could raise faculty salaries; and we had been appropriating money from general income back into scholarships, so that even with the higher tuition, students who had need could remain in the college. By projecting this forward for about fourteen or fifteen years, we could foresee a time when we would have to appropriate more money back into shcolarships than we would gain from the tuition increases. This forced us to take a long, hard look at our procedures; and instead of relying on outright scholarship grants, we began a financial-aid program which involves both loans and grants. Essentially, we appropriate from current income to loans, but this is simply a long-range capitalization of current income.

We were not the first to do this. We thought we had discovered it ourselves, but I am sure that other colleges had been planning ahead on a long-range basis and had discovered it earlier than we did.

As for the necessity of the independent, privately endowed colleges to expand, I grant that this is true. I think, however, that once a small institution is large enough to attain a degree of efficiency in its operation and to reduce its per-capita overhead sufficiently, it can do certain things for certain types of students which cannot be done in a larger institution or in a state institution. We need this diversity of institutional types, and if we all decide to expand four- or five-fold, this diversity will be lost—or, if it is not lost, the small institutions will be small merely because they lack quality.

There are other ways that private institutions can grow, aside from undergraduate enrollment. If your trustees are able, vigorous, successful men, and if your faculty is of high quality and caliber, these two dynamic groups will not be satisfied to stand still. In the past, they have found an outlet for their energies by growing physically or in numbers. But as president of Bowdoin, I have taken at face value the desire, so often expressed by the faculty and trustees, our constituency, that Bowdoin should keep its small undergraduate enrollment. In our long-range planning, I have sought to determine the paths in which these energies can be diverted which will be useful to Bowdoin, to higher education and to the educational system—paths which will not involve growth in numbers.

In our case, for our particular situation, I am convinced that this dimension of growth should be in graduate work in arts and sciences, providing twice the number of places for graduate students in 1975 that we need now. Higher education as a whole should not create these places by merely doubling the already large graduate centers. We should spread out the base for these graduate centers, and I believe that much of this work can be done in smaller centers of considerable quality.

This would be advantageous to the society, and it would be advantageous to us personally in attracting new faculty. It would mean an enrichment of the undergraduate program at the junior and senior level because the especially able student would be able to elect very advanced courses, which are not now available to him.

It would also mean an enrichment through contacts between our more mature undergraduates and the beginning graduate students. This plan has been successful in engineering and the sciences at the California Institute of Technology, with an undergraduate body of 750 and a graduate enrollment of 500. I think it can be successful in the arts and sciences as well.

This will not make our operations more efficient, and it will not increase our student-faculty ratio. In fact, it will do the opposite, which in turn means that the college president will probably have to raise more money. Fund raising, incidentally, is one of the less interesting aspects of the job for a person who has gone into college administration because he is interested in education. It is my experience that a $10-million capital-fund campaign is one quick way to kill a man's enthusiasm for the job of a college presidency. It is hard to survive this and maintain your enthusiasm.

With regard to increased efficiency in operations: we appointed a committee of our faculty several years ago, following the Ruml report, to carry out one of the most unusual studies undertaken in the last decade by any college. We had no foundation grant; we carried it out by ourselves.

The Committee on Academic Efficiency worked for a year, went through many arguments and hassles, wrote a report and persuaded the faculty to adopt the report. Many of the recommendations in the report adopted were put into effect. Among other things, we provided more clerical assistance for the faculty, reduced the number of courses in certain areas and converted our economics course from sections to a lecture course with discussion groups. We are more efficient than we were before.

The interesting part is that the gains we made here did not decrease our instructional budget, as we had intended; they showed up in a general improvement of the quality of our over-all program. This is something we had not anticipated, and it has perhaps not been anticipated elsewhere.

As for efficiency in plant utilization, serious problems are involved in the double standard which expects colleges to operate on a five-and-a-half-day week, while the rest of society is operating on a five-day week. We have to fight continually to maintain Saturday classes, primarily because business establishments have abandoned Saturday work. We cannot hire secretaries now if we tell them that they have to work on Saturday mornings, because the local businesses do not have them work on Saturday mornings. The same is true of our grounds and buildings staff: we recently had to put them on a five-day week because the local business establishments offer a five-days week. College faculties feel the same way about this, and so do the students.

Mr. Tickton's suggestions regarding classrooms as good collateral baffles me. It is difficult to make even dormitories good collateral. A few years ago, we looked into borrowing money for dormitories, particularly since many state universities say they can borrow money for dormitories and amortize their costs. We found that these are roughly the figures: if your dormitory construction is $6,000 per occupant, and if your loan to cover that is on a 30- to 40-year basis at three per cent (which is about as good as you can do), your amortization costs run around $210 to $220 per year. Our operating costs for a dormitory, including full loading of all charges, come to around $250 per year. The amortization and operating costs total around $450 a year, which you have to charge as room rent. Very few state universities or colleges, except Harvard, can get $450 a year from an undergraduate for room rent.

It is impossible to make new dormitories self-amortizing at present construction costs and present room rates. Institutions which have taken Government loans and have not rocketed their rents are not doing the impossible. Instead, they are taking all their old dormitories whose costs have been fully written off—there may be six or eight or ten or twelve—along with the one or two new dormitories, then pooling the income and amortizing the new construction costs out of that. There is nothing wrong with this at all; but if you do not say that you are pooling all your dormitory income, you are not telling the straight story.

The situation with regard to classroom buildings is still more difficult. Mr. Tickton suggests that students lined up at the doors are sound collateral, but this seems to me awkward to demonstrate, particularly if the college subsidizes every student and has to raise more money as its enrollment climbs.

Last, about the problem of cooperation among colleges: If the colleges are close together, they can collaborate to a certain extent, if they have relatively the same standards of faculty appointment and student enrollment. In Maine, however, we have one college seventeen miles from Bowdoin and another about forty-five miles away. If we appointed a man jointly with either college, he would have to make three round trips of either thirty-four or ninety miles a week during Maine winters. Naturally, he would prefer to teach somewhere else. The real solution is to share him through educational television, but first we must educate the faculty so that they are ready to work with this medium. We are cooperating on that, but it has caused a good bit of difficulty.

We also made a valiant attempt to cooperate on libraries, but one of the colleges does not believe in maintaining a research library, and the other is concentrating on building a basic collection of periodicals. We just could not get any real cooperation.

So there are lots of problems in this sort of cooperation, and they can be solved in only a very few cases.

REPLY BY . . . *Mr. Tickton*

It is essential to keep in mind that Bowdoin is atypical. As a matter of fact, most colleges in the northeast are atypical, as far as the rest of the country is concerned.

You must remember that the country has nine hundred private colleges and universities. Many of them face the same problems that the eastern colleges face, but they are not as fat. Bowdoin and two or three others have declining student-faculty ratios. The others cannot afford it, and the others that cannot afford it include some fairly rich colleges. They have decided that there are other things more important than having a declining student-faculty ratio.

Many institutions have concluded that they need to expand the coverage of subject matter, since there is more knowledge that demands to be covered. To make faculty available for this, they must take advantage of certain new techniques, which means having a student do many things for himself that he did not do before. This may not be ideal, but a great many institutions will have to do things which will make them less than happy. They cannot help themselves. They are stuck.

State institutions must grow to accommodate the rising demand for admission. Private institutions must grow because they cannot survive at their present size. A quarter of the colleges have 300 students or less; another quarter have between 300 and 800. In order to have a quality college, you need 15 to 17 departments, with at least three or four people in a department. This means 50 to 55 faculty members. For a faculty of that size, you must have a full-time president, a dean, a business manager and probably a development man. You must have a secretary to the president—and a Cadillac—

and somebody to cut the grass. You end up with about 75 people on the payroll, and to be viable you then need a minimum of a thousand students. You cannot make it work on anything less; projections that have been tried show that the fund raising is altogether too difficult. Therefore, many of the smaller colleges—those with far less than a thousand students—must grow. They don't want to grow; they may not be as good when they do grow. But under the circumstances, they have to.

There is also a serious question whether the smallness of the college makes much difference. For example, several years ago a committee at Amherst made a study of the future size of the college. Among other things, they took a survey among the students to find out what the advantages of the small college were. One advantage, it seemed, was contact between the students and the faculty outside of class; but they discovered that eighty per cent of these contacts were had by twenty per cent of the students—the big men on campus —and that fifty per cent of the students had one contact or less per year. Amherst decided that it might just as well go from 1,000 to 1,300.

This problem is bothering many private colleges. They will be doing things that will not make them as happy as they would like to be. But they cannot help themselves. Their problem is to stay open and to provide the best possible education under the circumstances. You can say, "Well, they don't give a good enough education," but the point is that they will be providing much of the education in the country.

This raises another huge problem: money raising. When we reach the point that only twenty per cent of the students are in private institutions—as a matter of fact, twenty per cent is a high figure—and when the presidents of these twenty per cent go out fund raising, from whom will they be seeking funds? They will be seeking funds from the graduates of public institutions. And these men will be asking a pointed question: "What kinds of excellence do private institutions offer that public institutions cannot match?" There is only one answer: they can provide church-related education. When you go beyond this, it is hard to find any excellence that is unique to the private institutions.

This is a difficult problem, and many administrators of public institutions are worried about it. As a matter of fact, in Kansas, one reason that the state institutions want to cooperate with the private institutions is that they are afraid they will be accused of driving the private institutions to the wall. In Kansas, the private institutions are terribly weak; there are too many of them, and they have too small constituencies. The public institutions are afraid of being blamed for their demise.

Many things will have to be done, not because anybody wants to, but because there is no other choice. For example, forty colleges and universities now have regular year-round programs that are designed to get the student through in something less than four years. Three years ago, the number was twenty. More than a hundred institutions have committees actively working on this possibility, and these are not the small institutions but the University of California, the University of Michigan, Illinois and so on.

The students are coming in torrents. You cannot build all the buildings you would need to house them all, and you cannot turn masses of them away. So you must do something with the property you have. It is not good to have students coming at night and on Saturday; but if you cannot help yourself, you do it. We did it with the veterans after the war, and if we have to do it again, we will.

Remember that educational institutions, whether public or private, exist because somebody either appropriates money for them or gives them money. If you run a business, you can do anything you want. You can run the place twenty-five hours a week or a hundred hours a week. You can have a Cadillac or a Ford for the president. You have no responsibility to anybody but yourself.

When you are an educational institution, you are criticized if you keep the plant shut, for you ask people for money. If you didn't ask them for money, you could do anything you pleased.

SUMMARY OF THE DISCUSSION

The general discussion delved into present problems and future possibilities:

Location: "Many of our institutions of higher learning," Mr. Tickton noted, "were located by missionary groups a hundred years ago, when there were few roads and communication was poor. They needed a college for a handful of students, and they simply took the students, went out to a plain where they happened to own land and set one up. Today they are out of the way and having a devil of a time keeping alive."

Colleges remain in the wrong locations for several reasons, including inertia and political pressure. As an example of the latter, President Coles cited the case of the University of Maine, which is located in Orono, more than one hundred miles north of the state's population center, the Portland-Lewiston area. Political pressures have forced the university to open a branch in Portland, but it "doesn't want the Portland branch to grow any more than it absolutely has to." Rejecting a chance to build a new Portland campus at a convenient spot within easy highway distance of the city—a location which would permit a growth to seven or eight thousand students—the university planners have met the inevitable expansion by cramming a new building onto the old, small campus in the middle of the city. "This is just plain political pressure, exerted by a well-established constituency in the Bangor area opposed to a new constituency in the Portland area."

Colleges in the wrong location are not only far from the students; they face many additional burdens, including the expense of bringing in supplies. Under such handicaps, few or none can survive. Only two possible solutions were suggested: let them move to the cities, where the demand for higher education is burgeoning, or let them merge. If a small institution merges into a large one, however, it will have to cease training its particular constituency. If small institutions of the same kind merge, they may be able to keep their distinctive character. "In Kansas," Mr. Tickton pointed out, "there are three small Presbyterian colleges and two small Methodist colleges. If these merged into one college of each denomination, they would be large enough to survive."

Private into public: The obstacles confronting private institutions were recounted, including the shortage of money, the inability to raise sufficient new capital and building funds, the inability to meet competition for faculty members, and the fact that government support tends to improve the position of public institutions vis-à-vis private institutions. Large private institutions will have to struggle; small ones will have to expand or die. "Some of them," Mr. Tickton observed, "will die anyway."

One significant new development, caused by these troubles, is the conversion of private into public institutions. During 1959-63, the University of Buffalo, the University of Houston, Midwestern University and the University of Kansas City were taken over by state or municipal governments. The discussants did not indicate whether this might be considered a national trend.

Smallness: The question of whether small enrollment may be an advantage was reopened briefly. Asked for a value judgment, Mr. Tickton asserted that he sees no particular value to society in small enrollments. (The questioner did not press for amplification.) President Coles, who had declared in his original comment that smallness does offer advantages, was asked: "What evidence is there to show that students entering small institutions are those who will benefit from these advantages?" He replied that self-selectivity tends to assure this, and there the matter was dropped.

Faculty salaries: Mr. Tickton's prediction of a steep rise in faculty salaries evoked some comment. He responded that "for the first time in many generations, well-trained college professors with publications and research experience are scarce commodities. You have to pay a high price if you want them. If you do not pay a high price, you do not get them." He cited the example of the University of Mississippi, whose low salary scale has forced it to hire the bulk of its new instructors from among its own graduates. This problem is becoming serious, and "as administrators pay more attention to it, salaries will move up faster than they otherwise would."

Related to the question of salaries is the question of faculty discipline. Traditionally, faculties have been underpaid and, in return, have been indulged in wasteful practices concerning course offerings, class sizes and class hours. As salaries climb, productivity in these areas will have to increase. "I know of no institution and no society that will permit the payment of adequate faculty salaries on the basis of operational slackness, such as has been followed by most institutions in the past."

Indeed, financial incentives and productivity should be more tightly geared. "To get faculty members to do things they do not want to do," Mr. Tickton said, "you follow the old economic rule: you pay them more. You pay them more to teach in the summer and at night, and they will teach in the summer and at night." Mr. Harris cautioned, however, that financial incentives are not infallible. "A lot of money has been spent to attract more students to the sciences, but the proportion of scientists among persons getting their baccalaureates has not changed in five years [1958-62]. Incentives do not always, apparently, have the desired effect."

New types of institutions: Robert W. Merry, professor of business administration at Harvard University, introduced another aspect of long-range institutional planning: "It seems to me that Mr. Tickton's presentation indicates, on the whole, an acceptance of the present kind of institution, except perhaps those with small enrollments. I would like to look beyond that.

"My own first three years in school were spent in a two-room schoolhouse. Then I moved to an experimental 'integrated school' run by the school of education at the University of Iowa. The school included classes at all grade levels, from first grade through graduate school.

"In the nation today, increasing attention is being given to curriculum changes, articulation and individual differences in learning ability—especially the fact that a student may be ready for advanced work in one subject while learning at an average rate, or less than average, in other subjects. In view of this awakening interest, there might be great value, it seems to me, in creating 'integrated schools' like the one I attended, so that students would have available classes in every subject at whatever level of challenge they are able to handle. Do you have any information about current thinking regarding this possibility?"

No information was forthcoming, but Mr. Tickton agreed that new types of institutions will be created. Experimentation with ungraded high schools is a straw in the wind. The most urgent pressure, however, is likely to be felt in technical and vocational training. "There are areas of the economy in which we have plenty of jobs but not enough people qualified for them. In the health services, to take just one example, we need nurses, occupational therapists, x-ray technicians, occupational therapists, medical secretaries—medical auxiliaries of all types. If the demand becomes great enough, we will create institutions to concentrate on training for these occupations. In industry we may have technical training institutes linked to industrial firms, in which the training can change rapidly to match changes in the industry.

"I expect that we will see quite a few new types of institutions, but I think they will be mainly under public auspices. Private institutions will not be able to raise the money. Unless you have some access to taxes, it is too tough."

12.   Forms and Functions
of Student Aid

John C. Esty, Jr.
Associate Dean, Amherst College

My speech might be titled "A Concentric View of Student Aid," which perhaps needs some explanation. In reading the reports of Mr. Harris' previous seminars, I have detected some sensitivity to the use of the language of economics in a group of educators. As a teacher of mathematics—and on the theory that the best defense is a good offense—I have borrowed vaguely from mathematics so as to make my title sound a bit mysterious and a bit threatening.

The innermost circle of my concentric vision comprises all the financial-aid students at my college; these students are my daily concern as a practicing financial-aid officer and dean. The next larger circle comprises the needy students who are prospective candidates for Amherst College. The outer circle is the universe of all students who should go to college (possibly Amherst) and who are financially disabled. I wish to discuss some of my observations and concerns in each of these three circles. But particularly I wish to call your attention to the perspective gained as one moves from the center outward.

First circle: Student aid in college

At its simplest, the task here is to determine the student's financial need and then help him meet that need by some combination of scholarship grant, loan and employment. The neatest way to determine need is to add up the student's financial resources and subtract the total from an over-all, projected figure for costs. The College Scholarship Service provides invaluable aid in determining the fair share of the parents' contribution. All the financial-aid officer has to do is find the aid money, create the jobs and decide how each individual student can best finance his education.

To do this he must seek the answers to such questions as: How much can students reasonably be expected to earn during the college year and during the summer vacation? What is the proper balance between loans and grants? And how do parents typically pay for their children's schooling? At Amherst we have begun to father some research to help with the answers, and I would like to share some of the results with you.

Student earnings: Many financial-aid programs guarantee a campus job for the scholarship student so that a need of, say, $1,000 can be met by a package of, say, a $500 grant, a $200 loan and a job worth $300. I consider this practice unsound. First, it may pre-empt all the available campus jobs and, in effect, bar the non-aid student from employment. And second, it may make an unfair demand on the recipient's time, especially in his freshman year. At Amherst, for example, the average job would require 300 hours of work for $300 compensation.

In 1961-62 we asked all Amherst students—there are 1000, of whom 320 are receiving financial aid—to fill out a chart indicating how much money they earn themselves, how they earn it and how much time they spend working. We found that 520 students earned an annual total of $70,000, or an average of $135, in campus employment. Moreover, 82 students earned an average of $120 a year in off-campus jobs; only 34 of these students were receiving financial aid. Clearly, a great many students help to pay their way by their own efforts, without asking for college aid funds. It would seem unfair to prevent them from doing so by pre-empting the jobs exclusively for aid students.

We also found that freshmen work an average of about 75 hours a year, while upperclassmen average 150. This suggests a certain maximum fair figure, which seems to be an empirical function of course load.

We have, therefore, concluded that it is not wise to include a guaranteed job in the financial-aid package. Instead, in reckoning the resources available to each financial-aid student, we assume a college-year earning potential of $75 for freshmen and $150 for upperclassmen. His remaining need is then met by some combination of grant and loan.

A more dramatic finding of our survey concerned the summer earnings of our students. During the summer of 1962, 829 students earned a total of $457,000, an average of about $550 per student. Sixty per cent of the total earned was saved to meet college expenses.

The amounts earned ranged from $8 to $2,400, the latter on a construction job repaving highways for the State of New York. One boy earned $1,000 baking bread in an assembly line; another earned $1,700 as a merchant marine seaman on an oil tanker; a third earned $1,800 as a truck driver. We had a singer and saxophonist with a twist band in Morocco, a translator of commercial documents for Credit Lyonnais in Paris, a roustabout in the Oklahoma oil fields and a boy who conducted research on the polarization of neutrons with a proton accelerator. Our students are not only willing to bear a large share of financing their own education; they also find fascinating jobs and worthwhile experiences in the process.

Loans and grants: Our experience with the loan aspect of our program should be encouraging to other institutions which are re-examining this form of student aid. In 1961-62, Amherst College awarded $336,000 in financial aid; loans comprised $45,000, or just under a seventh of the total. Each aid student is asked to take a progressively larger proportion of his aid each year in the form of a loan; sophomores may expect a 20 per cent in loans, juniors 30 per cent and seniors 40 per cent. (Freshman aid is typically a straight grant.) The grant part of the aid package is not contingent on acceptance of the loan; some students prefer to increase their summer earnings, rather than take the loan. Yet even though almost 90 per cent of our students plan to do graduate work, 86 per cent of the loans offered were accepted.

A further valuable factor in the loan program is its flexibility. We can and do adjust the loan-grant ratio to reward strong academic performance—the original point of a scholarship, from which higher education has strayed considerably. Students who stand at the top of the class receive all their aid in straight grants. The needy student who is performing poorly does not have his financial aid withdrawn, but he finds it necessary to take a greater portion of his aid as a loan. This is a direct incentive, but a gentle one.

Sources of financing: One of the more ambitious studies of how people pay for college was conducted in 1959-60 by Michigan's Survey Research Center, which interviewed 2,700 family spending units over the country with at least one child in college.[1] Through a series of inferences I was able to approximate similar data for the Amherst College population. The figures are matched in the chart below and provide an interesting comparison between higher education in general and a high-cost, northeastern, liberal-arts college. It seems noteworthy that with an overall cost 70 per cent higher than the average, the percentage from each major source of financing an Amherst education is about the same as the average. It is also somewhat surprising to note that while the Amherst students' financial-aid average (from all sources, not from the college's own financial-aid grants alone) is two and a half times that of the national sample, the percentage of the total cost which it pays is not greatly larger. Perhaps this will comfort those who feel uneasy about the apparent concentration of funds in a small number of rich, northeastern colleges.

	National sample		Amherst College	
Source of funds	Average amount	Per cent of total cost	Average amount	Per cent of total cost
Parents	$ 950	60%	$1740	66%
Student earnings	360	23%	500	20%
Financial aid	130	9%	310	12%
Other	110	8%	50	2%
Average cost	$1550		$2600	

Private colleges which expect to keep increasing their tuition are generally apprehensive that this will narrow the socio-economic base of their student body. In the past six years, Amherst has had three tuition rises. Each was accompanied by a statement that financial-aid funds would be increased proportionately, yet we have been surprised to discover that our average award has hardly risen in that period. Indeed, only about half the awards needed to be increased in the year following each tuition rise. In short, as we bring our tuition increases in line with general cost-of-living increases, we find that our average parent's ability to pay has increased proportionately. This would argue that tuition rises do not affect the student body significantly. But the failure of our average award to rise also suggests an undesirable corollary, which I shall discuss in a moment.

One final comment should be made. My daily experience suggests that for every financial-aid student who is especially hungry for the education he almost didn't get, there is another whose sensitivity about his award causes some anxiety and motivational problems. Student aid is not just a key to opportunity; it can be a burden also.

Second circle: Student aid in recruiting and admission policy

The financial-aid officer is typically a member of the admissions committee, and freshman awards are sometimes actually made by the admissions office. The major implications of student aid in admissions are obvious, especially in the competitive aspects, but again I would like to make some specific observations.

Amherst's experience, as I have said, is that the average scholarship award has not risen significantly after the last three tuition rises. The augmented funds have gone, rather, to increase the number of students on financial aid. In other words, as tuition rises, we have fewer large awards and, for whatever reason, fewer really indigent students. Mr. Harris has thoroughly reported the arguments for and against tuition rises;[2] but more and more studies of the problem are being made, and we shall soon have enough evidence for a new assessment. For example, in his introduction to the recent University of Illinois study of student economics,[3] President David Dodds Henry comments that although no interpretation of the data was made, "it seems clear to me . . . that any substantial increase in cost would keep many of these students out of college and impose great hardships on others."

My own feeling is that while cost rises do not seriously affect students already in college, they make the job of recruiting good, indigent students more and more difficult. As someone put it at one of these seminars a few years ago, when prospective students ask the recruiter how much it costs and hear the figure $2,600, "the long explanation about scholarships, jobs and loans somehow fails of its purpose . . . ; $2,600 is $2,600, and it may amount to more than half the family's income."[4]

I would like to add two other negative factors which are not often mentioned. First, for a poor boy, the sound of a high-cost figure may not even register in the economic sense. He may hear it purely as an index of the social tone of the college, and he may decide that it is not a good place for him, irrespective of the cost. Second, whether rightly or not, prospective college candidates perceive applying for financial aid as a supercompetition within a competition. Some may be scared off, even though they would have been perfectly acceptable.

But the major loss of good, indigent candidates for a highly selective college like Amherst does not result from rising costs. The explanation lies in the discovery that high-grade preparation for college is increasingly a function of family or community wealth. In 1946-47, seven per cent of the Amherst student body received scholarships (not counting the G.I. Bill); their academic average was 83, while the college average was 80. In 1958-59, the 26 percent on scholarship averaged 81, which was the same as the college average. Today I hesitate to work out the statistics. Though there has been no major change of financial-aid policy in this period, I am afraid that the scholarship group is now below the college average. This phenomenon occurs mainly in highly selective colleges, but it may account for the frequent observation that scholarships are not going to the neediest groups. The problem is that, in general, the neediest do not qualify for admission.

The attempt to recruit outstanding aid candidates has been helped immensely by the work of the National Merit Scholarship Corporation. One valuable instrument is the Financial Need Survey, published each May, which lists those semifinalists and commended students who said that they wanted to attend college but could not because they lacked financial resources. The 1962 survey lists about 3,000 names from the top 35,000 scores on the national test. (Ninety per cent of the nation's high school students participated in the program, and these 35,000 represent the top two per cent of those participating.) National Merit reports that in 1961 about half of the financially disabled students received offers of aid. Here is a rich field for those colleges, with some aid to spare, who have not already selected their freshman class by the middle of May.

One thing which strikes the college recruiter forcibly—especially the financial-aid man who wishes to use his funds to broaden the socio-economic range of an entering class and therefore visits high schools in the deprived areas—is the number of high-IQ students who are beyond his grasp because they are not in the college-preparatory curriculum. No amount of financial aid can get these people to college unless they would be willing to start over again in ninth grade. I have already written about this problem and proposed some possible new uses for financial aid to alleviate it,[5] but I wish to re-emphasize the point here: Much of our present financial-aid leverage is lost because the opportunity it represents is brought to the students' attention too late.

Third circle: Student aid and educational opportunity

The third concentric circle in my vision concerns the use of student aid to staunch the yearly loss of potential college talent and to equalize educational opportunity. No financial-aid officer can fail to be impressed by this problem, yet there is a curious frustration on the part of those who attempt to deal with it merely by interviewing students and offering aid. Money is simply not enough. We are now aware that a college-going pattern is a complex sociological and psychological phenomenon, as well as an economic one. Summarizing the recent research, one writer has stated that in general "the probability of a student's going to college is strongly related to his ability, his sex, and his parents' education or occupation. The nearness of a college also seems to exert a positive influence. These studies have not yielded much direct evidence on the influence of financial factors."[6]

In a new study, Brazer and David [7] have sought to isolate certain factors or characteristics of the heads of families which seem to correlate with the grade levels attained by the children. The main factors, in their order of importance, are: education, difference in education between husband and wife, occupation, number of children, north-south migration, need-achievement index and attitude toward work, peak earnings, and religious preference and church attendance. Values apparently play as much a part as economics. Indeed, other evidence suggests that the economic factor may be even more elusive. In a study entitled "Dropouts from College," [8] Summerskill lists the three major factors involved as lack of motivation, lack of ability and financial difficulty, in that order. He points out, however, that "the importance of financial difficulty in attrition is overestimated if students find this reason more permissible than lack of motivation or lack of ability."

The importance of motivation is underscored again and again in studies of college-going patterns. In presenting the findings of state-wide surveys in Arkansas, Indiana and Wisconsin, Beezer and Hjelm infer that "lack of motivation is probably the greatest single deterrent to college attendance by capable youth." [9] National Merit's Annual Report for 1961 puts it this way: "Many of the talented students have not been sufficiently motivated to apply for admission to college. Others are unfamiliar with scholarship opportunities or uncertain about their chances of receiving help. Because they fail to apply for admission, they are not considered for scholarships. As a result, scholarships offered by colleges are used mainly to support students who are already motivated to enter college."[10]

All of this research suggests that we cannot simply ask how much money is needed for scholarships and loans to provide fair educational opportunity. We must ask "how much money is required to cause a boy or girl at what ability level and under what family education and occupation levels to go how many miles to college when influenced by what community traditions and what counseling activities." [11] And we must ask how much money is needed to influence favorably each of these variables.

What I am proposing, then, is a new principle by which we can view economic factors and student aid as part of a wider attack on the problem of unequal chances for higher education. I call this new principle the *inertial principle*. Put grossly, it says that once a student is set in motion toward college, he is inclined to keep moving in that direction. Conversely, it takes a great deal of force to get an unmotivated student moving.

The implications of this principle for student aid are interesting. For example, it suggests that lack of aid may not deter the strongly college-bound student. In fact, Pasanella reports that in a sample of 276 colleges (228 College Board members, plus 48 non-CEEB members of the largely mid-western Association of College Admission Counselors), of every 2.39 aid applicants accepted for admission but denied aid, one registered at that college anyway.[12] Mr. Harris cites similar evidence,[13] but he takes this as an indication of waste of scholarship funds. Since more and more institutions are basing awards on a standard calculation of need, I should think the figures demonstrate not waste but the chance to make greater use of loans and to save scholarship grants for leverage in a different sector.

Another phenomenon that the inertial principle may illuminate is the migration of top students—under a free-choice, national aid program—to the prestige colleges. To use this migration as an argument for the undesirability of such a program may be spurious. They probably would have gone anyway.

The inertial principle not only suggests possible areas for the conservation of gift aid but also focuses our attention on the diverse factors in motivation toward college. It makes clear that the only dramatically successful program which uses student aid for inertial purposes is athletic scholarships. Every ninth-grader knows that a good high-school athlete can go to college. Here alone, I suspect, is the promise of financial aid widely enough recognized to make a substantial contribution to motivation to college. Why should there not be a similar understanding for good students? National Merit has done this for the all-stars, but we need the same impetus for the second-stringers, of whom there are a vast number.

After pointing out the strong influence exerted by the plans of a student's high-school peer group, Beezer and Hjelm suggest the use of sociometric techniques to identify leaders, who could then be singled out for special attention in college guidance in the hope of motivating a whole group.[14] Here again, the promise of financial aid would provide tremendous leverage. Perhaps college financial-aid officers should visit not the college guidance counselor for seniors but the counselors for the underclassmen—especially those responsible for helping eighth-graders to decide whether to enter the college-preparatory curriculum or not.

Th inertial principle does not deny the importance of economic factors in college attendance. It suggests that student aid is a necessary but not sufficient motivating factor. Hopefully, it can also suggest new forms and new uses for student aid, which even in its infancy as a professional field show signs of hardening of the arteries.

REFERENCES

1. J. B. Lansing, T. Lorimer and C. Moriguchi, *How People Pay for College*, Survey Research Center, Institute for Social Research, The University of Michigan, 1960.
2. S. E. Harris, *Higher Education: Resources and Finance*, New York, 1962, Part 2.
3. The University Committee on Student Economics, *Student Economics at the University of Illinois*, Urbana, 1961.
4. S. E. Harris, ed., "Higher Education in the United States: The Economic Problems," *The Review of Economics and Statistics*, Vol. XLII, No. 3, part 2, August 1960, p. 33.
5. J. C. Esty, "Does Financial Aid Come Too Late?" *College Board Review*, No. 44, Spring 1961.
6. S. J. Mushkin, ed., *Economics of Higher Education*, U.S. Office of Education, Washington, 1962, p. 374.
7. *Ibid.*, Chapter 2.
8. Reported in N. Sanford, ed., *The American College*, John Wiley & Sons, New York, 1962.
9. R. H. Beezer and H. F. Hjelm, *Factors Related to College Attendance*, Office of Education, Washington, 1961, p. 38.
10. National Merit Scholarship Corporation, *Talent; Our Prime National Resource*, Annual Report, 1961, p. 25.
11. E. D. West, ed., *Background for a National Scholarship Policy*, American Council on Education, Washington, 1956, p. 69. (In

a speech entitled "Background Revisited," delivered at the annual meeting of the College Scholarship Service on October 30, 1962, Mr. West outlined some of his findings for a new book on the same subject.)

12. A. K. Pasanella, "A Report on a Survey of Admission Statistics," College Entrance Examination Board, 1962, p. 6.

13. S. E. Harris, "Higher Education in the United States. . . . ," p. 209.

14. Beezer and Hjelm, *op. cit.*, p. 140.

Harold Goldthorpe
Specialist for Student Financial Assistance Higher Education, Administration Branch, U. S. Office of Education

I must preface my remarks with a couple of limitations. The first is to indicate clearly and plainly that I am not speaking for the Office of Education or for the Department of Health, Education and Welfare. By no stretch of the imagination can what I have to say be regarded as official doctrine. As a matter of fact, so far as I have been able to determine, there is no official doctrine on the question of student aid.

The second limitation is that I shall concentrate on the problem of student aid at the undergraduate level. This is a large enough topic to occupy our attention, without involving ourselves in the problems of aid to graduate students and advanced professional students.

In recent years, many responsible observers have shown an increasing concern over the nation's shortages of professional, technical and scientific manpower. Acute and alarming personnel shortages in many fields threaten to limit seriously our expanding economy and even to jeopardize the national security. At a time when the future of free institutions is threatened and the United States bears the responsibilities for world leadership, an educated and productive citizenship is more essential than ever before.

Part of the long-cherished American dream has been to make educational opportunities available to all able citizens, irrespective of race, creed, sex, status or national origin. This dream was substantially achieved by the expansion of secondary education during the past generation, and it was partially attained in higher education during the postwar period under the several G.I. Bills. Within the next decade or two, it appears almost inevitable (barring an atomic war) that the nation will materially expand its higher-education facilities and programs for young adults who have the requisite ability and interest. The national welfare—indeed, our very survival—demands such an expansion.

Congress recognized this situation and its own responsibilities in 1958 in its adoption of the National Defense Education Act. The preamble of this law includes the following significant statement:

"The Congress hereby finds and declares that the security of the Nation requires the fullest development of the mental resources and technical skills of its young men and women. The present emergency demands that additional and more adequate educational opportunities be made available. The defense of this Nation depends upon the mastery of modern techniques developed from complex scientific principles. It depends as well upon the discovery and development of new principles, new techniques and new knowledge.

"We must increase our efforts to identify and educate more of the talent of our Nation. This requires programs that will give assurance that no student of ability will be denied an opportunity for higher education because of financial need; will correct as rapidly as possible the existing imbalances in our educational programs which have led to an insufficient proportion of our population educated in science, mathematics and modern foreign languages and trained in technology.

"To meet the present educational emergency requires additional effort at all levels of government. It is therefore the purpose of this Act to provide substantial assistance in various forms to individuals, and to States and their subdivisions, in order to insure trained manpower of sufficient quality and quantity to meet the National defense needs of the United States."

The leaders of higher education face serious problems during the coming decade in raising vast sums to increase faculty salaries, educational services and plant facilities. A somewhat different financial problem, however, concerns us today: What does college cost students and their families? How do they raise the necessary funds? And what are the major research problems in this area?

I want to address myself to these questions primarily by presenting, in a series of tables, the basic statistical data on which any further discussion must be based.

Experience has taught us that these projections, which the Office of Education prepares, have, on the whole, been quite conservative.

Table 1A. Comparison of the number of 18-year-olds and secondary-school graduates, 1940-1970.

Academic Year	Estimated number of 18-year-olds	Secondary-school graduates	
		Number	As of percentage of 18-year-olds
Actual			
1939-40	2,438,400	1,221,475	50.1%
1945-46	2,384,300	1,080,033	45.3%
1949-50	2,202,300	1,199,700	54.5%
1953-54	2,121,500	1,276,100	60.2%
1957-58	2,306,000	1,505,900	65.3%
1959-60	2,567,000	1,860,000	72.4%
1961-62	2,769,000	1,890,000	68.3%
Projected			
1965-66	3,830,000	2,520,000	65.8%
1969-70	3,756,000	2,710,000	72.2%

Source: U. S. Department of Health, Education and Welfare, Office of Education, preliminary estimate and computations, October 1962.

If anything, we err on the low side. (In May 1962, for example, we revised our projections for 1970 and discovered that our estimated college-enrollment figure for that year was nearly a million larger than we had estimated in 1957. Then our estimate was about six million; now it is roughly seven million.)

Just two observations on this table: *First,* the number of eighteen-year-olds dropped slightly over 300,000 during the first fourteen years shown here. Since half of these were males, the drop was a matter of great concern to the Department of Defense some years ago. But since 1954 the number has been rising fairly rapidly. *Second,* the right-hand columns show the number and percentage of graduates from all secondary schools, both public and private. These figures have been growing quickly; the percentage will have increased close to fifty per cent in the thirty-year period. The puzzle, of course, is the dip shown in the percentage figures for the 1960's; they fall back from a high point in 1959-60 and barely recover the loss by 1969-70. I have been unable to get a satisfactory explanation of this from our research and statistics people. All I can say is that there is no error in our arithmetic computations.

Table 1B. Comparison of the number of 18-year-olds and first-time college students, 1940-1970.

Academic Year	Estimated number of 18-year-olds	First-time college enrollments		
		Number	As a percentage of H.S. graduates	As a percentage of 18-year olds
Actual				
1939-40	2,438,400	417,539	34.2%	17.1%
1945-46	2,384,300	474,894	44.0%	19.9%
1949-50	2,202,300	594,126	49.5%	27.0%
1953-54	2,121,500	663,070	52.0%	31.3%
1957-58	2,306,000	721,547	47.9%	31.3%
1959-60	2,567,000	929,823	50.0%	36.2%
1961-62	2,769,000	1,026,000	54.3%	37.1%
Projected				
1965-66	3,830,000	1,415,000	56.2%	36.9%
1969-70	3,756,000	1,569,000	57.9%	41.8%

Source: U. S. Department of Health, Education and Welfare, Office of Education, preliminary estimates and computations, October 1962.

These figures have only a very crude utility, mainly because the Office of Education does not have precise data on the composition of entering freshman students. We do not know what percentage of first-time college students are eighteen years old. The figures in the center column include, of course, the veterans of World War II and of Korea. They also include a substantial—and probably growing—number of sixteen- and seventeen-year-olds. Entering college freshmen are certainly not all eighteen.

A second important caution is that these figures include a substantial component of part-time students. Until 1961 we did not ask the registrars of colleges and universities to provide separate tabulations of full-time and part-time students. As nearly as we can estimate, roughly thirty per cent of the entering freshmen are part-time students; the percentage is virtually the same for the total college enrollment. The percentage has been growing, so that the climb in first-time enrollment is not quite as steep as the bare figures suggest. Even so, the total first-time enrollment will have nearly quadrupled in the thirty-year period—a really dramatic increase in any terms.

Table 2A. Comparison of median income of families with heads aged 35-56, the Consumer Price Index and mean annual institutional charges, 1949-1961.

| Year | Median income of families with heads aged 35-56[a] | | Consumer Price Index[a] (Annual average) | Mean institutional tuition and required fees[b] | | | |
| | | | | Public institutions | | Private institutions | |
	Amount	Per cent relative to 1949		Amount	Per cent relative to 1949	Amount	Per cent relative to 1949
1961	$6,618	195%	128	$216	193%	$1,045	225%
1960	6,450	190%	127	207	185%	938	202%
1959	6,140	181%	125	194	175%	890	191%
1958	5,772	169%	124	179	160%	820	176%
1957	5,560	164%	120	168	150%	741	159%
1956	5,383	159%	116	155	138%	690	148%
1955	4,987	147%	115	147	131%	638	137%
1954	4,719	139%	115	135	121%	590	127%
1953	4,735	140%	114	130	116%	565	122%
1949	3,393	100%	100	112	100%	465	100%

[a] Summarized from reports of the U. S. Department of Commerce and the U. S. Department of Labor and from an article by Lanore G. Lewis, "Median Family Income, the Cost of Living and Tuition Charges," *College and University Business*, Vol. 27: 19-21 (December 1959).

[b] For the academic session beginning in September of the years indicated. Mean tuition charges of 196 representative institutions for 1949 and 1954 are taken from "Trends in Tuition Charges and Fees," *Annals of the American Academy of Political and Social Science*, Vol. 301: 148-64 (September 1955), by Herbert S. Conrad and Ernest V. Hollis. Data for 1955 through 1961 are calculated for the *same* institutions.

The family group whose income is charted here is the group that most families are in when they have children of college age. As the table indicates, family income in this group has nearly doubled, but the implications of that are not quite as cheerful as they may seem. I shall return to these figures in a moment.

The data on average tuition and required fees are not drawn from all colleges and universities in the country. They are based on a study of 196 institutions, which accounted for 55 to 60 per cent of the total college enrollment in the country. The minimum enrollment of these institutions, when the study began, was about a thousand students.

Note especially that the average charge at the public institutions has, in recent years, increased almost parallel with the rise in family income, while the average charge at private institutions has risen a good deal more sharply. These relationships are perhaps more apparent when the same data are presented in the form of a graph:

Table 2B. Data of Table 2A plotted in graph form.

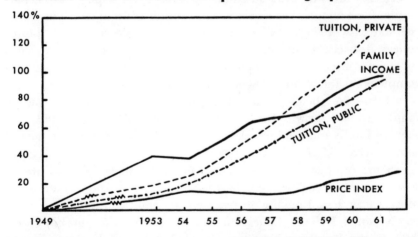

There is little reason to expect any marked change in these trends (with the possible exception of public junior colleges) before 1966 or 1967—and probably not soon after that, though I am not rash enough to make any formal projections so far ahead.

Let me return briefly to the figures for median family income and point out a further correlation which bears on the problem of anticipating how many needy young people may be candidates for sizeable scholarship and loan programs. This is the correlation between the *size* of families and their family income.

The 1960 census showed 1,134,000 families with six children or more under eighteen years of age. Sixty per cent of these families had family incomes of less than $5,000. Another, slightly smaller group (1,081,000) had five children; half of these families had incomes under $5,000. About 2,514,000 families had four children, and 38.5 per cent of these children came from families with incomes under $5,000.

In short, the nation had 4,729,000 families with four of more children, 46 per cent of whom came from families with incomes under $5,000 a year. This is probably a group that many of our institutional scholarship programs are not now reaching, at least in sufficient numbers. It is, therefore, an important group of talented young people to whom we should be addressing ourselves.

A substantial group of this category, of course, are now enrolling in public junior colleges—especially in the western states, where a larger number of public institutions are supported by tax funds and where they are well distributed and accessible to the population. California, for example, has about seventy junior colleges distributed over the state; by 1970 it expects to cover the whole state with junior-college districts. California is apparently going to repeat, at the junior-college level, the development which most states and cities have completed at the secondary-school level.

Table 3A (below) offers a slightly different perspective on the family-income factor. Incidentally, between 1960 and 1961, the median family income increased over $100, from $5,620 to the median shown here, $5,737.

Some comparisons between the two percentage columns are instructive. About 31 per cent of all families are in the income group of $4,000 or less. Roughly 40 per cent of those who borrowed under the National Defense Education Act came from this income group. And as the interquartile range shows, half of all borrowers under this program came from families with incomes between $2,350 and $6,108.

At the other end of the scale, only 3.5 per cent of the loans went to families of top income, who comprise 16 per cent of all families in the country. Even this low percentage requires some explanation. Family income is only one factor used in assessing the financial strength of a borrower and his family. The other factors include not only family assets but also the family's obligations and the number of children. Moreover, these loan figures include graduate students and students in professional schools, who are more mature and less disposed to depend on their families. Unfortunately, the data on undergraduate students alone were not readily available in this report.

The loan program is expanding rapidly to serve an increasing number of borrowers. The figures in Table 3A are for the fall of 1960. Two years later, there were 170,000 borrowers in approximately 1,560 colleges and universities. The average loan was just over $500, a total of close to $90 million. Our increasing loan total reflects the consistent support of the Congress, which has thus far always granted our requests.

Table 3A. Comparison of national family-income distribution with family incomes of National Defense Student Loan Program borrowers.

Family income group	Family income, 1961[a]		NDSLP borrowers, fall of 1960[b]
	Number of families	Per cent of total	
Under $2,000	5,889,000	12.7%	⎱ 40.1%
$2,000— 3,999	8,424,000	18.1%	⎰
$4,000— 5,999	10,284,000	22.2%	30.4%
$6,000— 7,999	8,945,000	19.4%	15.1%
$8,000— 9,999	5,375,000	11.6%	6.3%
$10,000—14,999	5,219,000	11.3%	⎱ 3.5%
$15,000 and over	2,205,000	4.7%	⎰
Total number	46,341,000 families		86,216 borrowers
Median family income	$5,737		$4,471
Interquartile range	$3,360—8,450		$2,350—6,108

[a] Defined as all money income prior to deductions for taxes received by the civilian, noninstitutional population.
Source: U. S. Department of Commerce, Bureau of the Census, *Consumer Income; Average Family Income Increases in 1961.* Current Population Reports, August 28, 1962. (Series P-60, No. 38) .

[b] 3,093 borrowers (3.6 per cent of the total number) reported "No parents or guardians."

Source: Robert C. Hall and Stanton Craigie, *National Defense Student Loan Program; Student Borrowers, Their Needs and Resources.* Department of Health, Education and Welfare, Office of Education, 1962.

By way of comparison, here is a summary of undergraduate scholarship grants by colleges and universities, public and private, in a recent ten-year period:

Table 3B. Growth of institutional undergraduate scholarships.

	1949-50	1955-56	1959-60
Number of institutions that awarded scholarships	1,198	1,341	1,559
Total value of scholarship grants	$27,000,963	$65,736,950	$98,157,498
Number of students awarded scholarships	124,223	237,370	288,521
Average scholarship grant	$217	$277	$340

Source: U. S. Department of Health, Education and Welfare; *Annual Report, 1961*, page 285.

One caution is in order: We cannot document this readily, but we think that many institutions were holding back on their own scholarship money in 1949-50 because the Federal Government, under the G. I. Bill, was subsidizing a substantial proportion of the male enrollment. The total value shown for that year is, therefore, probably not typical, and the apparent increase in the course of the decade is probably in some measure spurious.

The two following tables provide some data for determining the number of superior high-school students who are not entering college primarily for economic reasons. This is, of course, a key group whom the Federal loan program should be reaching, in pursuance of the preamble of the National Defense Education Act.

Table 4. State and national estimates of the percentages of superior high-school graduates (upper 30%) who entered college immediately following graduation.

Study and class	Boys	Girls	Total
ETS-NSF National Study, class of 1955[a]	75%	60%	68%
Minnesota, class of 1950[b]	64%	56%	60%
Upstate New York, class of 1956[c]	80%	71%	75%
Kansas, class of 1956[d]	—	—	65%
Wisconsin, class of 1957[e]	72%	59%	66%
Arkansas, class of 1957[f]	60%	50%	56%
New Hampshire, classes of 1955, 1956, 1957 (upper 25%)[g]	72%	44%	53%
National estimate, 1960, Donald S. Bridgman[h]	80%	65%	73%

[a] Educational Testing Service, *Background Factors Relating to College Plans and College Enrollment Among Public High School Students,* 1957.

[b] Ralph F. Berdie, *After High School—What?* University of Minnesota, 1954.

[c] New York State Education Department, *Needs and Facilities in Higher Education in New York,* 1957.

[d] Alex A. Daughtry and Richard C. Hawk, *Report on the Post-Graduation Activities of the 1956 Kansas High School Graduates.* Kansas State Teachers College of Emporia, 1957.

[e] J. Kenneth Little, *A State-wide Inquiry into Decisions of Youth About Education Beyond High School.* University of Wisconsin, 1958.

[f] Francis Stroup and Dean C. Andrew, *Barriers to College Attendance; A Study of Factors Related to Educational Discontinuance of High School Graduates.* Arkansas Southern State College, 1959.

[g] Margaret R. Cusick, *The Upper Quarter; A Study of Education Beyond High School for the Upper Fourth of New Hampshire High School Graduates.* New Hampshire Council for Better Schools, 1959.

[h] Donald S. Bridgman, "Where the Loss of Talent Occurs and Why," *The Search for Talent.* College Entrance Examination Board, 1960.

This table needs little comment, except that there is a need for more —and more up-to-date—studies of this character.

Perhaps the most interesting aspect of the data is the rise, as evinced by the two national studies, of the proportion of superior students who enter college immediately after high school. The variation from state to state is worth noting also, from two out of four students in New Hampshire and Arkansas to three out of four in upstate New York.

Table 5 is more immediately significant:

Table 5. Reasons why superior high-school graduates fail to enter college.

Principal reason	ETS-NSF study[a]		Upstate New York[c]		Kansas[d]		New Hamp-shire[g]
	Boys	Girls	Boys	Girls	Boys	Girls	Total
Economic and financial need	32%	31%	19%	28%	58%	50%	32%
Lack of interest	29%	48%	13%	34%	14%	21%	27%
Military service	—	—	46%	1%	18%	—	5%
Marriage	—	—	1%	12%	—	22%	11%
Family or social pressure	21%	15%	—	—	—	—	12%
Personal inadequacy	18%	6%	—	—	—	—	6%
Other reasons	—	—	21%	—	10%	7%	7%

[a, c, d, g] See notes to Table 4.

This table is based on small-sample studies, a number of which are several years old. It is pitiful that we do not have a recent, nation-wide study of this extremely important subject.

A few observations: Note the sharp variation between boys and girls in their response to the first two reasons, as indicated by some of the studies. In the response to "Lack of interest," this variation is partly explained by the fact that many girls enter short, intensive courses in private business schools and in hospital schools of nursing. That group, which we estimate at about five per cent of all girls graduating from high school, would not be classified as college attend-ants in this table.

With regard to the figures on military service, keep in mind that these studies were made at a time when the military and the draft were taking sizeable groups of high-school graduates. Please do not ask me how to account for the difference between upstate New York's 46 per cent and New Hampshire's 5 per cent.

As of 1960-61 our conservative estimate was that between 50,000 and 60,000 superior young people were not entering college primarily for economic reasons. But this is a complex situation, involving mul-tiple causes and motivations, and a precise determination is extraor-dinarily difficult to make. We do know, however, on the basis of a number of state surveys, that within a few years after new junior colleges or four-year colleges have been established, there is a sharp increase in the number of high-school graduates in the immediate area—say, within a radius of forty to fifty miles—who enter college. This factor of accessibility is important; the problem is not just a matter of financial need.

Turning now to the actual costs involved:

Table 6. Major items of a student's mean current expenditures, 1952-1953, and actual estimates for 1961-1962.

	Publicly controlled institutions		Privately controlled institutions	
	1952-53	1961-62	1952-53	1961-62
Mean total current expenditure	$1,120	$1,425	$1,676	$2,470
Major item				
Tuition and required fees	$151	$216	$546	$1,045
Room rent	102	190	146	240
Board (regular meals)	270	380	301	430
Clothing	130	150	149	160
Books and supplies	51	85	52	90
Other expenditures	416	404	482	505

Sources: Data for 1952-53 are computed from Tables 3 and 4 of *Costs of Attending College* by Ernest V. Hollis and Associates; Bulletin 1957, No. 9, Office of Education, U. S. Department of Health, Education and Welfare. Estimates for 1961-62 are based upon the increase in mean institutional tuition and fees since 1953 (Table 2A) and data in the Office of Education Circular 685, *Basic Student Charges, 1961-62* by W. Robert Bokelman and Louis A. D'Amico.

These figures cover only the student's cost of entering college and his running expenses. They do not include capital outlay items, such as the purchase of a typewriter, a radio or a car. The figures for 1952-53 are based on a stratified sample of the expenditures and income of about 16,000 students enrolled in 110 colleges and universities. It is therefore a national study. We then extended these figures, on the basis of our annual bulletin on basic student charges, in order to derive our estimates for 1961-62.

The salient fact revealed by this table is the widening gap in costs between public and private institutions. In 1952-53 the private institution cost $556 more; in 1961-62 it cost $1,045 more. I shall not at this point ask whether the difference is justified or not, from the student's point of view.

Table 7. Major sources of student income, 1952-1953.

Source of funds	Per cent of total income	Mean amount received by all students
Family (parents and other relatives)	40.5%	$647
Long-term savings	20.0	695
Term-time earnings	17.0	413
Summer earnings	9.3	395
Scholarships	4.8	310
Veterans and vocational rehabilitation benefits	4.3	894
Loans	1.5	400
Other sources	2.6	133
Total	100.0%	$1,462

Source: Summarized from Table 8, page 48, of *Costs of Attending College.* See Table 6, "Sources."

To recapitulate the major sources briefly: families were responsible for about two-fifths of the cost, long-term savings for about one-fifth and the student's own earnings (term-time and summer) for about one-fourth. These three sources provided 86.8 per cent of the funds.

College and university scholarships accounted for less than five per cent of the funds. The average scholarship amount—this is a national average—was $310. By 1959-60 it had risen to only $340 (see Table 3B), still no more than the frosting on the cake. We have no data on the number of students receiving grants in excess of $1000, but considering the low average, the number cannot be large.

Grants under the Veterans Administration programs, though large in dollar amount, are small in proportion because they reach relatively few students. The programs are being phased out. That is one reason why some of us in the Office of Education were so anxious to get a general, noncategorical scholarship program under way.

Loans, at the time this study was made, provided only 1.5 per cent of student income, but since 1957 there has been a striking increase in the number of students borrowing and in the average amount borrowed. We are inclined to take some credit for the Government program for having opened that new market, though there are still large sums—some tens of millions of dollars—being lent out of institutional loan funds.

Loan programs are also being facilitated by the states in diverse ways. Some are appropriating the money out of public funds and lending it directly to the students. Others provide guarantees to banks for loans made to students. North Dakota, in a very interesting variation, uses the profits of the Bank of the State of North Dakota as the principal for its state-administered lending program. These state programs are being extended and often liberalized to meet the increasing demands.

The facts presented in these tables make it evident that we are facing a serious problem: how to get qualified young people into our colleges and universities with the help of scholarships and loans. This problem will be with us for at least a decade; as far as we can see at the Federal level, it will be with us much longer than that. And it will come at a time when most of our resources will be severely stretched to raise the funds necessary to operate these institutions, let alone to build new facilities and to improve faculty salaries. I am very much afraid that the situation will get worse before it gets better.

We see some other problems in this area, notably the problem of administering these student-aid programs. Many institutions are now asking whether, when the loan program of the National Defense Education Act comes up for renewal, it will be possible to get administrative funds to ease the burden on the institutions. We make them do the dirty work of assessing need and deciding who gets what; it takes the responsibility off the bureaucrats. All we do is to provide the funds—ninety per cent against the institution's ten per cent. We make no grants for the cost of administration.

This question is being raised particularly by some of the smaller institutions which have had little or no experience in handling student aid. You can imagine what the problem will be in another three years, when they have to start collecting these funds back from the borrowers. This will be a new type of operation and a new responsibility for many institutions. But whether Congress will be willing to advance Federal funds to help administer what is essentially a Federal program—that remains to be seen.

A third problem that we see arising is the tendency on the part of many institutions to use an increasing share of their general support money, their general revenues, to support scholarships. One of our studies indicates that about sixty per cent of the money that is passed out in the form of scholarship grants originated in general revenues, either earnings from the endowment or gift money that has been contributed to the institution. Some of us are beginning to wonder what faculty members will say when they realize that they are helping to subsidize, in the form of lower salaries, the increase of students year after year. The question is going to be raised: "Why do we need scholarships to bring these people? Why can't they come in on their own?"

These are just some of the larger problems it seems to me, that we have in connection with student aid.

SUMMARY OF THE DISCUSSION

The general discussion polarized around four topics:

Recruitment: There was full agreement that a number of actions should be taken quickly to motivate more students toward college and to help them qualify for admission. This process must begin long before the eleventh or twelfth grade, probably by letting every student know from the time he enters school (or, at the very latest, from the time he chooses between a terminal and a college-preparatory track) that scholarship aid will be available for qualifying students. At the high-school level, the importance of intelligent college counseling, both by guidance counselors and by college representatives, cannot be over-estimated.

For high-school graduates with undistinguished academic records who wish to test themselves on college-level work, a junior college within commuting distance of home may be a boon. For a relatively small expense the student can experience two years of college; if he likes it and can handle the work, he can then transfer to a four-year institution. The low costs involved mean that scholarship aid can be stretched much further than usual. Concern that the junior-college training is not adequate preparation for upperclass college courses seems to be ill-founded. Studies in California indicate that such transfer students do slightly better than so-called native students. The junior-college system is now working excellently in California, Texas and other states. There is good reason to expect it to spread in coming years.

One discussant asked about the possibility of providing financial aid for students who are talented in nonacademic ways and who would benefit from a college education. Must all aid be reserved to students whose talent is readily quantifiable? Mr. Esty noted that nonacademic factors are, of course, weighed in considering applicants for an essentially academic institution such as Amherst. No one else responded directly to the question.

Grants vs. loans: As the relative advantages of grants and loans were assayed, the grants were recognized to have one indisputable advantage: they can be used to attract and retain promising students from families in very depressed income groups. These families, who suffer from intermittent employment and are often heavily committed on installment payments, are reluctant to assume new loan obligations even under generous repayment terms. A recent study of a group of NDEA loan holders from poor families confirms that the first- and second-year dropout rate is significantly lower for those who have some straight grants than for those who have none, quite apart from differences in academic achievement. "You have to buy them," said one man, "if you want to keep them."

For more well-to-do families, however, grants are at times a temptation not easily resisted. Though given primarily for need, they are taken generally as an indication of academic superiority; and as a status symbol they are occasionally sought by families which have no real financial need. The result may be falsified figures on scholarship application forms. To protect themselves when there is reason to doubt the figures, colleges resort to various means of verification, including credit checks (which are distasteful and not very productive) and asking for certified photostats of income-tax returns. The percentage of dishonest applications is small, but the problem does exist.

A loan program allows some flexibility in meeting this problem. If an application is suspicious, the college can offer a greater proportion of the financial aid as a loan and see whether the student accepts it. Mr. Esty suggested that "this provides a natural escape valve." The applicant might even be invited to specify the proportion of his aid which he could take as a loan; this option might result in fewer unreliable applications.

Two possible disadvantages of a loan program were examined. The first was the alleged danger of an increasing number of defaults; there was unanimous agreement that all available evidence points toward a remarkably low default rate, perhaps only about one per

278 EDUCATION AND PUBLIC POLICY

cent.* The second danger is more serious: the burden of administering the loans, the offer rate and the repayments may lead to a virtual strike in the bursar's or the treasurer's office. The loan policy may be sound, but the funds may pile up. This is, of course, a problem of internal management, but it is not lightly to be dismissed.

Coordination among sources of aid: There was agreement that student-aid funds could be used much more productively if the many sources of aid coordinated their efforts. At present no one knows the total value of grants and loans offered by sources other than colleges and universities. (A committee at the Office of Education is trying to develop the statistics but is encountering difficulties, including the reluctance of students to admit their sources of outside aid.) As a result, over-all planning for the most effective use of these resources is impossible.

The cumulative weight of small grants and loans from outside sources is impressive, as those colleges which have investigated the matter have learned. In 1961-62 university scholarships to freshmen at Tufts represented only 55 per cent of all the scholarships they were receiving. In the same year a survey at Amherst showed that, in addition to $80,000 of outside aid which the college knew about (from the National Merit Foundation, the Sloan Foundation and so on), its students were receiving almost $40,000 that the college had *not* known about. These funds were from smaller sources, such as local Kiwanis Clubs and PTA's. They had never been known because the fifty or so students receiving them had not asked for aid from the college itself.

Since the aid from diverse sources is uncoordinated, the possibility for waste is distressing, and instances of waste can be embarrassing in the extreme. One case was mentioned in which the student received both a maximum grant from a state program and a very large Navy ROTC award. Neither source knew about the other's grant until a separate investigation accidentally turned up the facts. The student had not only covered all his colleges expenses with the grants; he had been putting money in the bank.

Two remedies seem to be called for. "First," said Professor Grant E. Curtis, director of financial aid at Tufts University, "there must be a thorough exchange of information among all sources of student aid, big and small, so that each will know to whom the others are providing financial aid. Once this is established, the timing of the

---

*By 1965, defaults had become more troublesome.—Ed.

awards should be phased. The universities and colleges should make their grants and loans earliest; when this information has reached the other sources, those that give moderate-size aid should make theirs; and finally the agencies that give small awards should fill in the gaps. This way we will be using our financial-aid resources to help more students—and to help them more wisely."

Role of the Federal Government: Two possible forms of Federal participation in student aid were discussed, in addition to the NDEA loan program. One was Federal sponsorship of a summer work program which would assure college students of employment if the labor market cannot absorb them. The consensus was that the labor market is, in fact, absorbing them and paying a good deal more than a Federally sponsored program could pay. There are also job opportunities which enhance a student's total education but which are hard to fill from the regular labor supply; the job of orderly in a mental hospital was mentioned as one example. The immense complexities of administering and policing a Federal program must also be considered.

Considerably more enthusiasm was shown for the possibility of a Federal scholarship program, which might well begin at a moderate size until the administrative kinks were smoothed out. The preference seemed to be for direct aid, rather than tax allowances; and it was assumed that Congress would prefer a modest maximum stipend, which would encourage students to attend colleges in their home states. There was agreement that the country can afford such a program; there was some doubt that the Congress would approve it.

Mr. Esty cautioned, however, that a scholarship program in itself will not be enough. "We have to find out why these kids are not going to college. Money is one reason but not the only one. After we find out why they are not motivated, we can decide what the remedies might be and what the Federal Government can do that local school boards, for example, cannot do."*

---

*The 1965 proposals of President Johnson provide up to 140,000 scholarships—the President points out that 1 out of 3 from low-income families goes to college and 4 out of 5 from high-income families—and also work-study programs that will yield as much as $950 per year.—Ed.

Part IV:
Economic Issues:
Government and Education

13. Allocation of Resources to Education

Michael S. March
Assistant to Chief (Legislative and Program Analysis), Labor and
Welfare Division, U. S. Bureau of Budget

Let me just say at the beginning that I am on my day off and that
nothing I say should be taken as representing the views of the fine
institution with which I am associated.

In approaching the question of the allocation of Federal resources
to education, we might first take a quick look at the total amount
of money which the Federal Government presently spends on education. This quick look, however, turns up a curious problem: there
is no single definition in the Federal Government of what "education"
is.

The budget of the United States Government shows a total expenditure of $866-million for education. Some reports by the Office of
Education show a total of about $2.7-billion.* The essential difference
is that the budget figure relates largely to the Office of Education,
the National Science Foundation and the college-housing program,
while the Office of Education figure is based on a much broader
definition. That definition includes money for surplus property which
the Federal Government turns over to institutions; Defense Department funds of $300-million or so for basic research and development;
some Labor Department money for apprenticeship programs; certain
State Department expenditures for cultural and educational affairs;
some Atomic Energy Commission money for biological research; about
$400-million of Veterans Administration money, which is classified in
the budget under veterans' affairs; and about the same amount in
Department of Agriculture funds for such things as school lunches
and special milk programs. (The Bureau of Census figures, inciden-

---

*The most careful survey (1963) yet made put Federal educational outlays for
F.Y. 1962 at $2.2 billion. House Doc. No. 159, *The Federal Government and Edu-
cation*, p. 115 (by John Morse).—Ed.

tally, shows still another total, about $700-million. Obviously a third
definition is being used there.)

Despite this confusion, it seems clear that the amount spent by
the Federal Government on education has increased significantly over
the last generation, though an attempt to determine precise statistics
leads again to some confusion. By one reliable definition, the total
national expenditures on education—by Federal, state and local governments and by private institutions—rose from about $3-billion in
1940 to about $9-billion in 1950 to about $24.6-billion in 1960.*
During approximately the same period, the Federal expenditures
shown under the Budget Bureau definition rose much more steeply,
from $68-million in 1945 to $866-million in 1960. Under the Office
of Education definition, the total increased only slightly, from $2.5-bil-
lion in 1945 to $2.7-billion in the fiscal year 1963. Nearly all of
the 1945 total, however, went for payments by the Veterans Administration under the G. I. Bill. Such payments now account for barely
one seventh of the total.

(Unfortunately, neither of these Federal figures is computed on
a definition strictly comparable to that used above for the total economy. The trends are clear, but the exact relationship between Federal
and total-economy spending cannot be defined on the basis of these
figures.)

The Federal Government, then, is involved in aid to education
in a major way and to an increasing extent. We are now, I think,
at the threshold of a major evolution—or perhaps a revolution—in
the financing of education which will take the Government's responsibility more formally into account. Questions of how to raise and
allocate funds, under such a Federal commitment, are being discussed
seriously at responsible levels within the Government.

According to the Office of Education, the Federal Government
as a whole is spending $2.7-billion on education in fiscal 1963. At
virtually no point in the Government, however, are these expenditures
reviewed as a whole. The basic decisions are made in several agencies
and by administrators of a vast number of separate programs. It may
be instructive to illustrate this fact in some detail.

The Office of Education has long been charged, by law, with

---

*The 1963-64 estimate is $33.7 billion. The 1964-65 figure was substantially higher.
President Johnson's budget for 1965-66 calls for $1.5 billion of new obligational
authority and the F. Y. 1966 education budget calls for appropriations of 4.1 billion dollars.—Ed.

responsibility for promoting education. Of the \$2.7-billion in Federal spending, however, less than one-fifth is administered by the Office of Education. But the budgetary and legislative proposals concerning even this half a billion dollars or so are not subjected to an expert scrutiny as a whole. The proposals originate in three separate compartments, for lower (elementary and secondary), higher and vocational education. These are coordinated at the commissioner's level, but I think it is fair to say that the program-planning resources of the Office of Education are not very strong and that they tend to draw almost exclusively on professional educationists, rather than on a broad assembly of authorities in various disciplines. For example, the Office of Education does not have a single high-level economist on its staff to analyze the economics of education.

At the next highest echelon, the budgetary requests and the legislative proposals are reviewed in the office of the Secretary of the Department of Health, Education and Welfare. They have a small legislative staff and an embryonic program-analysis staff, but I believe that it is again fair to say that the coordinating and analytical resources of the department are not strong. Yet it is in this department that one would expect to find the principal respository of information, analysis and advice on which the President must rely if he is to discharge properly his responsibilities to the nation in the general area of education.

The department's proposed budget goes to the Budget Bureau, which is organized in five principal divisions. This department, along with the National Science Foundation, is assigned to the Labor and Welfare Division. We also have a Resources and Civil Works Division, which handles Agriculture and Interior, including their school-lunch and Indian-affairs programs. We have a Military Division, which has very substantial cognizance over the outlays that the military makes in training and other areas. We have a Commerce and Finance Division, which handles, among other things, the Housing and Home Finance Agency, including its college-loan programs. Even within the Budget Bureau, then, supervision of Federal spending on education is dispersed.

These divisions perform the basic work on both the budget and legislative proposals submitted by the agencies and departments assigned to them. The budget proposals, by and large, are not very flexible. It is the legislative proposals that are of major significance in forming and developing policy.

The budget proposals of the various divisions are coordinated by an Office of Budget Review; the legislative proposals are coordinated by an Office of Legislative Reference. There is, of course, close liaison between these two offices at the level of the Director of the Budget Bureau, but they are still separate offices. The budget and legislative proposals are brought together for scrutiny only in a very general way, at what we call the directory review. (Science expenditures, by the way, are studied as an entity, though educational expenditures are not. So it can be done.)

The completed budget is re-examined "across the street," as we say, in the President's office. He, with a few assistants, must make the final decisions as to how much money he will request from the Congress and which legislative proposals he will recommend.

In the Congress, the appropriations requests are considered by the appropriations committees in the House and Senate, though for working purposes these have subcommittees which act practically as independent committees. Legislative proposals are not handled so uniformly. On the House side, for example, they are sent to some ten committees which deal with educational matters. The Rules Committee also enters in in a significant way. Even in Congress, therefore, there is no over-all review.

What does it all mean, this dispersal of decision making? In the first place, it should lay to rest any fear of Federal control over education. I think it is fairly clear that the Federal Government, at least as of now, has no consistent policy toward education. It has, rather, a whole series of policies relating to specific agency missions.

At the same time, it seems clear that we must not rest content with this confusion and uncertainty. We must quickly compile an accurate picture, total and in detail, of the Government's present support of education. We must do this partly as a basis for determining what the Government can and should contribute in the long run. We must develop some consistency among the objectives of our educational programs, so that their total results can be more efficiently controlled without misplaced emphases and waste. We must have searching analyses of such economic factors as the contribution of education to national growth* and the marginal returns of Federal programs in education.

This entire subject is ripe for advanced economic analysis. Such an analysis is, in fact, long overdue.

---

*See Chapter 16, "Education and Economic Productivity."—Ed.

Senator John E. Powers
President of the Senate, General Court,
Commonwealth of Massachusetts

The subject matter of this meeting is the allocation of resources to education. Professor Harris has suggested that, as a representative of the General Court [Legislature] of the Commonwealth of Massachusetts, it would be pertinent and appropriate for me to discuss how the Legislature determines allocation of state resources to education. Although I accepted the suggestion, I hope you will not keep me strictly bound to it, particularly since the Legislature plays only a secondary or subsidiary role in the allocation of state resources.

Please allow me at the very outset to clarify my role among you. I dare say that I am the only person present who has not pursued his formal education beyond the secondary school. At an age when most boys and girls today are eagerly looking forward to an exciting and rewarding college life, I had been working for several years, helping to support a widowed mother and younger children. But, as is often the case, my awareness of the advantages which I did not enjoy as a youth has imbued me, throughout my public career, with a desire to make them available to all in our Commonwealth, particularly to the children of our Commonwealth. And, to the best of my knowledge, every member of the General Court shares that desire.

I am not here either as a champion of or an apologist for the Massachusetts Legislature, although our record in the past session [1961-62], especially in the field of education, is one of which I am very proud. I am here merely to lay before you certain facts from which you must draw your own conclusions.

All allocation of state resources is made by the Governor. The Constitutional Convention of 1917, 1918, and 1919 approved Amendments 45-66, inclusive. These were submitted to popular referendum and adopted. Among them, the 63rd, ratified on November 5, 1918, reads in part as follows: *"Article 63, Section 2. The Budget.* Within three weeks after the convening of the General Court, the Governor shall recommend to the General Court a budget which shall contain a statement of all proposed expenditures of the Commonwealth for the fiscal year . . . For the purpose of preparing his budget, the Governor shall have power to require any board, commission, officer or department to furnish him with any information which he may deem necessary."

Clearly, therefore, it is not only the prerogative but the duty of the Governor of the Commonwealth to allocate the funds required by each state department. This includes, of course, the Department of Education.

In actual practice, the Governor must rely almost completely upon his department heads for budget estimates. Rarely does a department head receive as much as he requests. Here undoubtedly lies a weakness in the budget systems of Massachusetts, the Federal Government and most of the other states of which I have knowledge.

The department head naturally and instinctively wants the finest of personnel, buildings and equipment for his department. He wants better salaries, more key people, expanded facilities. He may urge the institution of new programs within his department. But all these things cost money; and department heads, no matter how able and conscientious they may be, cannot possibly have an over-all and accurate picture of the state's economy.

The Governor, on the other hand, has before him the financial facts of life as presented by the Commissioner of Taxation, the Budget Commissioner and the Comptroller. He knows what the state's income will be and how much he can spend without increasing taxes. Accordingly, when all department estimates are presented, he is invariably compelled to pare them. And the story doesn't end there. Once the Governor has trimmed all estimates to fit into a net package called the budget, it must then be approved by the General Court.

Here, we, for the first time, take an active part in the allocation of state funds. Although this part is only secondary, it is, nevertheless, authoritative and important, because we can cut still further or we can increase.

Since the budget is a money bill, it must first go to the House of Representatives. There it is referred to the House Committee on Ways and Means, which slashes, changes or adds. The committee's final product is then debated fully on the floor of the House, where it is again subject to cuts or increases. Then, having passed the House, it is sent to the Senate. Here the same procedure is followed: referral to the Senate Committee on Ways and Means, followed by debate on the floor of the Senate. At each step in this branch, more budget changes are in order.

The practical and experienced department head knows all this. He realizes well that his estimated budget must encounter all the hurdles—Governor, House Ways and Means, House, Senate Ways and Means, Senate and final approval by the Governor. Can he be blamed, therefore, for adding a little fat here and there, in the hope that only the fat will be cut? Who must bear the responsibility if, in its winding course, a budget ends up with the fat intact but some of the best meat removed?

In any event, this is how the system works, for education as for all other departments. It is not perfect by any means, but it has evolved through trial and error and experience into what I believe to be the best method yet devised for the allocation of public funds.

Let us see what this system did to the budget for the Massachusetts Department of Education for the fiscal year 1962-1963.

Roughly, the budget is divided into two main areas called "state purposes" and "local aid." State purposes include all state colleges, community colleges and other state schools. Local aid refers to such local programs as vocational schools, transportation, lunches, adult classes and school-building construction, among others.

For state purposes the Department of Education requested $48,-655,000; for local aid it asked $55,725,000. The Governor [John A. Volpe] reduced these amounts to $38,171,000 and $50,632,000, respectively. The Legislature, in turn, shaved these figures slightly to $37,618,000 and $49,816,000.

In other words, the Governor chopped a sizable $15.5-million from the department's estimated needs, from over $104-million down to less than $89-million; while the General Court reduced the Governor's total by another $1.3-million. Therefore, although this discussion is certainly nonpolitical in character, and without attempting to assess the justification for reductions, if any onus is to be attached for alleged failure to support Massachusetts education, such onus must fall upon a Republican governor rather than a Democratic legislature.

Of course, it can be argued that the General Court could have restored the Governor's cuts. And in some quarters, both the Governor and General Court have been applauded for their actions. But these arguments are all rather academic. You are interested primarily in what funds were allocated to education and how they were allocated. This is a factual report of exactly what happened. Whom to blame or whom to credit is somewhat beside the point.

It is often claimed that Massachusetts does too little for education. That may well be true, although I personally believe that statistics can almost always be utilized to bolster any side of any argument. In point of fact, the $87.4-million allocated in this year's state budget for education represents approximately 17 per cent of the entire budget. Except for the highway program, which is financed by the gasoline tax, the item for education is the largest in the entire budget.

The amounts distributed for local aid are triple what they were only ten or twelve years ago. From 1950 through 1963, appropriations for capital outlay for state educational institutions will total $140-million. Operating appropriations for those same institutions have risen from $5-million to $17.5-million in the past decade. I do not contend that these sums are sufficient. Perhaps they are not even adequate, but they certainly represent a sizable effort.

There can be no question that amendments are warranted in our program of local aid for education. That program is based on formulas which are obviously antiquated. In general, their most important elements include assessed valuations of 1945, plus current school-age population.

The School Building Assistance Law also requires adjustment. It now provides for new construction grants, but nothing for repairs and renovation. Because of population losses, our larger cities have done little in the way of new school construction but have borne substantial costs for repairs and renovation, all without state assistance. On the other hand, our suburban areas, with doubling and tripling populations, have been forced to erect new structures on both the primary and secondary level. For these new schools the local communities do receive state funds. Taxpayers in the cities are thus being called upon to support small-town school systems while receiving little or no help for their own.

Before closing, I believe it pertinent to discuss briefly the positive steps taken by the General Court this past session in the field of education. After a quarter century in the Legislature, I agree with many experts that these steps constituted the most momentous educational advances in this century.

First, we increased the minimum salary for public-school teachers from $4,000 to $4,500 a year. We also passed a mandatory provision for equal salaries for men and women teachers. Both measures met with considerable Republican opposition; the second was passed over the Governor's veto.

Second, we created a state medical school to be associated with the University of Massachusetts at Springfield, Worcester or Boston. I have no intention of abusing the hospitality extended to me here, but it is common knowledge that Harvard, as well as the other two medical schools in the Commonwealth, have long-established admission practices which militate against Massachusetts students. In some instances these practices have included quota systems against certain students on the basis of creed or color. In others, they have favored students from outside the Commonwealth. Whether these practices still continue—and if so, to what extent—is no longer of any consequence, for in about ten years the first medical practitioners from our new school will be ready to grapple with the increasing medical needs of an exploding population in Massachusetts. The only requirement to be demanded of these doctors is that they be qualified both for entrance to medical school and for the practice of medicine.

Third, the General Court granted fiscal autonomy to the University of Massachusetts. This means that once the university budget is approved, the trustees can expend it in any way they see fit. They can transfer funds from one account to another, and their academic employees will not be subject to the minimum and maximum salary schedules applicable to other state employees.

University officials had long urged such a step by the Legislature, on the ground that without it they could not obtain the best teaching personnel. The Democratic leadership in the General Court, whose spokesman I am today, finally went along.

Frankly, I have some misgivings about this action on our part, praised though it has been by educational experts everywhere. I recognize the logic behind the proponents of fiscal autonomy—that is why I supported it—but it does create other problems, and it certainly raises other serious questions. For instance, if the state colleges and community colleges request the same autonomy, should they receive it? If not, won't we eventually be faced with a deteriorating morale among professors of the state colleges, who will be receiving smaller salaries than professors at the state university doing the same work? Or suppose that the Departments of Mental Health and Public Health demand the same treatment, so that they can obtain the services of doctors whom they badly need . . . These and other questions must be raised, and I certainly do not have the answers. But at least we took a bold and decisive step forward. Let us see how it works.

Finally, the General Court approved the creation of a special commission to study all facets of education in the Commonwealth. The commission, which has already been appointed, consists of three state senators and seven members of the House, plus eleven private citizens, at least six of whom must have either teaching or administrative experience on the grammar-school, secondary-school and college levels. The commission is empowered to rent quarters, travel within or without the state, hold hearings and hire a recognized expert as secretary. And to show that we mean business, we have granted the commission the generous sum of $250,000 for its work.

The commission is to report to the Legislature by December 1963.* I sincerely anticipate that all the questions raised here will be answered in that report, and many others as well—whether the state is contributing sufficiently to local education; what the formulas for state distribution should be; whether fiscal autonomy for the university is warranted, and whether it should be extended to other state educational institutions; whether more or less emphasis should be placed on the sciences in our grammar and secondary schools; how to provide higher salaries for teachers; what to do about regional schools; and how to build schools by the most efficient and least expensive methods.

The commission has the personnel, the finances and the ability to answer these questions and a score of others. If even more money or more time is required, I am sure that the Legislature will lend a favorable ear to requests for either or both.

In any case, we have finally embarked on a program which should, in a reasonable time, result in expert and authoritative answers to all the issues which face us in education. I have no doubt whatsoever that your General Court will accept the commission's recommendations and that the educational prognosis for Massachusetts is brighter than ever before in its history.

Kermit Morrissey
Chairman, Massachusetts Community College Board;
Assistant to the President, Brandeis University

Many complex political issues are involved in the allocation by the Commonwealth of Massachusetts of funds for education. I want now to discuss only one aspect of this allocation: state budget support for post-secondary-school education. And in this connection, I want to examine primarily the very important factor of immediacy.

State support in this area is an immediate problem for Massachusetts. Policies, legislative authorizations and execution must be completed rather rapidly to compensate for the very long delay, only recently overcome, in recognizing the need for expansion. The immediacy of this phase of education development is intensely pragmatic;

---

*The commission has reported.—Ed.

it is influenced very little by political rivalries or by the religious division within the electorate—factors which have severely limited local school aid by the state government. There are, of course, differences in approach between the parties: Democrats tend to be uncritically sympathetic to proposals for new schools and enlarged public responsibility, while Republicans are less inclined to move rapidly. However, the need for expansion of collegiate facilities is widely accepted inside the legislative organization of the state government.

The major pressure affecting budget allocations in this area is, in my judgment, the widespread public concern about the need for expanded educational opportunity. This pressure is reflected in the inchoate public expression of need, the popularity of education expansion and the apparent unpopularity of the contrary position. Educational exposure for young people is popularly equated with the benefits of a New Frontier "welfare state." Post-secondary-school training (including college enrollment) has become, quite simply, a bread--and-butter issue of Massachusetts politics. This single, well-advertised feature of the current educational scene has stimulated the political environment and has created a hospitable climate for increased public spending to provide more student places.

The expression of need in this area is very personal and pressing to politicians. For example, one major legislative leader, a man who is very powerful in the Legislature and whose previous position on education had been largely negative, recently came to the Executive Office and expressly requested permission to put in the budget an authorization to establish a regional community college to service his district. His rationale was very direct and simple. He had been harassed by innumerable phone calls from people in his district, asking about college opportunities for their children. "There just aren't enough spaces," he said, "and I have to get out from under."

Immediacy, as in this case, may be felt as direct personal knowledge by a legislator or an office holder about specific people who need assistance. The politician, in such cases, is not inclined to review patiently and technically the measures that promise to relieve him of his frustrations. Rather, he commits himself to very large expenditures on the basis of accumulating pressures from individual constituents in his own district.

Immediacy in Massachusetts is also affected by the national publicity campaign about education during the last six or seven years. The needs have been repeated continually through all media, and being "for" educational improvements and expansion has become a reflex action for most Massachusetts public officials.

The significant observable fact in Massachusetts is that these immediate political pressures for post-secondary-school expansion and improvement are reflected directly in the political process—and in a very positive way. Note the recent series of educational bills and programs, all of which have been accepted without furor. These provide for new colleges, a new medical school, fiscal autonomy for the University of Massachusetts, a salary of $25,000 for the president of the university (the Governor's salary is only $20,000) and so forth. Each of these measures has been achieved without fanfare and without major political struggle. No major educational goal has failed. Indeed, most of them have been readily accepted by groups in the Legislature whose previous position on educational development had been negative.

A new style of political service is in vogue. Education is linked to life chances, and politicians in Massachusetts are reacting to the immediately expressed needs of their constituencies. This is the major political fact governing resource allocation for education in recent years.

One form of pressure that influences who gets what in the state budget is competition—in this case, competition among the six boards charged with responsibility for post-secondary-school education. (There is one board for the University of Massachusetts, one for the nine state colleges plus the College of Art, three for the three technical institutes, and one to establish a new system of regional community colleges.) This competition poses a serious problem of balance, since the units offering the most rapid expansion—that is, the most immediacy—have a marked political advantage in the division of the spoils. This advantage is not related to quality, and it has little to do with the total educational enterprise within the state. It is a stark fact of political arithmetic, which channels funds into a rapidly expanding enterprise without considering what other desirable goals must be postponed or abandoned as a result.

For example, what are the relative advantages of establishing two or three new community colleges, as against enabling the university to establish a special research fund with an appropriation of $200,000? This type of question is virtually never posed. Instead, specific decisions have been made by recourse to extremely general political and economic preferences.

Legislators of the dominant Democratic party are led, in fiscal matters, by the chairmen of the House and Senate Ways and Means Committees. These chairmen bear a relationship to their fellow members analogous to that of the Rules Committees of the U. S. Congress. Their predilection it so happens, is to favor an inevitable expansion of public higher education at bargain rates. They are inclined to be guided largely by the unit costs of different types of public higher education, and they attach a disproportionate significance to the cheapest unit. The two-year community colleges have been given a splendid start as a result of this myopic view, but at the expense of the state university and the four-year state colleges. This lopsided trend does not represent a long step forward in rational planning or resources for higher education in Massachusetts.

In 1962 a law was enacted that asked the various boards of higher education to agree on the percentage of the total appropriation that each board should receive. This was an effort to create a buffer. The Ways and Means Committees were saying, in effect, "We've been taking it on the chin. Now let them make the tough decision." This move reflected the extreme frustration of the appropriations committees. They are asked for funds that cannot ever be provided in full, and if they balk, they may be labelled "anti-education." They cannot win, and they dare not lose.

I predict, however, that the six separate educational boards will not submit an agreed limit to their own appetites. This would violate the first law of political expansion. Instead, the boards will initially support all educational requests; and later, when the legislative committees have to square hope with reality, they will press their individual requests through a variety of formal and informal devices readily available to them. The most effective of these devices are the introduction of their needs by individual legislators, favorable comment on their needs by sympathetic newspapers and, in extreme cases, the organization of a full-scale program designed to polarize public opinion.

It was indicative of the present uncertainty in allocations for educational developments in Massachusetts that a new commission with adequate financial support was created to review the conduct and organization of all education in the state. This action was in response to a substantial publicity campaign by a major newpaper in Boston, and the proposal enjoyed strong legislative support. It will, under optimum conditions, produce better order and more effective coordination of effort. Such a commission, however, cannot make ugly facts pleasant; and the long neglect of reason in the state budget for education will make a more rational plan difficult to sell in the political market place.

A final note should be sounded on the expansionist psychology which now controls the scope and direction of political pressures in Massachusetts relating to education. The state's bookkeeping procedures make it possible to project an annual budget surplus, but this is only a political stunt. In fact, the state has been expending in excess of income for many years, and the present policy of expanding higher education and authorizing new colleges annually cannot be continued unless some new resources are made available. This situation is well-known, both to elected officials and to those charged with developing education programs and budgets for their support. Yet the latter group increase their demands annually, secure in the knowledge that history and immediacy are on their side. The legislators bend in response to political demand. They are disturbed by the apparently endless upswing of educational spending, but they are unable to provide meaningful obstacles or alternatives.

In this setting, the possibility of waste and duplication of effort is maximized. Each educational board has its own mission, unrelated by law or temperament to those of other boards engaged in comparable activity. The office of the Governor is relatively weak and, in view of the brief two-year term, is in poor position either to plan educational development or to apply priorities to the rapidly expanding enterprise. The Legislature is most sensitive to immediate issues; it is most vulnerable to exposures of neglect and oversight; and it is most in need of dramatic evidence of concern for the public welfare.

This troubled situation appears to be unpromising, but we must keep in mind the fact that education has been severely neglected in Massachusetts during the last decade. Much of what is being done should be done; perhaps it should be done even more swiftly. But the absence of over-all plans and goals makes the present system inherently unstable.

One is reminded of the starving man who, when suddenly confronted with ample food, killed himself through excess indulgence. Political pressures in Massachusetts today invite such over-indulgence. Political immediacy is both a promise and a threat. Only major fiscal reshaping of education, from grade school through college, will make the promise real and the threat remote.

SUMMARY OF THE DISCUSSION

A brief, general discussion followed the reading of each of the three papers.

The discussion of Mr. March's paper was led by Francis Bator, associate professor of economics at the Massachusetts Institute of Technology. Mr. Bator described the Federal Government's present share in education as "appallingly small" and asserted that there is a strong case for much greater Federal involvement in the allocation of resources to education. He rejected economic arguments as a basis for policy decisions on the issue, since "propositions derived from general principles of economic efficiency or similar factors are of extraordinarily little relevance, given all the political restraints." Rather, the issue must be decided on the basis of "some very crude gut-judgments as to what constitutes a good society."

Mr. Bator stated the argument for minimum Federal involvement: "If the local community's parents decide that they do not want to educate their children well, why should that be anyone else's concern?" The answer, he pointed out, is that education within any community has a significant effect on all other communities in the nation. "The quality of the political society in which my children will live ten years from now will be affected by, say, West Virginians. West Virginians will elect Federal congressmen and two senators. And my children's world will be benefited by the physicists, lawyers, composers and novelists—and even the economists—who will develop among West Virginians if the education there is good rather than sloppy." It follows that "the nation as a whole has a stake in influencing the level of resources being allocated to education in particular segments of the nation."

A corollary, Mr. Bator noted, is that the doctrine of equal opportunity "leads to a very strong presumption in favor of the richer states making transfers of resources to the poorer states." Massachusetts, for example, ranks relatively high in per capita personal income; and it would probably resist a large Federal program because the net transfer of resources is likely to be away from Massachusetts. "Precisely this reluctance, I think, justifies a large Federal program."

There was general agreement that in debating this issue, as Mr. Bator defined it, economists are no more qualified than any other citizens. The issue calls for value judgments and is a matter for general public concern.

The discussion of Senator Powers' speech was sparked by Mr. Harris' observation that, according to a study made a few years earlier, Massachusetts ranked lowest of all states in the proportion of its personal income that is spent by the state on education. "That is not a good record for a state that, in the nineteenth century, ranked first in education."

An attempt to trace the reasons for this low rating led to a consideration of several factors, beginning with problems of taxation. To increase spending means to increase taxes, Senator Powers noted, and Massachusetts already has the heaviest burden of direct taxation of all the states. To impose more corporate or property taxes would discourage industry, and taxpayers are opposed to higher personal taxes. A withholding system is one possible solution.* A sales tax might also be acceptable if it were called frankly an educational tax and if the revenues went exclusively to education according to a fair and fixed system of allocations.†

A second factor, Mr. Morrissey explained, are certain religious and political facts that influence state spending on education. "At present about 919,000 children are enrolled in our public schools. Another 205,000 are enrolled in parochial schools. Thus approximately 18 per cent of the total enrolled student body are from families which must pay a dual charge for schools. Inevitably, a substantial segment of the population is divided on the crucial issue of state aid for local schools." This split is reflected primarily among legislators of the Democratic party, which has a generous legislative majority. The Republicans, at the same time, favor rigid spending limits on local communities as a matter of political philosophy. The combination poses a major obstacle to an increase in state aid.

Domination of the Legislature by suburban and rural communities was mentioned as a third important factor. Senator Powers summarized the history of the equalization formula under which state funds for education are allocated to various communities. After World War II this formula, which was then quite fluid, was revised to favor the small towns, since these were encountering an extraordinary population increase with a consequent need for new school buildings. Now those schools are built, and the money is needed for repair to older schools in the larger cities and towns, but the legislators from rural areas will not permit a new revision of the formula. Senator Powers

---

*Since introduced.—Ed.

†A sales tax seems on the way in 1965.—Ed.

anticipated that reapportionment decisions by the U. S. Supreme Court would help to correct this imbalance.

The role of the Governor as a fourth factor came in for some debate. Senator Powers had indicated that the Governor has the power to shape his budget. This was qualified by Mr. Morrissey, who noted that Massachusetts is a "weak governor" state and that the Governor's power lies largely in his ability to persuade his department heads and the Legislature of the wisdom of his proposals. With real determination, he can achieve many of his goals, even in the event of legislative hostility. He has, however, relatively little direct power, and it is not infrequent for boards and departments to reverse the Governor's budget decisions by direct appeal to the legislative leaders. In some instances, the Governor is virtually an innocent bystander.

A fifth factor, in Senator Powers' view, is the experience and psychology of the average legislator. A representative or senator must deal with policy in many areas, and it is impossible for him to become expert in them all. Not many have served long enough to understand in detail the issues and implications of state support for education. The legislator is also "in the unfortunate position of being elected rather than selected." If he must run for re-election by explaining why he voted to increase taxes, rather than why he voted to lower them, he is placing himself in an almst indefensible position.

A number of other related topics were discussed somewhat inconclusively. These included the possibility of a Federal education tax; the contribution which Massachusetts makes to education by its complete tax exemption of private educational institutions; and the political significance of the sharply rising number of students enrolled in public institutions financed by the state.

"We are an old state," Senator Powers observed, "and we have problems that have not yet caught up with many of the other states. I think that the others will find, as the years go along, that their problems will be not much different from ours."

The discussion of Mr. Morrissey's paper opened on the question of the extent to which states can solve their educational problems alone, without recourse to Federal financial support. Mr. Morrissey suggested that the amounts that would be available to Massachusetts under any proposed Federal law, though they would be welcome, would be far from adequate to the state's needs. Only the poorest states have reason to wait for enlarged Federal support before beginning to improve their educational facilities. All other states should —and can—set to work immediately with their own resources.

Mr. Harris offered statistical encouragement for this position. "If state and local governments continue to increase their expenditures for the next decade at their present rate, the total might rise from $50-billion to $100-billion, enough to cover almost all their needs. This allows for the rise in prices in each area, so that it represents a tremendous potential. I have always argued, as most good Keynesians have, that the Federal Government has a better tax structure and can do the job with less general sacrifice. But nobody could have anticipated the amazing increase in state and local revenues, especially from property taxes, since 1950."

These increased resources are actually being released for educational purposes, Mr. Morrissey noted, largely because of the immediacy of the issue. "The sheer political force of education as a value can now be brought to bear in the Ways and Means Committees and with legislative leaders. You no longer have to go with your hat in your hand. You are talking about the life chances of boys and girls in every legislative district. The politicians know that and welcome the chance to support appropriations that will go in part to their own districts." Industry is also showing immediate concern about the level of education in communities where it is contemplating expansion or new location, and this concern is a powerful incentive for increased state support.

One other question of general significance was examined in this discussion: the possibility that the six educational boards will gradually become coordinated, perhaps in a single general board of higher education. Mr. Morrissey suggested that this would happen, "though whether in one master board or two or three, I have no way of knowing. There are many alternatives." But it will not happen quickly, partly because of the expansionist psychology of the boards, partly because some of them are resentful of others.

The expansionist psychology, he explained, is essentially healthy; the boards must not be willing to settle for the present inadequate facilities. But the resentment is not always rational. A board may, for example, see $1-million allocated to another board and conclude, "That money might have gone to us." More objectively, that money probably would not have gone to education at all if an aggressive board had not successfully pressed its demands.

14. Training Manpower in Relation to Needs

Howard Rosen
Assistant Director for Manpower, Automation and Research,
Office of Manpower, Automation and Training,
U. S. Department of Labor

On March 15, 1962, President Kennedy signed the Manpower Development and Training Act. I would like first to discuss some of the reasons why this Act was passed and then tell you a little about the problems we face in its operation.

The Manpower Act was passed against the background of a 5.5 per cent unemployment rate. At the time, about 4-million people were unemployed, with a sharp rise in those who had been unemployed long-term (fifteen weeks or more) and very long-term (six months or more). We could also identify special groups in the labor force who had a persistently high unemployment rate, much higher than the rest of the population. These groups were mainly young persons, older workers, Negroes, workers attached to declining industries such as the railroad industry and mining, workers located in depressed areas and unskilled laborers.

Another factor which contributed to the passage of the Manpower Act was the basic, postwar shift in employment in the United States from goods-producing activities (manufacturing, mining and construction) to service-producing activities (transportation, finance, public utilities, trade and government). In 1947, about 26.7-million people were employed in producing goods; by 1962, this number had dropped to 25.3-million. During this same period, the ranks of people employed in service activities rose from 25.4-million to 35.2-million. While this is a recent development, it appears to be a definite trend.

A third and collateral factor which led to the passage of the

Manpower Act was that white-collar employment is increasing at a much faster rate than blue-collar employment. In 1956, when the balance actually shifted, the fact did not create much excitement, but from 1958 to 1962 the trend became increasingly obvious. More and more people are being employed in professional, technical, sales and managerial jobs—in jobs as proprietors, engineers, teachers, technicians and nurses—than in jobs as construction craftsmen, semiskilled workers or laborers. There has been a decline especially in the number of unskilled jobs, calling for people whose contribution to the labor force is a strong back and not necessarily much education and training. The jobs which have increased most radically have been those requiring higher levels of education and training.

A fourth factor in securing passage of the Act was the number of people who are unemployed or underemployed because their skills are obsolete as a result of technological change and changes in consumer demand. Many of these people have worked in coal mining, railroading, textiles and tobacco, among other industries.

A fifth factor was that, during the 1960's, about 26-million new young workers are expected to enter the American labor force—the largest such influx of any decade in our history. Many of these youngsters will enter the labor market direct from high school; they will be seeking jobs without attending college or receiving further training of any sort. In fact, about 7.5-million of this group will consist of the so-called dropouts, who will not have completed even a high-school education.

A sixth factor was the fact that the labor market frequently does not operate efficiently. While the Act was being considered, Congressional committees visited some of the depressed areas. In Wheeling, West Virginia—to offer just one of the most striking examples—they found that the city had a very high unemployment rate, with thousands of able-bodied men in the prime working-age group unable to find jobs. Yet a visit to the local employment service revealed that there were unfilled job orders for workers—in this case, for people able to repair automatic transmissions. Some of the unemployed workers were automobile mechanics, but when they learned the trade, there were no automatic transmissions around, and their training had not kept pace with the technological change. It quickly became obvious that the workers who most needed training or retraining could least afford to pay for it themselves. Congress drew the conclusion that the Manpower Act could help to make the labor market operate more efficiently.

Let me describe very briefly how the Manpower Development and Training Act operates. The local Employment Service office is supposed to examine the local labor market and develop a job inventory. That is, it is supposed to go to employers and ask them, "Do you have any job vacancies now, or do you anticipate any job vacancies?" and then convert this data into a listing of current and potential vacancies. Next, the office calls in either the unemployed or the underemployed workers and, after testing and counseling some of them, selects those who cannot be expected to find jobs unless they are retrained. The workers who are thus selected are sent to local vocational education schools to be trained for jobs for which—this is a quotation from the Act—there is a "reasonable expectation of employment." That word "reasonable" can be interpreted in several ways.

A man who is the head of a household or the head of a family and who has had a two-year attachment to the labor force is eligible for a training allowance under the Act. The allowance is equivalent to the average unemployment compensation paid in his state and can be awarded for up to 52 weeks. The training, in theory, can extend beyond 52 weeks, but the training allowance cannot.

After the worker has been trained in the local vocational school for an occupation selected by the local Employment Service office, he comes back to the office for counseling and placement. This is where the Act pays off. The ultimate objective of the Act, of course, is to place unemployed workers in jobs, and its success or failure will depend not on how well we train people, not on how well we select them or counsel them or guide them, but on how successful we are in placing them. (There are special provisions in the Act for training young people, farm people and so on, but I shall not go into that here.)

The Act is not a cure-all for unemployment in the United States. That vast problem will not be resolved by its passage. The real hope in this Act is simply to get a better matching between unemployed workers and job openings by enabling those people who can least afford training to be trained. Yet, in my opinion, this Act is a major step forward in the economic maturity of the American people. Prior to this, if a man lost his job in peacetime, we either did nothing or we put him on welfare or on unemployment compensation. We were doing nothing positive to get him employed again. The welfare reports from Cook County, Illinois, showing the existence of second- and third-generation welfare recipients, indicate the futility of that approach. The Manpower Act at least turns us into the right path. It cannot solve the unemployment problem, but it does contribute to a solution.

Let us look at some of the very early problems under the Manpower Act. One which became obvious very quickly is illiteracy. About 3.1-million men and women in our labor force are classified as funtionally illiterate; they have not had education above the fifth grade. We have not yet learned how to devise effective training programs for these people, though I shall describe in a moment an effort in this direction at Virginia State College. Most of the people in our training programs, however, have a high-school education; relatively few have not attended high school at all.

A second immediate problem is the concentration of unemployment in certain areas, such as Pennsylvania, West Virginia, Massachusetts and Puerto Rico, combined with the immobility of many unemployed workers. The Act is oriented to the local labor market, not the national labor market—a fact that will present more difficulties as time goes on.

A third problem is the age distribution among the unemployed. The Act was supposedly aiming at the hard-core unemployed, and people over 45 are among the most difficult cases, but we are still not reaching a large proportion of these people. Only about eleven per cent of all those enrolled for training have been 45 or over; most have been in the so-called prime working-age group, between 22 and 44.

A fourth and fundamental problem is the variation among job prospects in different industries. We have been happily surprised, on the one hand, by the variety of occupations in which openings are anticipated by the local Employment Service offices. On their recommendations we are training people to enter vocations as draftsmen, practical nurses, clerks, stenographers, typists, cooks, waiters, nurses aides, turret-lathe operators, welders, sewing-machine operators, pipefitters, machinists, automobile mechanics, automobile body repairmen, electronic mechanics, electronic assemblers and so on. Our record of placement in these jobs has been good.

On the other hand, in the light of the occupational projections which the Department of Labor has developed over the years, we realize that we are training many workers for occupations which are not among the fastest growing. We cannot take an unemployed miner, for example, and train him to be a mathematician, an electronics technician or a physicist. We are necessarily training for many semi-skilled and service jobs, for which the number of job openings anticipated in future years is relatively limited.

Fifth and last, a problem more diffuse than the others but no less crucial is the lack of motivation among many unemployed workers to undertake training. We encountered this, for example, with a training program that is part of a very interesting research project in Norfolk, Virginia. There was a large layoff at the Norfolk Navy Yard some time ago, and most of those affected were unskilled Negroes. Anticipating this layoff, the commandant of the yard asked the Virginia State College division at Norfolk, which is a Negro institution, to find some way to help these people. It so happens that some of the faculty members there have national reputations as authorities in developing teaching techniques for helping illiterates to become literate quickly. The college devised an interdisciplinary research project combining occupational and literacy training; the project is being subsidized by both the Department of Health, Education and Welfare and the Department of Labor.

When the college tried to get the unemployed workers to come in for training or retraining, it discovered the publicity through newspapers, radio and televisions could not do the job. Faculty members learned that it was much more effective to go to the churches, both the store-front churches and the larger churches, and ask the ministers to spread the word. The faculty went also to the barbers and the operators of pool halls and asked them to pass along the news that unemployed workers could be trained at the college and that money would be available for training allowances. At first, entrants were scarce; but as those who enrolled went home and reported that the rumors were true, Virginia State became overwhelmed with applicants. All were Negroes; whites in the area would not participate in an integrated program.

The sociologists on the faculty, meanwhile, taking note of the matriarchal society among Negroes, recommended that the wives of the trainees be directly involved in the training program. For example, when the full quota of trainees had enrolled, a dinner was held to which all the wives were invited, and the program was explained at that time to everyone. This was especially important because, for most families, the training allowance was less than the man's income through such odd jobs as he had been able to find. Since the regulations then forbade trainees to work even part-time—this has since been changed—the training period entailed an economic loss, and the wife knew that she would have to carry more of the burden of supporting the family than she had before.

By way of conclusion, let me note five propositions which suggest the philosophy of the people who framed the Manpower Development and Training Act:

First, everyone can be trained. We must not be hasty in deciding who can be trained, or who should be trained, or who is capable of being trained. Many more people can be salvaged and made employable again than we have believed until recently.

Second, at some time or other, everybody needs to be trained or retrained. In all probability, many people in our labor force will have to be trained and retrained throughout their working lives, for as long as technological change continues at an accelerated pace, we will have much more occupational mobility than we have had in the past. People should therefore consider training and retraining, not as a peculiar process suited to a handful of people, but as a definite part of the entire career of every working person.

Third, every geographic area, whether it is an area of economic expansion or of decline, needs training or retraining programs and facilities. Training should not be confined only to depressed areas.

Fourth, all vocational education given under the Manpower Act must be of the highest quality if the Act is to succeed.

Finally, we must, above all, maintain our democratic framework and our concept of democracy, allowing people a free choice of occupation, if this Act is to be successful and contribute to the reduction of unemployment in the United States.

COMMENT BY . . . *John Dunlop*
                        Professor of Economics
                        Harvard University

I should like to offer three observations, not meant in any way to depreciate the MDTA program but designed to help put it in perspective.

First of all, we ought to see the program in its true magnitude. It is really a relatively small program. At the present time [April 1963] America has 600,000 or more people who have been unemployed for at least 26 weeks; nearly as many more have been unemployed between 15 and 25 weeks. Thus well over a million people are experiencing long-term unemployment. So if we are talking about training 100,000 or 200,000 people, we are talking about a relatively small proportion of even the so-called hard core of unemployment. Let us get that point clear.

The second observation is that, as Mr. Rosen has well said, a large number of new jobs are coming in the professional and technical fields for which this sort of training is quite inappropriate. Since the Manpower Retraining Administration has not yet gone into training college teachers, engineers and so forth, there is a significant group of jobs that it does not touch.

The third observation is, I think, most important: We must be very cautious in deciding what share of America's training and retraining needs is to be met by the Government and what share is to be met by private parties, especially by industry and labor unions. In the past, the largest share of our retraining has been done outside our formal educational system; it has been done by the individual companies and the individual unions. The pipefitters, for example, have an agreement with the national contractors under which two or three per cent of the payroll is deducted and turned into a national fund which is used to retrain existing journeymen to handle new processes and new technologies. Six hundred instructors are engaged full-time year-round in this retraining process. The electricians' union has a similar program which, though not quite as elaborate, is in many ways just as good.

This preventive approach, it seems to me, is an indispensable measure in coping with the problem of unemployment. Existing employees must be continuously trained to handle a wider range of duties, so that as one type of job disappears, they will be capable of doing another. It follows that the Manpower Act must be administered so as to stimulate, rather than deter, this kind of training. Thus a series of fundamental questions arises: To what extent are the MDTA appropriations used to subsidize training programs already under way? To what extent are they used to develop new programs? To what extent do its programs replace training which a company would have done anyway? How much are they a net addition to training?

If we are going to train 100,000 or 200,000 people a year, when more than a million workers have been unemployed over 15 weeks and additions to the labor force are coming in at a torrential rate, this Government training program at its present scale can have only a small impact on the total situation. What the Government really needs to do is to stimulate the intensification and broadening of training programs which companies, unions and other private parties in the community can carry on. My hope is that the Manpower Act effort will be used to stimulate and support such activities by private groups. Unless that is its main impact, its effect on the challenge of unemployment may be very small.

SUMMARY OF THE DISCUSSION

Five topics were examined in the general discussion:

Problems in determining manpower needs: "No one knows how many job vacancies exist in the American economy. We have been pressing the Department of Labor vigorously to carry out a decent study of current vacancies." This remark by Mr. Harris triggered a sharp exchange of ideas on the difficulties in determining both immediate and long-range manpower needs.

With regard to immediate manpower needs, two practical problems were identified. *First,* the local Employment Service offices are ordinarily not well informed, even about their own areas. One discussant asserted that "most private businesses prefer to deal with private employment bureaus. A number of employers do not even bother to contact the state bureau except to fill extremely menial jobs."

Second, unemployed workers are not effectively informed of appropriate job openings in other states and regions. Mr. Rosen observed that the Manpower Act was specifically designed to train workers for jobs in their own cities or states. It would be a violation of the law to train a man for work elsewhere, and certainly no funds have been provided to help workers relocate after they have been trained. The research office of the Department of Labor does, of course, gather data on employment opportunities across the nation and does provide guidelines on significant developments to all local Employment Service offices.

The difficulties in determining long-range needs were more to the point of this session, primarily because the Manpower Development and Training Act requires that workers be trained for jobs in which there is a "reasonable expectation of employment." It thus becomes necessary to determine accurately what jobs will be open *in a given city or state* at the conclusion of a given training period and presumably well into the future. The discussants were in full agreement that this is harder than it sounds.

Determining long-range needs on a national scale is an intricate process and full of pitfalls, but it can be accomplished with some confidence, Mr. Rosen explained. "Let me speak as one who has worked in the manpower area in the Bureau of Labor Statistics and helped to develop the national projections of manpower needs. In preparing the Occupational Outlook Handbook, which comes out every two years, we first determine the number of people employed in a particular occupation. Then we apply a death-and retirement rate based on the age distribution in the occupation. We relate these data to productivity, to technological change and to various special factors—in the case of automobile mechanics, for example, to the number of automobile and truck registrations by state over a period of years, to the scrappage rate of automobiles and trucks, to the projected number of new automobiles and trucks, and so forth. From these and other data we estimate the number of automobile mechanics we think will still be employed in the labor force in 1970.

"But I am not worried about the fact that there will be change and that jobs will always become obsolete. I believe that we should welcome change and adjust our work habits, our training habits and our whole thinking toward it."

Projections of long-range needs in local areas, on the other hand, are often uncertain. In the first place, Mr. Rosen explained, the managers of plants in large corporations may have no accurate idea of their national offices' development plans; any estimates they provide locally may be hazardous to rely on.

A strategy which seems to have been successful is to form committees of large employers in particular cities and ask them to estimate the skills they will need in six months, in one year and in two years. The Connecticut studies developed through this strategy, Mr. Rosen reported, are "exceptionally good. They provide a sound statistical basis on which to plan." As a general rule, however, such studies require extreme caution. Mr. Dunlop noted two dangers: (1) companies estimate their future growth on different bases, not all of which are equally dependable; and (2) a company which is laying off people may estimate its need as zero, when in fact it will have a minus impact by adding to the pool.

Regardless of the strategy employed, Mr. Dunlop declared, any local determination of "reasonable expectation of employment" is suspect because no study has been made of the theoretical basis for such projections. "I think it is very important to begin to analyze the concepts involved, the assumptions that are implied, the administrative procedures that are being established, the kind of computations that are being made." At present the reasonable expectation may be enough greater than the number of trainees to provide a margin of safety; but sooner or later, if we are not to train people for jobs which fail to materialize, the concepts of local estimating will require careful study.

Broad vs. narrow training: Pivotal to any manpower training program is the decision whether to provide narrow training, which prepares a worker for a particular job, or broad training, which prepares him to adapt to a range of related jobs. The former is obviously faster and cheaper. The latter is more costly in the short run, both in time and in money, since the worker must be taught more technical knowledge and more skills. The discussants were agreed, however, that broad training is far more desirable—and probably less costly to the nation in the long run.

This issue, Mr. Dunlop noted, "is one of the big areas with which collective bargaining has been concerned, though not always directly. In general, employers have been in favor of narrow training; and in general, unions have been in favor of broad training. There are a few unions in some localities which prefer to minimize the amount of training available in order to restrict entry to the union; but in the skilled crafts generally, the principal restriction to entry is that the employers do not want to bear the cost, even when they have the variety of operations that lends itself to general training. If they can get a skilled man to do a job, why pay a high rate for an apprentice?"

The advantage of broad training, Mr. Dunlop explained, is that "a more broadly trained man is more able to adapt to technological change when it takes place." The importance of this fact can best be understood in terms of "the internal labor market"—that is, the dynamics of promotion and job security among those already employed in a craft or industry. "In any enterprise there are limited points of entry, from which rise lines of promotion. A man can be hired as a laborer or as a maintenance mechanic, say, but not as a drill-press operator. For the skilled jobs, openings are normally filled by promotion from within the enterprise."

If management looks far enough ahead, it knows that it must build into its work force a stock of broad training, so that someone will always be available to fill a vacancy in a skilled job. To hire a man trained by another employer may be cheaper, but it is not always possible. Conversely, when a particular machine or operation is eliminated, the broadly trained worker need not be laid off; he can be channeled through a labor pool into another type of skilled job for which his training has prepared him. Unfortunately, not every employer looks quite so far ahead.

Carrying Mr. Dunlop's logic a step further, one discussant suggested that perhaps the Manpower Act training programs should not attempt to train men for particular jobs or even for specific crafts and industries. "I wonder if we might not be better off—this idea is a bit radical—by—paying the trainees the same allowances and giving them some plain, basic education. This would simply be enlarging our concept of the broadly trained man." Mr. Harris agreed enthusiastically: "This is such a dynamic world that a general education is terribly important if we are to adapt to the great changes taking place all around us." No other discussant picked up the suggestion.

Training within industry and unions: Mr. Dunlop's advocacy of broad training within industry and unions led to two questions: How effective is apprenticeship training? And what impact will the Manpower Act have on private training programs?

Mr. Rosen stated:

"The apprenticeship system, on the other hand, is an excellent way to train craftsmen. If it were to use the most modern methods and techniques, and if the number of years of training were fairly related to what people are being trained for, I think that apprenticeship programs could contribute tremendously to raising the level of skill of the American labor force. I think we are making a mistake in not using it more extensively.

"But there are reasons why it is not more fully utilized. It costs employers money; and many young people have no motivation for it. It entails years of hard work at salaries below the beginning salaries in many unskilled occupations. A bachelor apprentice finds it very difficult to support himself; a married man finds it practically impossible. Not many people take the long view and are willing to make such an investment for a later return."

Mr. Dunlop dissented from this assessment by challenging the premise on which it rests. Acknowledging that "Mr. Rosen is quite right in saying that the crafts vary widely in the proportion of manpower recruitment through the apprenticeship system," he declared that several crafts—the electricians, sheetmetal workers and pipefitters, among others—supply half their new workers through formal training programs. The conflict between the two sets of figures was not pressed.

As for the impact of the Manpower Act on private training programs, Mr. Rosen explained that "the Manpower Act does specify that we should try to stimulate training by private groups, but this requires some judgment. The importance of a net addition to training, which Mr. Dunlop called for in his comment, is very strongly entrenched in our thinking."

Vocational guidance in schools: Some observations on vocational guidance were elicited by a question by one discussant: "In what ways are the surveys of employment opportunities in cities and states being passed on to the local schools?" Mr. Rosen replied:

"The entire question of whether the people who are doing vocational guidance in school systems are aware of occupational and employment changes would, I think, make an extremely interesting Ph.D. thesis. All I know is that the Bureau of Labor Statistics has for many years published the Occupational Outlook Handbook, which is one of the most sensational buys in the country. For $4.75 it provides occupational information for some 600 occupations. Well, the Bureau of Labor Statistics believes that it has accomplished a miracle if it sells 42,000 of those handbooks every two years.

"The Department of Labor also carries on a very extensive informational program, trying to get this information out to the vocational guidance people. How well it is used and what impact it has is difficult to say. Knowledge of what is happening in the world of work is, in many cases, quite limited.

The Manpower Act in operation: In the course of the discussion, questions were raised about various aspects of the actual operations of the Manpower Development and Training Act. The following points were made:

On the selection of trainees: (1) There is a basic dilemma in the policy on selection criteria. The groups which have the most difficulty finding jobs—illiterates, for example—are those toward whom the Act is directed. But these groups are also the most difficult to train for jobs with a "reasonable expectation of employment." An attempt is sometimes made to strike a balance by lowering the usual criteria for the available jobs, and possible solutions such as the Virginia State project are commanding close attention. But the dilemma remains.

On the training program: (1) "A good deal of the vocational education in the United States is directed toward the manpower requirements of the past. The Manpower Act, in contrast, is geared to manpower requirements current and future. In the area of agriculture, for example, we may train people to be tractor operators or repairmen, arborists or vineyard experts; but we will not teach them to be farmers." (2) Training may be provided to meet special needs, such as instruction in English for Puerto Rican workers in New York City, where the ability to speak English is a requirement for most jobs. "This is a real problem," said Mr. Rosen, "but the Act hamstrings us in attempting to deal with it fully." A comparable challenge is teaching work disciplines to people who have never been in the labor force. "There are people who have to be taught about going to bed early at night so that they can get up early the next morning to go to work." (3) Since all training is to be of high quality, there may be a serious problem of locating sufficient teachers for the number of people who should be trained, if the operations get into high gear.

On the cost of training: No precise estimates were given, even under questioning, of the expected cost of the training program; but Mr. Harris observed that the program is bound to be far more economical than any effort to achieve the same result through deficit financing. "In a recent three-year period we had a $60-billion rise in Gross National Product and an increase of 3-million in employment. If the Manpower Act were a deficit-financing program, we might roughly assume that a deficit of about $30-billion would be required to create another $60-billion rise, so that each of the 3-million resulting jobs would cost about $10,000—far more than the direct outlay for training under the Act. There are intricacies and provisos, of course, but still the savings are mainfest."*

* The talk by Mr. Rosen preceded the December, 1963 and April, 1965 legislation on Manpower. In the period since Mr. Rosen gave his paper, there have been many changes in legislation and administration. (See the *Manpower Act of 1965*). Thus the number of years of attachment to the labor force need be only two, not three years; it is permissible to give as much as 104 weeks of training; the allowance for training can exceed unemployment compensation by $10 per week. The basic amount of the training allowance may be increased by $5 per week for each dependent in excess of two up to a maximum of four additional dependents.

In no sense whatsoever does Mr. Rosen write for the Department of Labor. The editor appreciates his able contribution all the more because he substituted for Mr. Seymour Wolfbein who was prevented from coming to Cambridge because of an unexpected development.

15. Womanpower and Education

SUMMARY OF THE DISCUSSION

No formal papers were presented at this session. The extended general discussion was devoted to five main topics:

Statics and trends: To set the scene for the discussion, Mrs. Esther Peterson, U. S. Assistant Secretary of Labor, offered a synopsis of the current situation in the employment of women. Over 24-million women are now working, she reported; this is about one-third of the total labor force. By 1970 there are expected to be 30-million—an increase of 25 per cent, as against an over-all increase of 20 per cent. The unemployment rate for women, however, is a little higher than that for men.

Over half of all working women are married; this is a new and highly significant development. The other half is divided about equally between single women and those who are widowed and divorced. Roughly 4.5-million working women are heads of families, and a number of these are their families' sole support. Another participant added that "the rate of married-woman participation in the labor force has doubled within the last two decades. The same change has not occurred among single women."

The average age of the working woman today is 41, Mrs. Peterson continued. The stable part of the female labor force is in the thirties and forties.

There has also been a shift in the occupations which women enter. Formerly, most working women were domestic workers; today the largest group (thirty per cent) are in the clerical occupations. One-fourth are service workers. Only one-seventh are operators, chiefly in factories, and only one-eighth are professional and technical workers. Within the professional area, teaching offers and will continue to offer women the greatest opportunities, but considerable demand is also expected for social scientists, social workers, home economists, dieticians, psychologists, counsellors and librarians. New jobs are also opening up for public relations and publicity writers, mathematicians and recreation workers.

The percentage of professional and technical workers in the female labor force is increasing, Mrs. Peterson noted. However, Mrs. Joan Burstyn, of the Harvard Graduate School of Education, observed that between 1930 and 1960, the percentage of women among all professional and semiprofessional workers dropped from 50 to less than 35 per cent. "While the total number of professional women rose, their share in the total professional force declined. This is important, especially because this sector will supply a large number of the new job opportunities expected in the next twenty years. I suggest that one reason for the decline is that women have taken jobs in clerical work, partly because it relieves them of the necessity to compete with men."

There is no question that women can handle a vast array of jobs from which they are now generally excluded, Mrs. Peterson said. "During World War II there were tremendous increases in the number of women working as surveyors, engineers, draftsmen, radio operators, chemists, airplane pilots, accountants and technicians. Today there are relatively few, but the skills that were used during the war years still exist." Mrs. Burstyn added that women are generally excluded even from many jobs which were considered "women's jobs" a generation ago. "Men seem to have entered these occupations from the top—as principals and superintendents of schools, as chief librarians and so on."

In addition to the 24-million women in the regular labor force, several millions more are part of the marginal group who float in and out of the labor force as the supply of jobs attracts them. Most of these marginal workers are in seasonal and part-time jobs and in the soft industries.

Should women work: The discussants were unanimous in asserting that women ought to feel free to work. The traditional belief that a women's place is in the home was dismissed abruptly by Mrs. Mary I. Bunting, president of Radcliffe College: "As long as the world was underpopulated and the problem of continuing the human race was critical, there was a genuine need to emphasize the special functions of women and to build up a value system that would support a woman's role as mother and in the home. Now the situation has changed, and I think that much of our ambivalence about working women is related to our general confusion about the unsolved problem of overpopulation." This change in the woman's role at home has been reinforced, Mrs. Burstyn added, by the mechanization of house-keeping during the last generation.

The greatest obstacle to the employment of women, the discussants agreed, is the current high rate of unemployment and the economy's failure to create enough new jobs to outweigh the effects of automation and the population explosion. "Where once there was a need to work as hard as we could, just to keep going," Mrs. Bunting declared, "now the burning question for many people is whether they will have a chance to work. There are breadwinners in our society, some women as well as men, who feel threatened by the prospect of a whole new segment of the population competing with them for jobs." The highest rate of employment of women, Mrs. Peterson noted, is in the nation's industrially developed and growing areas.

Two strong arguments were advanced for a greater acceptance of women in the labor force. The first was America's indisputable need for more skilled workers in vital sectors of the economy. Julian Hill, executive secretary of the committee on educational aid of the Dupont Company, offered a case in point: "The need for people with advanced education in the sciences is perhaps greater today than it has ever been. To increase the number of men in high levels of science is bound to be a slow process. It means influencing the career choices of students at the age of twelve, or fifteen, or whatever the critical age might be in each case. It means tapping the culturally deprived groups, which in time—but it will take time—are sure to make a real contribution. The most immediate undeveloped source is the bright girls who have made some beginning toward a science education."

The Dupont Company, Mr. Hill said, has made " a small gesture" toward encouraging such girls to pursue advanced science studies—"a gesture that we hope will carry the message that women are really wanted and valued in the top atmosphere of science, industry, education and the Government. This gesture is a fellowship to be awarded to a girl with an outstanding record in her first year of graduate work in a physical science or mathematics. It provides twenty-four months of additional full-time graduate study or the equivalent in part-time or interrupted study spread over perhaps six years." It thus takes account of the fact that the educational plans of a superior woman student may be altered by marriage. In this it differs significantly from National Science Foundation fellowship program, in which any student who is forced to study part-time is automatically dropped. (The first of these Dupont fellowships was to be awarded to a girl enrolled in the Harvard Graduate School of Arts and Sciences.)

The second argument for increasing the freedom of women to seek employment was advanced by John Riley, vice president and director of social research at the Equitable Life Assurance Company and formerly professor of sociology at Rutgers University: "A massive change that is taking place in our society is the change in the life cycle of the family. In each family today, the husband and wife both remain alive for an average of fifteen to twenty years after their youngest child has left home. Not much over a generation ago, the chances were better than even that the wife would already be a widow. Surprisingly little attention has been paid to this phenomenon and its implications, but I think it is here to stay.

"Three factors, by and large, are responsible: (1) There has been a slight narrowing of the gap between the median ages of husbands and wives. (2) There has been a drastic reduction in mortality in the middle years. (3) Most important, there has been a change in childbearing. While the median age for marriage has remained constant over the past generation—just under 23 for males, just about 20 for females—the family is formed in a much more compressed time. The first child is no longer postponed for several years; the median age for the mother today at the birth of her first child is just about 21. Furthermore, the spacing between children has been reduced, and the incidence of large families has been sharply reduced. As a result, the wife is about 26 and the husband about 29 when the family is complete."

Mr. Riley did not extend his argument explicitly beyond this point, but one clear implication—to which other discussants later responded—is that the wife is in her mid-forties when her youngest child graduates from high school and that she may have an eager desire to find useful employment in order to share an active and constructive life with her husband. Such a desire on a national scale must be recognized as profoundly important, morally as well as economically, in any concern over the issue of womanpower.

Combining marriage with a career: In point of fact, an increasing proportion of married women are either continuing to work, with brief interruptions for childbirth, or returning to work after their children are grown. Those who continue to work, said Mrs. Peterson, are in two groups (1) "a very small group of professional women who can afford to have mother substitutes and day care for their children" and (2) "women whose husbands earn low wages and who must work from economic necessity." This distinction led to a brief controversy over the economic motivation of the first group.

Miss Constance Smith, director of the Radcliffe Institute for Independent Study, observed that educated, well-to-do women must work in order to help provide for their children an adequate higher education, comparable to their own, at today's very high tuitions and costs. This is especially true in view of the more closely spaced families, in which "the children are all in preparatory school or college at the same time and the economic drain is enormous." This group, in short, may also be said to be motivated by economic necessity.

Three discussants disagreed. Mrs. Burstyn pointed out that such a view of economic necessity would be incomprehensible to families in lower income groups. David Riesman, Henry Ford II professor of social sciences at Harvard University, suggested that many well-to-do women are taking jobs partly to escape the incessant demands to which they would be subjected as housewives and from which they would otherwise have no adequate shield. Mrs. Matilda Riley (John Riley's wife) noted that these women give economic rationalizations largely because "it is not a norm for educated women from upper-income families to work. If this becomes a norm, they may no longer find it necessary to talk in economic terms."

Mrs. Burstyn attacked directly the widespread notion that a woman must make an either/or choice between her marriage and a professional career. "It is false to think that women are professionally oriented at one age and marriage-oriented at another. These roles are not mutually exclusive. Professor Achenfelt of New York University has commented that men have always played many roles without feeling any concern, but women who have several roles to play become very perturbed over what they think is a conflict. She wonders whether women could not learn to accept this as a natural way of life."

This vexing problem of role expectations had been the subject of a research study conducted by Mr. and Mrs. Riley among a few hundred upper-ability high-school juniors and seniors in New Jersey. They had searched into the student's attitudes toward the idea of women working; and Mrs. Riley commented in some detail on the girls' attitudes toward their own futures, "whether or not they wanted to work when they finished their education, and why they thought they might like work or might not. It was a very limited study, but I think it suggests a lot of interesting clues."

In this group, she explained, "hardly any girls thought of themselves as becoming unmarried workers. They all expected to marry and have children, and the only question in their minds was whether it would be possible to combine a career with marriage or not. Something like half of our sample thought that it was possible and planned to do it; the other half thought that they either could not or did not want to accomplish it.

"There were a number of major differences between those who accepted the idea and those who did not. We found, for example, that the higher a girl planned to go in education, the more eager she was for a job. This difference was very striking: something like 20 per cent of those who did not plan to go to college thought they would have careers, while something like 75 per cent of those who planned to go to graduate school thought that they would have careers.

"We looked into this a little further and discovered that there is a great difference between these two groups in the concept of a job. Those who were ending their education with high school stressed that they would work to raise the family's standard of living. Those who planned to seek a higher education stressed self-fulfillment: they wanted to work in order to make use of their interests and abilities. It was very clear that this expressive, noneconomic need was facilitating their acceptance of a job.

"This divergence reminded us, of course, that women's work has traditionally been considered an economic affair. The institutionalized, societal image of the working woman of a couple of generations ago was a poor creature whose husband is inadequate and defaults in his male role, so that the poor soul has to go out and do washing in order to support the children. Consequently a stigma was attached to a woman's job; it supposedly revealed that her husband was an inadequate provider. Apparently this 'hard life' stereotype of the working woman is with us still. On the other hand, the on-coming generation of would-be educated girls are thinking in very different terms. For them a job is part of the good life. It will enable them to earn money, of course; but far more important, it will add to the enrichment of their lives. Well, more and more educated women are coming into the labor force all the time. Could it be that the predominant concept of a job is changing? Could it be that the 'good life' view, which correlates with the tendency to seek higher education, will gradually take precedence?

"To check our findings, we went to larger sets of data and discovered, in some 1957 issues of the monthly *Labor Review*, tabulations of two major factors in motivating women to work. One factor was the woman's education; the other was the husband's income. The latter, of course, is very important: the less income the husband has, the more likely his wife is to work, and as the husband's income goes up, the proportion of wives who work falls off. But education proves to be equally determining: for any given level of husband's income, the higher the education of the wife, the more apt she is to work. Since the better-educated women tend to marry the higher-income males, this suggests that in one whole segment of the population, the women are under a tremendous set of role pressures. Because they are well-educated, they seem to want to work; but because their husbands earn a lot of money, the traditional pressures operate to discourage them from working. Only a trend toward the 'good life' view can gradually resolve this dilemma.

"If the concept of a job as primarily self-fulfilling, rather than economic, were to become institutionalized throughout the country, we could expect a much higher proportion of educated wives in high-income families to enter the labor force. It would also have a deep impact among low-income families, for if a working wife is not a stigma to a family but a symbol of an expressively successful home life, a woman can work without feeling guilty, and a man can encourage his wife to work without feeling inadequate. Moreover, if the wife has a broader occupational experience than that of housewife, she may understand better the problems which her husband and her growing children face in the larger world, and she might be able to perform even better her primary functions as a wife and a mother."

In response to questions, Mrs. Riley explained that boys seem to be much slower than girls to accept the "good life" view of the working woman. She suspected two probable reasons on the basis of this study of an admittedly small sample of high-school students. *First*, "while parents seem to encourage their daughters to look forward to a highly enriched life, including higher education and a career, they seem to encourage their sons to look forward to wives who will not be as well educated and who will certainly not have jobs outside their homes." *Second*, apart from what the parents say, the sons apparently want wives who resemble their mothers, who are themselves imbued with the traditional "hard life" view of the working woman.

At what should women work? Granted that it is desirable for women to work, their actual entrance into the labor force is governed not only by the general employment situation but also by several special factors. One is the widespread reluctance to hire women because their terms of employment are always unpredictable and often short. Mr. Hill reported, however, that "our laboratory directors give me the impression that, qualification for qualification, a girl is at no disadvantage in seeking employment, even though they know there is a chance that she may stay only two or three years. In part this impartiality results from the scarcity of applicants with advanced scientific training. In part it arose because we have had some very bright girls whose work we respected highly."

One solution to the choice between full-time employment and no employment is part-time employment, which Mrs. Burstyn set in a new perspective. "There is a need to have women accepted as part-time workers who can maintain their professional status vis-à-vis the men, with rights of promotion, tenure and fringe benefits in fair proportion to those of full-time workers."

A second factor governing the employment of women is the prevailing attitudes toward women's essential nature or temperament. Here the discussants exemplified our society's troubled ambivalence. Some asserted that women tend by nature to prefer jobs in which close personal relationships are of central importance, as in psychology, sociology and some of the guidance professions. "In such areas," said Mrs. Peterson, "women have an inside track." She also indicated that women tend naturally to pursue occupations which are extensions of their work in the home. "Women work at home as nurses, hairdressers, waitresses, clerks, cleaners and teachers, and they follow these jobs out into the community."

In contrast to this assumption that certain types of job are natural to women, the point was made that little or no reliable evidence exists to support any assumption that men and women have inherently different work traits. Mrs. Peterson recalled the bewilderment of a group of Russian women who were visiting various industries in America. "At an electronics plants they found women doing very intricate wiring under extremely narrow tolerances. When they asked why only women were doing the work, they were informed that only women had sufficiently great finger dexterity. Soon afterwards they visited a neurological institute where men were performing very delicate neurosurgery. When they asked why no women were employed, they were informed, 'Women couldn't do this work. They don't have the dexterity.'"

With regard to women's tendency to choose service jobs or jobs with close personal contact, explanations were offered which did not rely on assumptions of inherent traits or traditional bents. Mrs. Burstyn noted that women historically entered the service occupations through economic necessity and that they considered such work an extension of the drudgery they accepted as their lot at home. An unidentified member of the audience suggested that women seek work with close human relationships largely because "the woman's experience as a mother and homemaker is most easily validated and legitimated in these jobs. When she re-enters the labor market, she is asked what she did since her last employment, and she knows that her experience in the home will be considered most applicable to these jobs." She may take them not through instinct but by default.

Male chauvinism is a third factor which governs women's points of entry into the labor force. The discussants agreed that while this remains a severe problem, the shortage of skilled workers in some traditionally male occupations is creating a few small fissures in the wall which, for the most part, shuts women applicants out.

The challenge of determining whether any particular occupations are especially appropriate for women—and if so, what these occupations are—will probably not be resolved on a national economic or a psychobiological scale. An unidentified member of the audience observed: "Quite apart from motivations, there appears to be a mismatching between job vacancies and the available womanpower. The jobs are not in the right places. Judging from recent analyses of small-city labor markets, I suspect that a very resilient group of women workers is available if industry would only develop there. This problem requires a great deal more analysis and specific questioning."

The implications for education: "The median education level of American women today," said Mrs. Bunting, "is 11.6 years of school. This is a very impressive figure; but as soon as one mentions it, one remembers the 3- or 4-million women who are functionally illiterate, and one's mind goes back and forth between these facts." More women than ever before are entering college, but the percentage is still far below that for men. "In 1961," Mrs. Peterson stated, "41 per cent of all girls graduating from high school went on to college, as against 56 per cent of the men. This is very important because the jobs of the future are jobs that require advanced training and special skills." The proportion of women who graduate from college falls off very sharply, and many college graduates find it financially impossible to return for graduate training after their children are grown.

These quantitative challenges must be interpreted in part according to their impact on women's working careers. The most obvious and urgent challenge is that of the functional illiterates. Unskilled, repetitive jobs are becoming relatively scarce, Mrs. Peterson warned, and these women must be educated to the point where they are trainable for jobs which require some specialized knowledge and skills. At the college and university level, the number of women students must be increased. The curricula provided—and the rationales for those curricula—must also be keenly re-examined.

"Historically," Mrs. Burstyn explained, "women's education was a consumer commodity. Men educated their daughters, in large measure, so that the daughters would be 'well endowed' and so more marriageable. Few people expected them to utilize this education once they were married. Men have begun in recent years to calculate their education objectively as an investment. It seems to me that women today are changing in this direction. They are no longer prepared to think of education as a mere frill to their accomplishments. They are thinking of utilizing it in some way."

It does not follow, however, that a woman's education, including her higher education, must be geared to preparing her for a profession or occupation. Such narrow training is certainly one possibility, the discussants noted, but they were unanimous in declaring the need for flexibility in a woman's preparation for employment. Two major reasons were given:

First, in our restlessly mobile society, men may be transferred on short notice or may be compelled to move to other cities in order to find better jobs, regardless whether their working wives can find good jobs in the new locations. The wives' education, therefore, must have prepared them to be flexible; they must be able to adapt to the best possibilities among the jobs they find available.

Second, women who re-enter the labor force after years of absence often find that their interests have been radically altered by their experience as wives and mothers. (This redirection of interest is common among men also, but it manifests itself gradually throughout their working lives.) The shift tends to be horizontal rather than vertical: women are drawn to different and more congenial jobs, rather than to jobs with greater status and income. If their earlier education has been too narrow, it may no longer stand them in good stead.

16. Education and Economic Productivity

EDITOR'S PREFACE

Readers who are not professional economists may want to skip this chapter. But an intelligent layman should be able to absorb most of it. The issues are important.

The substantive conclusions of Mr. Denison's paper are:

Education: According to Mr. Denison's estimate, the improvement in the quality of the labor force as the result of additional education was very important to the nation's economic growth in the period 1929-57. (It accounted for 23 per cent of the growth rate of the total national income and for 42 per cent of the growth rate of the national income per person employed.) However, it does not always contribute to growth at a constant rate, partly because of changes in the rate at which education is improved and partly because there is a long time lag before the education of the young shows up as a characteristic of the labor force.

In the next twenty years, education will tend to decline slightly as a source of growth unless we can improve radically the *quality* of education. The reason is that we cannot continue to increase, at the same rate as in past years, the amount of time an individual spends in school. In the long run, however—say, over the next fifty years—even adding one year to the amount of time spent in school would increase the growth rate significantly. This long-range growth deserves our closest attention.

Advance of knowledge: By Mr. Denison's assessment, this factor per se has been virtually insignificant in its effect on the growth rate in recent years. One can assume that it has contributed to the growth rate very slightly (rather than retarding it) and that its contribution will increase minutely in the future. A greater financial investment in research and development activities would probably not be very productive. More promising would be a wider dispersion of such activities throughout American and world industry.

The substantive observations in the comments which followed are:

Mr. Solow: Education has not only an economic value; it also has a consumption or amenity value, in that it makes good citizens and enriches life. Moreover, Mr. Denison's analysis (as he himself noted) involves some guesswork at a very crucial point. Until we can determine exactly the actual rate of return from our investment in education, we cannot decide, even on purely economic grounds, whether it makes sense to invest proportionally more in education or not.

Mr. Eckstein: There may be only slight room for lengthening the school year (it should immediately be lengthened by thirty days, to match the school year in western Europe and Russia), but there is much more leeway for lengthening the school day. Also, now is a good time to begin adding a full year to each person's schooling, since the unemployment rate is high and those in school for the extra year would not be economically productive in any case.

Discussion: The substantive matters dealt with in the general discussion will be found in the summary under three headings: "Educational input," "Education as an investment of resources" and "Advance of knowledge."

Edward F. Denison
Economist, Committee for Economic Development and
Brookings Institution

Let me begin with a few general remarks about a study which I recently prepared for the Committee for Economic Development, *The Sources of Economic Growth in the United States and the Alternatives Before Us,* which was intended to throw some light on three questions concerning economic growth. Please keep in mind that I measure economic growth by the real national income or real net national product and that I am concerned with long-term growth of the economy's capacity to produce. This means that questions concerning the adequacy of aggregate demand to purchase the goods and services which the economy can produce are essentially outside the study, although I do consider them and acknowledge their importance.

The first of the three questions I set myself is: What, quantitatively, have been the sources of actual economic growth in the United States in the past? For the years 1929-57, the period with which I am mainly concerned, the growth rate of our real net national product was 2.93 per cent a year; that of real product per person employed was 1.6 per cent a year. I attempt to allocate these rates among the sources of growth.

The second question—and to me the least interesting—is: What is our future growth rate likely to be if we continue to follow essentially the same policies that we have been following, with no major conscious effort either to accelerate or to slacken the rate?

The third question, that which interest me most, is: What would be the effect on the growth rate in the future of adopting any measures which we may visualize in an attempt to raise it? This is important because almost anything which will materially raise the growth rate also imposes costs on the economy. Any rational decision, therefore, requires some quantitative appraisal of both the benefits and the costs. The benefits, of course, may be primarily something other than growth, and that has to be taken into account.

The study was intended to look comprehensively at all the factors which seemed likely to have anything important to do with this subject. My effort was to start with an open mind and to arrive at some results with no preconception as to what was important or unimportant. When I speak today about the contributions of education and of what I call the advance of knowledge, I am just pulling them out because they happen to be the subject of the seminar.

Any classification of growth sources obviously requires the use of factors whose definitions are somewhat arbitrary. No matter what classification one may adopt. one could always go behind it; for example, if one concluded that the increase in capital that actually occurred contributed at a specific rate to the growth rate, one could then ask, "Why did the capital stock increase at that and not some other rate?" This need for firm definition has particular relevance to the distinction I make between the contributions of education and the contributions of the advance of knowledge.

I approach education through its effects on the quality of the labor force, and I approach it quantitatively in terms of time spent in school. As for the effects of the fact that more is known now to teach in school than was taught twenty or thirty years ago, I include these not as a contribution of education but as part of the contribution of the advance of knowledge. One could, of course, argue that the two factors are interrelated: an increase in education contributes to the increase in the number of scientists, for example, and thus contributes to the rate at which knowledge advances. This is true, but my distinction stops without imputing back the advance of knowledge to education.

Let me say just a few words about my general approach in that part of the study which is concerned with sources of past growth. It is essentially a marginal-productivity approach, which starts with the assumption that total output increases for two reasons—because we increase the amount of resources that we put into production, and because we increase productivity.

As a first approximation, one may suppose that if we increased by one per cent the quantity of labor, capital, land and entrepreneurship—that is, of all inputs, according to whatever classification you like—output would be one per cent higher, other things being equal. In my study I actually assume that, because of economies of scale, we get little more; taking the economy as a whole, a one per cent increase in all inputs would actually yield a 1.1 per cent increase in output during the recent period in the United States. In my estimates for the past, I just let that extra amount ride separately as a contribution of economies of scale, rather than counting it in the contributions of labor, capital and so on. When I come to my third question, however—what would be the effect, let us say, of increasing the quantity of labor?—I do count in an allowance for scale economies.

Let me now turn to my evaluation of the contribution of education and take it up in terms of the three questions I have posed. First, let me indicate briefly the methodology I use in trying to get at the contribution of education to past growth, and let me stress certain assumptions that are involved in the evaluation. I work from three types of data: (1) Distributions of earnings of the male labor force by years of schooling, cross-classified by age. My general approach is to assume that the contribution of broad groups of individuals to production is in proportion to their average earnings. (2) Distributions of the labor force by number of years of education. I obtained these from the census for the period since 1940 and developed them myself back to 1910. (3) The numbers of days of actual schooling each of these years represented. This is necessary because a year of schooling has not meant the same thing over the last half-century; the number of days has increased greatly.

It is not ideal, of course, to assume that the amount of education is the only characteristic that distinguishes a group which has an eighth-grade education from one which has a high-school education and another which has a college education. There is a strong presumption that those with more education have also more innate ability, energy and application, and that other sorts of variables may also be correlated with education. But there are no adequate data to tell us how much of the observed income differentials is due to each of these factors. This is the biggest unknown in the whole procedure.

After looking at all the data and deciding that there is no way to assess these factors definitively, I made as assumption. I took the average earnings of people with an eighth-grade education as a base of 100, and I computed the earnings of those at each other level of education as a percentage of the earnings of those with an eighth-grade education. On this scale, I assumed that three-fifths of these observed differentials are due to education and two-fifths to other variables, and so I reduced the observed differentials by two-fifths. The resulting distribution suggests that if a person with an eighth-grade education can contribute 100, then one with no formal education can contribute 70, one with a high-school education 124, and one with a college degree or better 181. These results (which are only key points on the full scale) are intended to measure the difference in earnings due to education.

Next let us trace the rise in the amount of time which members of the labor force spent in acquiring education. In 1957 the average member of the labor force had spent four-fifths again as many days in school as his counterpart in 1929 and two and a half times as many days as the average worker in 1910. This amazing change resulted from large increases in both the number of years of school attendance and the number of days attended per year.

The process is, I think, obvious by which one can use the income differentials to standardize over time so as (1) to calculate how much earnings would have changed if nothing had changed except education and (2) to develop the contribution of education from that.

One should not be surprised, given the huge increase in education and the importance of education to earnings, if it turns out that education has made a rather large contribution to growth. The numbers I have just given imply an average annual increase of two per cent a year in the amount of education of the members of the labor force during the period 1929-57. After the income differentials have been applied, the implication is an increase of .97 per cent a year in the average quality of the labor force, as reflected in earnings, as the result of additional education. Finally, one must take account of the fact that labor is only one factor of production, which accounted for about 73 per cent of the national income over this period.

Ignoring here some minor adjustments, I take 73 per cent of .93 per cent and conclude that the improvement in the quality of the labor force as the result of additional education contributed .67 of one percentage point to the growth rate of the United States national income in this period. This is equal to 23 per cent of the growth rate of the total national income and to 42 per cent of the growth rate of the national income per person employed.

In the period from 1909 to 1929 the contribution was only about half as large. Education, therefore, is not a stable source of growth, partly because of changes in the rate at which education is being improved and partly because there is a long time lag between changes in the education of the young and the resultant education of the labor force. The benefits we were getting in the 1930's and 1940's, in terms of the composition of the labor force, were primarily the consequence of school extension much earlier.

Let us now go on to the second question: What contribution to the growth rate can we expect from education in the period 1960 to 1980?

The Census Bureau has made projections of the likely distribution of the labor force by education over the next twenty years. (Actually, there are two, slightly different projections. I have used the higher.) The same statistical approach used for the past yields a projected contribution to the growth rate from additional education, during the next twenty years, smaller than that realized from 1929 to 1957: .64 per cent as against .67 per cent. The retardation would be more substantial except for two offsetting factors: (1) the shift in the age distribution towards the younger age groups, which are better educated, and (2) the fact that as we move into higher levels of education, an additional year of education adds more to earning power than it did in the past. If we were measuring the retardation simply in terms of time spent in school, it would be substantially greater.

Looking beyond 1980, I think it is fairly clear that education must be a declining source of growth unless we can improve radically the quality of education. It seems impossible to continue to increase the quantity of education—the amount of time individuals spend in school—at the rate we have in the past. We have almost doubled the number of days per year spent in school, and there just are not enough Saturdays, holidays and vacations left, or enough absenteeism left, to double it again. Even with respect to school years we are limited; we cannot spend all our lives in school. So if we are to continue the same contribution of education to growth, we must work for quality. And we must remember that, if there has been improvement in the quality of education in the past, as I believe although my numbers do not measure it, what is required is an even faster improvement.

Finally, I come to the third question: What would be the contribution of still more education? Suppose that for the next fifty years we were to give everybody one more year of schooling than he otherwise would get, what effect could we anticipate on the nation's economic growth?

There are three points to consider: *First*, this would cost something—about .3 or .4 per cent of the national income. This would not be a deduction from the growth rate, since education counts as part of the national income, but it does mean that less would be available for other uses. However, I omit this cost from the following calculation. *Second*, we would have a net benefit in improved quality of the labor force. And *third*, we would have an offsetting cost, since the people attending school would not be working.

The effect on growth, therefore, appears to be approximately as follows: At the end of ten years, the growth rate would be *lower;* only a small fraction of the labor force would have received the increased education, and the benefits to that group would be more than offset by the loss of the work of the students then in school for the extra year. In twenty years, however, we would be ahead, and for twenty years after that we would get a contribution to the growth rate of about .07 of a percentage point. About fifty years from now, the whole labor force would have had the benefit of this extra education. Over that time-period as a whole, we would get an increment of about one-tenth of a percentage point to the growth rate. This means that the national income, fifty years hence, would be about five per cent higher than otherwise.

To summarize this examination: (1) Education has been a major factor in growth in the past. (2) It is likely to be a declining factor in the future, though the decline will be slight over the next two decades. And (3) because of the very long time lag between the investment and the full return, it cannot be used to increase growth except over rather long time-periods. But since the long-range growth is what we should be interested in, this time lag is no bar.

Let me turn now to the contribution of the advance of knowledge, which is probably the most difficult of all factors to get at. And let me begin again with the first question: What has been its contribution to our past growth rate?

My estimate is that the advance of knowledge contributed .58 of a percentage point to the 1929-57 growth rate. Quite frankly, I arrive at this estimate as a residual of what is left over after accounting for everything else. Every other economist who has approached this problem has done the same thing, but I have tried to estimate the contribution of everything else much more comprehensively, and so I arrive at a much smaller residual. This does not mean that it is right; it just means that it is reached after a more complete over-all evaluation. Certain other residuals, for example, have been fairly carefully described by their authors as including the contribution of education and many other things, along with that of advances in knowledge, yet they have often been used as if they measured simply the contribution of technological progress or something of the sort. Sometimes even the authors seem to get a little careless.

There is one other interesting distinction, though I shall not try to make it terribly precise. It concerns the new knowledge which makes more efficient production possible, if everybody knows about it and uses it in the most economic way. Since not everybody does, one can identify, as a separate factor in growth, the lag of the average firm or other producing unit behind the best.

It seems to me unlikely that any change in this lag can have been of much significance during the years 1929-57 in the United States. If our ability to produce increases .6 per cent a year, and if we can shorten the lag of average practice behind the best by one year, this would add .6 per cent to the national income. But over a thirty-year period, this becomes merely .02 per cent. Even shortening the time lag by two or three years would not result in a very big change. Furthermore, in so far as one supposes this lag to be determined by how new or old equipment is, it can be measured by the average age of capital—and that is not very large.

By essentially this line of reasoning, I concluded that the change in this lag, if any, and its effect on the growth rate must have been small. I put it down as .01 per cent, but this means only that I consider it unimportant.

Let me take a little time to point out that the meaning of the advance of knowledge in this context is highly dependent on the

way the national product is measured. First, for a considerable segment of the economy—government employees, nonprofit organizations, domestic servants and on-site construction work—the national-
product estimates assume that no change in productivity occurs for
any reason. Hence, nothing that occurs in these sectors is reflected
in my estimate of the contribution of the advance of knowledge.

Second—and very important—I must draw a distinction which
arises from the behavior of the price indexes that are used to deflate
the national product. This distinction is extremely difficult to explain
briefly, so let me instead offer an illustration. Even though new products are developed and old products are improved, the national income is not changed as long as the amount of resources going into
production is not changed. The national income will be the same,
for example, whether we decide we prefer to engage in moon exploration or to raise wheat. If we opt for moon exploration, it will be the
same, assuming we invest the same resources, whether we reach the
moon or not.

The advance of knowledge, therefore, plays a rather limited role.
It really refers only to new knowledge that can reduce the unit costs
of producing products; it does not include the benefit to the consumer
of having a choice among more and better products. This is not
a peculiarity of my estimate but an aspect of the measurement of
the real national income, and it is very important in deciding whether
a figure of .6 per cent seems reasonable on a priori grounds or not.

The contribution of the advance of knowledge to the future
growth rate is, I think, wide open. Looking for some precise indication
I examined three factors: patent statistics, research and development
expenditures and—the factor on which I would rely most strongly
—the past trend in the contribution of the advance of knowledge
to growth. Unfortunately, this last factor is one of those games whose
results are greatly dependent on which time-periods one chooses for
comparison. The annual contribution is virtually the same in three
recent periods: 1929-41, 1941-48 and 1950-57. In 1948-50, however,
there was a huge jump in productivity. Some people include these
two years in the later postwar period, while others consider it a reaction to World War II. Depending on what you do with it, you can
conclude that there was or was not an appreciable increase in the
growth rate of productivity in general—or in the contribution of
the advance of knowledge in particular—in the postwar period.

(There has also been an above-average productivity increase very recently.)

My own guess—and it is only that—is that the contribution from the advance of knowledge is likely to be a little higher, but not radically so, in the future than it was in the past.

Finally, are there ways to increase the future growth rate by accelerating the advance of knowlege? This is a very difficult question, but a few observations might be made.

Advances in knowledge, first of all, come not only from the United States but from all over the world. Only a fraction is subject to our control. Moreover, some of those advances in knowledge that contribute to production are created incidentally by people as they work and think and act. This process cannot be regulated by the conscious application of resources to research and development. Finally, scientific and technological research are only a part of what is relevant; management techniques, broadly construed, are also very important.

One quantitative step that seems available, if we wish to increase the contribution of the advance of knowledge to growth, is simply to augment the resources going into technical research and development. However, this may not be very productive. My estimate is that all kinds of advances in knowledge in the past contributed around .6 per cent to the growth rate. This includes the benefits of managerial as well as technological advances, those of foreign as well as domestic origin, and those which were incidental as well as those which resulted from research and development programs. Possibly a quarter of the whole contribution might be identified with conscious physical research and development; this would be .15 of a percentage point. To add a large amount to the growth rate by this route would require a tremendous increase in the amount of resources going into the effort, even if doubling the input would double the output, which appears unlikely. Moreover, it requires that additional skilled individuals be available, which they are not without a considerable time lag.

One other important possibility is dispersion. The whole research and development effort is now narrowly concentrated in a small part of the economy. Industries making up two-thirds of the national income account for less than .1 per cent of the total expenditures. It seems a priori likely that a broader dispersion of research and development effort would yield more overall results.

COMMENT BY . . . *Robert M. Solow*
Professor of Economics, Massachusetts Institute
of Technology

One of the most important products of anybody's research is questions
for further research, and I would like to point out a few questions
that seem very clear and very important as a result of Mr. Denison's
work.

The first of these, which has occurred to other researchers as
well, is the relative weight to be given to education per se as against
other factors which are statistically associated with it—innate talent,
energy, drive and so on. Mr. Denison guessed that the income differentials should be attributed sixty per cent to education and forty per
cent to the other factors, but so far as I know, there is no body
of fact available at the moment to verify that guess. Mr. Denison
would, I think, be the first to agree that we ought to generate some
facts which will throw light on this question.

This would undoubtedly be a long, hard job, but it could be
done. It would require some kind of longitudinal study, probably
through a state university which has a good school of education and
a good body of historical statistics relating to individuals—or which
would be willing to generate such a body of information—and can
then follow these individuals through time. It must be possible to
take fifth-graders or sixth-graders or eighth-graders and make accurate
measurements of their native ability; to correlate this data with their
educational attainment and performance and, ultimately, with their
life patterns of income; and in this way to measure the true marginal
product of education as a contribution to income-earning ability. I
do not know what the prospects are of getting this work done, but
I should think that a foundation could be interested, and it certainly
ought to be done.

A second question for further research, it seems to me, is whether
the number of days spent in school—or even the number of hours
spent in school—is an adequate measure of educational input. It may
be the only measure which is currently available, but I wonder
whether it is appropriate.

Everyone who has been to school knows that lots of different
things go on there from handball games to mathematics lessons. To
take the total number of hours or days spent in school as a measure
of educational input is, implicitly, to assume that the allocation of
educational time among alternative subjects is, in a rather precise

sense, optimal. It means assuming, for example, that the marginal contribution of an additional hour of education spent in learning high-school chemistry is approximately the same as the marginal contribution of another hour spent in learning English literature.

I see no reason to suppose that an optimal allocation of a fixed total of educational hours, in fact, occurs. On the contrary, there are at least two reasons to believe that it does not. In the first place, the market on which the allocation is determined is hardly a perfect market; with the best will in the world, it is governed very largely by convention and other noneconomic influences. It seems possible that a truer measure of educational input could be identified and could be considerably increased, without increasing the aggregate number of days or hours spent in school.

A second reason to believe that the allocation may not be optimal is that education is a consumer good as well as a capital good, a producer's good. The allocation of educational effort may be strongly shaped by the consumer's preferences for education in different subjects, for different methods of instruction and so on. This impact of consumers' preferences tends not to be measured in the national product, unless you suppose a priori that the cost of education does, in fact, measure the marginal utility of hours spent learning languages, sciences and other subjects.

There is another related point that needs to be made, a point with which Mr. Denison would surely agree. Because growthmanship is a popular pastime these days, we think it is natural to be interested in such quantities as the contribution of education to the growth of the measured national product. And since we take it for granted, rightly or wrongly, that more rapid growth of the measured national product is a social goal worth achieving, we conclude that we ought to have more education—or even that we *need* to have more education.

But the proper criterion for the allocation of resources of education, as distinct from the use of resources in other industries, is not simply its contribution to the algebraic rate of increase of the Gross National Product. There is also a consumption or amenity aspect of education. We value education, not only because it helps to increase the GNP, but also, I have heard tell, because it makes good citizens and enriches life and accomplishes a couple of other minor things.

Furthermore, on the purely economic level, the allocation of real resources to education is a form of investment or savings, depending on which end one looks at it from. Before one can make a rational allocation of resources among education and other uses, one must know the rate of return on social saving devoted to education. Is it two per cent per annum, or four per cent, or six per cent, or what? Only then (speaking now entirely from the point of view of production, leaving aside the consumption uses of education) can one know whether it would be wise for society to invest more in education, as against consuming more or as against investing more in other things, like plant and equipment.

To make this decision, one must compare the per annum rate of return on resources devoted to education with two other rates: (1) the per annum rate of return available to society from the devotion of resources to physical investment—that is, to investment in such things as plant and equipment, inventories and government buildings; and (2) what one could call, for want of a better word, the social rate of time preference. Mr. Denison emphasized that education is a classical investment; it involves abstention from consumption now in favor of increases in potential consumption, which will be spread over a rather long period of time and may not even begin to appear in any quantity until a long time has passed. One can legitimately question whether the rate of return on investment in education or anything else is sufficiently large to justify, from society's point of view, the postponement of the enjoyment of resources.

Some people tend to argue that a rich society, like ours, ought not to be interested in investing—or, at least, ought not to be *so* interested. They reason that since our per-capita income is already so high that increments can hardly be worth very much, we ought not to exercise ourselves very much to increase per-capita income in the future. That argument seems to me superficial. One can argue, for precisely the same reason, that we should be putting a low value on the present consumption that we have to forego in order to achieve higher consumption in the future.

One cannot, then, simply by some horseback rule, decide rationally whether current rates of investment in education are roughly optimal or not. One has to know about the rates of return.

I should like as a last comment, to point out another and rather different research problem which Mr. Denison's work suggests. We now look at what we call technological change in at least two ways. One is the historian's way: what historians mean by technological change is change in what happens inside factories. In one century iron ore was converted into wrought iron by puddling; today it is converted into steel by the Bessemer process. Or one year, as you drive across Nebraska, the alfalfa trains are being pulled by beautiful steam engines; a few years later, the same alfalfa trains are being pulled by dull, ugly diesel locomotives. This is the sort of change that the historian records as technological change.

The second way is the economists' way. The economist really need not know at all what it feels like to be inside a steel plant, or what it looks like to watch an alfalfa train cross the horizon. He quantifies technological change by making measurements of output per man hour, or output per unit of this, or output per unit of that.

I think it would be useful research to take lines of production, industries, and try to draw up parallel records of these two views of technological change—one which describes the actual production process, and another which deals with statistics of input and output —and to try to see just what the relationships are between changes in production technique and changes in productivity, as we measure them.

COMMENT BY . . . *Otto Eckstein*
                            Professor of Economics, Harvard University
                            and Member President's Council of Economic
                            Advisors

I have been spending the last two weeks lecturing about Mr. Denison's book to my undergraduates. We quarreled with a few points, and I tried to explain one or two, and there are one or two that I shall ask him to explain to me. But when we finished our scrutiny, I told them that I thought this book, almost single-handed, had changed the nature of the discussion about economic growth in this country. Mr. Solow's earlier studies had told us that there is a large residual, that the input of labor and capital does not explain the rate of growth. Mr. Denison has taken this enormous residual and split it into several components, and anybody who addresses himself to the question of economic growth from here on will have to look at it in the same sort of detail. His book is probably the most important thing that has happened in this problem—and perhaps in this field—in the last few years.

It is also, in a way, a very heroic work. Economists have always managed, somehow, to banish this residual into qualitative, mysterious segments called knowledge, technology, education, and so on. Mr. Denison has tried to spell out what it could really mean if one looks at it in detail.

Having said that, let me raise a few questions about the book, particularly those sections which he took up today, though they are really a little difficult to evaluate unless one is familiar with the structure as a whole.

First, it seems to me that the effect of education could be bigger in the future than Mr. Denison suggested. If he computed the education input per hour instead of per day, he would find much more leeway for increasing it. It may be true that the school year can only be reasonably lengthened another thirty days, and of course it should be lengthened. (As I understand it, the western European countries and Russia have a substantially longer school year than ours, which is still attuned to the old days, when the children had to go out and help bring in the harvest.) But there also is a lot of room for stretching the school day, so I would not necessarily assume that the rate of increase of education need slow down.

My second question concerns Mr. Denison's rather pessimistic conclusion that providing an extra year of schooling for everyone would actually depress productivity for more than ten years because of the loss of output while people are in school. If this is approached as a programing problem, there is surely some timetable for adding a school year which will always give a positive result. There is no need to increase education across the board, one year for everybody, from this day forward. There must be another, more gradual method which keeps us always substantially ahead.

Furthermore, one really should not assume full employment in judging the issue. On the contrary, this may be a very good time to add a full school year, since we have plenty of unemployment and the people who would be in school for the extra year would not have jobs anyway—or, if they did, would be taking the jobs from others in the labor force. So we would not lose a year of work for every person who stays in school a year.

Those questions were on education. Now let me turn to the advance of knowledge, where I must raise a question about the methodology of the whole study.

Mr. Denison discovers the effect of the advance of knowledge as a final residual. Now, if he had wanted to, he might have taken the estimated total input into nongovernmental research and development and assumed, if business is rational, that the rate of return on this is as high as the rate of return on manufacturing. If he computed this, it is not inconceivable that he would explain the entire residual. In fact, I think it is not impossible that he would wind up with a negative residual. Or, if research and development does not do it, we could find some other chunk whose marginal productivity would explain more than the total residual.

The residual method, then, as one gets to finer and finer points, becomes less and less reliable. When Mr. Solow estimated that about two per cent of the growth rate is not explained by labor and capital, he must have been roughly right. But when this residual is down to .64 per cent and I can account for at least half of that by the return on research and development, surely I can find other chunks that will reduce the residual to nothing. All I am really doing is performing a kind of consistency test to see whether resource allocation and the economy are rational and whether the sum of the marginal products add up somehow to the total.

But apart from this, I think Mr. Dension may be a little too pessimistic about the impact of the advance of knowledge. As he indicated, most quality improvement is overlooked in computing the Gross National Product, and we know that most of the quality improvement has to do with know-how and knowledge. I see no present alternative to using the GNP framework; but if we had a better method of measuring quality change, our GNP growth might measure substantially higher, and most of that extra would be attributable to the advance of knowledge.

Finally, two other methodological points. *First,* the method is an adding-up scheme, and this makes it difficult to trace the impact of interaction. For instance, would the impact on education be greater if there were also more research and development? It seems obvious that if the Government spends more on research and development, it drives up the salaries of scientists, so the reward in education goes up. This is an essential matter for investigation. *Second* and more generally, the composition of final demand has an impact on the payoff on these factors; and if we are moving into an era of sending men to the moon or Mars and so on, the composition of demand may very well raise the rate of return on education.

SUMMARY OF THE DISCUSSION

Mr. Harris opened the discussion by describing Mr. Denison's book as "a very significant study," largely because of its broad scope. "It goes beyond education to discuss the contribution of many other factors which I think are very important. Those of us who teach tend to exaggerate the contribution of education as against, for example, the contribution of health." (Inevitably, some of the other factors were touched on briefly by the discussants. Those remarks are not included in this summary.)

Five questions dominated the general discussion:

Educational input: There was unanimous agreement that no way has been found to achieve an accurate measure of educational input. Tabulation of time, whether by hours or days per school year, is clearly inadequate, since it ignores the uses made of that time. One alternative, said Mr. Denison, might be to use the number of teachers. "This figure, which is actually used in computing the national product and a lot of other series, assumes that each teacher creates a uniform amount of educational input." It seemed to him no improvement. The only other objective statistic which might be functional is the pupil-teacher ratio. "This may have something to do with the quality of education, but I do not know how to work it in."

Even though no other measure is available, he added, "I have nothing but apologies for using the number of school days. I suspect that it really understates, for several reasons, the increase in the real amount of education."

Two complicating factors were indicated by other discussants. *First,* as parents become more educated, the home influence becomes a significant source of educational input. And *second,* on-the-job training is indisputably part of our educational system, especially in the teaching of technical skills. Evidence of this is the linkage between job seniority and promotions (and see "Income differentials" below). Studies are now in progress to determine the extent of industry's investment in formal job training; it may turn out to approximate—or even exceed—the expenditures for formal education.

"A new man on a job," said Professor Wassily W. Leontief, Henry Lee professor of economics at Harvard University, "is forced to study not only the job skills but also the relevant aspects of a general education which he may have missed. Thus a man who goes directly into industry and learns on the job becomes, in a sense, a specialist, somewhat like the Soviet workers who are trained in special schools. Of course, our approach is normally more general, and from the consumption point of view it is obviously far superior."

Mr. Eckstein's suggestion of lengthening the school day was contested on the ground that the students, though exposed to more subject matter, might not be able to absorb more than at present. However, improvements in the efficiency with which the input is used are feasible and desirable. Three were specifically proposed: devising better curricula and methods, eliminating small school districts for better utilization of the staff and minimizing the number of competent students who do not receive a higher education.

Contribution of education: "The biggest unknown in the whole procedure," Mr. Denison had said, is the relationship between education and such related variables as innate ability, energy and application. In the discussion he explained that anyone who disliked his assumpton (three-fifths education, two-fifths other factors) could readily adjust it. "If you like four-fifths rather than three-fifths, simply take four thirds of my result, and instead of .67 you will have .89." All of the extra, however, comes out of that final residual, the contribution of the advance of knowledge.

A few major studies now under way, notably Project Talent in Pittsburgh, are seeking to determine the relationship among innate ability, environmental factors, motivation, education and final achievement. Though promising, Project Talent is a long-term study, and its results will not be available to economic analysts for many years. Nor will all the changes based on these results be immediately effective. Even if racial discrimination, for example, were suddenly eliminated, the effects of past discrimination would continue to be felt for some time to come.

Income differentials: In this study Mr. Denison assumed that the contribution of education to the growth rate can be traced through the quite large differences in the income earned by groups with different amounts of education. This assumption was sharply disputed on the ground that quantitative norms are very limited measures of educational output. A man working for the Federal Government at $20,000 a year, for example, could move to a Wall Street job at $40,000, but would this increase in income signify any change in the worth of his education? "In fact," said Mr. Solow, "a little extra education may ruin you for the really high-paying positions."

Mr. Denison replied that his study merely assumes that the relative importance of nonmonetary incentives has not changed during the years covered by the study. If the assumption is correct, the changes in income remain a reliable index. (The challenge seems really to have been directed at another of his assumptions—that earned income is a fair measure of one's contribution to national productivity. But the question was not pressed.)

Mr. Harris noted that while the absolute differences in income according to education continue to rise, there has been a slight decrease in the percentage of these differences. "The decline has been surprisingly small, considering the change in numbers, but it is definite." This may portend a considerable reduction in the marginal contribution of educated people in future years; as a higher percentage of people become better educated, each one's education will have less impact on the nation's productivity.

Mr. Denison responded cautiously. "The fact that any change has been slight is remarkable, for it suggests clearly that the pattern of demand for people with different abilities has been changing at the same rate as supply. It is not apparent which is the cause and which the effect, but obviously they interact on each other. However, if the decline becomes greater—which it well might for the college graduate—my projection might prove too optimistic." (The projection relied heavily on the premise that an additional year of education adds more to income at higher grades than at lower ones.)

Mr. Denison had taken groups of the same age, sorted them according to the amount of education and observed a corresponding increase in income. This information was the basis of his analysis of the contribution of education. He pointed out that the procedure can be reversed: one can take groups with the same amount of education and sort them according to age. The increase in income shows up again and is of the same order of magnitude. He ascribes this primarily to experience on the job.

"I regret that I did not do much more carefully what I did crudely—that is, deal with men, women and children as discreet kinds of labor and consider them in more detail, especially the remarkable change which has occurred in the experience level of women workers. In effect, aside from a special adjustment for women, I assumed that the amount of experience within each group did not change between 1929 and 1957. It would be interesting to re-examine this, though the effect of any change would be small unless there has also been a radical change, which I am not aware of, in age composition."

Education as an investment of resources: Mr. Solow had called for an assessment of education as an investment, as against other possible uses of national resources. Mr. Denison pointed out that his study had been formulated in such a way as to avoid the question, which is important only when a policy decision must be made.

"One might ask: shall we spend $10-million on education, or shall we spend the money on some other form of investment? In some countries, especially the underdeveloped countries, these are genuine alternatives, but in the United States I think they are not. When we invest more in education, we take a little away from each of the other alternatives: we invest a little less, we consume a little less, we probably have a little less government expenditure, and so on. Only a small fraction of the offset is in investment or other growth-supporting expenditures. This means that the rate of return on education would have to be a great deal lower than the rate of return on physical investment for us not to increase the growth rate over the long run by spending more on schools.

"Furthermore, I am not one who thinks that maximum output is the only—or even, necessarily, the most important—goal of society. There is a legitimate question, to which the answer is not obvious, whether there is sufficient reason for us to try to accelerate our growth rate. My personal view is that for students who are willing to live as we did when we were students, and who have the interest and ability to benefit from education, the consumption-citizenship yield is sufficient to warrant the whole cost, and whatever contributes to growth is a free good. But this is purely a statement of taste."

Advance of knowledge: The contribution of the advance of knowledge was discussed only in one aspect, the investment of funds and scientific manpower in space research. Mr. Harris reported a general impression that "an excessive amount of money is spent on engineering as against the basic expenditures," and he cited the concern of an eminent and knowledgeable scientist "who believes that one reason we have so little growth is that we are devoting too much of our manpower to space and similar programs. Very little gets into the industrial area, and so we have considerably less output than we would otherwise have."

Both assertions were rebutted by Mr. Leontief: "I once computed what the space program actually implies in demand for technical, engineering and scientific manpower. I spent some time on it. And I discovered that, contrary to the common assumption, the space business is just a manufacturing industry. It is incredible how large a proportion of the expenditures are typical of factory expenditures; and the scientific competence involved, apart from the military aspects, is not much higher than in many other advanced industries. The reason is that each space vehicle travels just once, making a terrible manufacturing problem. The physical content and the workmanship content must be much greater than any scientific content.

"Also, the scientific manpower is spread through the supply industries, and the byproducts of the research will contribute to the civilian economy. In fact, they will probably contribute as much in the long run as if the research were directed primarily at civilian products. At least, that was my impression."

Mr. Denison observed that "if the object is to increase the growth rate, certainly the concentration of research and development in a small part of our economy is damaging, regardless what share of this goes to the space programs. But a policy decision is involved: is a high growth rate more important than getting to the moon? It is a matter of objectives, a matter of choice."

Clarifications: In the course of the discussion, which centered on these five questions, Mr. Denison clarified certain points in his study. On the contribution of education to past growth, he observed that the massive change has occurred at the elementary- and secondary-school level, though colleges are playing an increasing role and will continue to do so.

On his assumption that the time lag in the application of research was almost static during the period he studied, he emphasized that the Gross National Product recognizes only those research applications which lower the unit costs of production. There may well be a considerably faster use of qualitative research which develops new products and improves old ones. This would include the great bulk of organized research and development, but it would not show up in his computations.

On the impact of unemployment on his projections, he explained that it depends on whether one assumes that the unemployment rate will continue to be excessive. If the rate becomes lower, then adding permanently an extra year of schooling will not be costless to the society.

Finally, on the role of "little numbers" in his calculations, he declared: "I think that .01's are important. Over a long period of time, they add up to a lot of money. After all, we have only 160 of these .01's in our past growth rate of output per person employed." (In his speech, referring to the contribution of the change in the time lag, he had declared: "I put it down as .01 per cent, but this means only that I consider it unimportant." None of the discussants asked him to resolve the apparent contradiction.)